7-27-73

MOVERS
AND SHAKERS

MOVERS AND SHAKERS:
American Women Thinkers and Activists 1900-1970

June Sochen

Quadrangle/The New York Times Book Co.

Library of Congress Catalog Card Number: 73-76290

International Standard Book Number: 0-8129-0360-9

1758925

*To Julie, Sarina, Abby, and Adam—
the movers and shakers of the next
generation.*

CONTENTS

PREFACE

Historians of the Western world have traditionally written about, and thereby preserved in print, the spectacular events, actions, personalities, and thoughts of human history. But with notable exceptions. Their idea of spectacularity has been governed by their cultural views: most especially, their inherent assumption that man, rather than woman, is the maker of history and culture; and that the white man, rather than the black man, is the noteworthy participant in history. In addition to these significant exceptions, all historians operate within their particular frames of reference, their unique regions, genetic makeup, family upbringing, and social experiences. Thus, the records of history are indeed fragile expressions of white male historians' limited perspectives.

The human restrictions upon historians, of course, cannot be overcome entirely, but many of them can be controlled. The liberation movements of women and blacks during the 1960's and 1970's have made all Westerners more aware of the serious prejudices that have governed society's treatment of these groups. Historians, among others, have been faced with the need to redress the legitimate grievances suffered by women and blacks in their written records. Histories and studies of women, along with black histories and black studies, are all part of the academic scenario in the 1970's.

The history books are slowly being rewritten to include these heretofore forgotten groups. Historians, as well as other people, discover (once they look) that women thought, wrote, and acted upon many of the same (and also other) subjects that men thought, wrote, and acted upon. This is not to suggest that women's (or black Americans') participation in history has been morally superior or ideologically preferable to white men's, but simply that women and blacks did participate in history and should be given their rightful place.

Women worked in the abolitionist movement, for example, as well as in all major reform movements in American history; yet they have not received their due recognition in the recorded annals. One of the prime historical tasks of the 1970's is to reexamine the past in light of the present's new-found awareness and to insert into the record the neglected deeds and beliefs of women and blacks.

The following study is a modest effort in the area of twentieth-century women's history. It is a study of selected women intellectuals of this century whose participation in the life of their time was significant and worthy of recognition. One of the basic assumptions that informs this work is that a minority of human beings, men and women, step to their own tune, while the majority march to the dominant melody. Historians have recorded male-minority thoughts and actions, and now the women-minority are entering the pages of history.

Women intellectuals and activists have existed in every generation. They have usually been members of the same class as male intellectuals—the middle class—and in this century they have often been college educated. Jane Addams, the woman exemplar mentioned in most history books, had a great deal of female company in the settlement house movement and the peace movement; during the Progressive era every reform venture, in fact, had women articulators and participants. But Progressives Lillian Wald, Belle Moskovitz, Pauline Goldmark, Grace Abbott, Crystal Eastman, and Charlotte Perkins Gilman are not known to students of history; whereas Lincoln Steffens, Walter Lippmann, John Reed, Herbert Croly, Walter Weyl, and John Dewey are familiar names in the history of that era.

This study is a highly selective, partial effort in the direction of acquainting the general reader and the specialist in American history with the names, thoughts, and actions of some women intellectuals and activists. A further restriction also prevails: this study concerns itself primarily with American women who consciously thought, wrote, and acted in an effort to elevate the status of women or to explore the dilemma of women. Included are selected women writers and feminist intellectuals who groped and struggled with the narrow definition of woman's role imposed by society. The women of this century who transcended cultural taboos and assumed roles designated as "male" (and there were many of these) are not treated, precisely because they privately resolved their dilemmas according to societal precepts. Whether they married and had a successful career or whether they became unmarried professionals, they operated within the cultural standards of our society.

Only those women who agonized externally, who shared their concerns with others, who organized similarly disposed women, and who wrote down their thoughts are the subjects of this historical study. And even all these self-conscious women cannot be adequately treated. Hopefully, this study will be the beginning—however modest, partial, and tentative—of a fuller, more comprehensive treatment of women leaders, thinkers, and writers. Some attention will also be given to the interaction between the feminists and the times in which they lived: the feminist response, like all reform responses, has been very much affected by the climate of opinion of the period in which they lived. Thus the thoughts, programs, and plans of the feminists of the twenties are different from those of the sixties. The movers and shakers described in this book reacted to, and acted upon, the particular environment in which they lived.

I would like to take this opportunity to acknowledge some of my debts: to the National Endowment for the Humanities for a research grant for the year 1971-1972 that enabled me to work on this study; to Northeastern Illinois University for a sabbatical leave during 1971-1972; to the archivists of Wayne State University library for their aid and cooperation in my study of the Mary Heaton Vorse papers; to a number of graduate students whose research and discussion aided me greatly: Ellen Sherman, Paula Pfeffer, Dorothy Cizmar, Corinne Goldstick, Ruth Aronson, Jeanette Blum, and Paul Linzer; and, finally, to Anne Saberman, Joan Allman, and Paula Wolf for their careful typing of the manuscript.

MOVERS
AND SHAKERS

1

The Feminist View

SO LONG AS ANY WOMAN IS DENIED THE RIGHT TO HER
OWN LIFE AND HAPPINESS, NO MAN HAS A RIGHT TO
HIS; AND EVERY MAN WHO WALKS FREELY IN HIS
MAN'S WORLD, WALKS ON AN IRON FLOOR, WHERE-
UNDER, BOUND AND FLUNG INTO HER DUNGEON, LIES A
WOMAN-SLAVE.
    —Floyd Dell, "Confessions of a Feminist Man"

NO MORE MAN'S OUTWORN CHIVALRY WHERE ASKED,
BUT EQUAL RIGHT TO LABOR AND BE FREE
TO LOVE BECAUSE OF LOVE, TO CHOOSE OUR TASK,
TO HALVE THE BURDENS OF HUMANITY.
    —Harry Kemp, "A Feminist Song"

Throughout recorded history, there have been women who
questioned the cultural definition imposed upon them. Abi-
gail Adams asked her husband John why women were not
included in the Declaration's famous statement, "All men
are created equal." Englishwoman Mary Wollstonecraft was
so inspired by the French Revolution that she wrote a fiery
document vindicating the rights of women. Indeed, a revolutionary time has always been a natural and logical time for
intelligent, sensitive women to wonder why the public fervor
for social justice and human equality never included their

1

sex. As women gained education, became conscious of other, similarly disposed women who shared their concerns, and were freed from frequent pregnancies—in other words, as women became part of the middle class in the Western world, and particularly in the United States— they organized, wrote charters, signed petitions, and demanded their rights as human beings. This did not occur, however, until well into the nineteenth century.

The force of the women's arguments was particularly apt in America; after all, this country was conceived precisely to grant liberty, freedom, and human rights to deprived Englishmen. And yet half the population was excluded from the fruits of victory. In the eyes of the law, American women were treated as chattels of their husbands or fathers; they received minimal instruction in the domestic arts from their mothers, and if they went to a formal school, it was for a short period of time *after* their brothers had been instructed. The institutions created in colonial America to deal with women fitted the cultural view of women: that is, that the main function and role of women were to be dutiful wives and mothers, subordinate to the commanding male in their lives. Cotton Mather, the famous and influential Puritan, sympathized with the husband who complained of a disobedient wife. God had surely punished this man, noted Mather. Duty, obedience, respect were the virtues taught to girls so that they would grow up to be pliant, obliging wives. Classical education was clearly unnecessary when this view prevailed. Indeed, a formal education that would raise a woman's self-image and increase her life expectations would hamper her performance as a wife and mother. It would create frustration, unfulfilled longings, and frequent headaches—for both sexes. Similarly, women did not need legal or political rights because their domain of life was the home and not the marketplace. Women could not manage business affairs, it was argued, and did not have the temperament or knowledge to participate in political matters. Thus the vote, property ownership, and the right to sit on juries were superfluous, if not actively harmful, for them.

There was an ample biblical and classical tradition to support this general view of womankind. Adam created Eve as a helpmate, but her wily nature caused unending grief, as did Pandora's curiosity in the Greek version of this myth. Children were essential to the continuation of the species; women were biologically (and, implicitly, culturally) equipped to produce and care for their own offspring; men were the hunters and providers. This is the way it had been in most human societies from time immemorial, and the English colonists, transplanted to a new world, did not believe that the basic pattern needed changing. Englishmen all knew that talk of woman's equality and natural rights was not to be taken literally. After all, no one thought that Indians (or later black slaves) were included in the category of equality, so surely women and children could be excluded as well. "Woman's place" became the accepted and approved way of describing the wifely and motherly roles of all women. If a young woman was unfortunate enough not to find a mate, she was labeled a spinster, lived in her father's or her brother's house, helped with the children, and possibly taught school. The spinster's life was considered incomplete and unfulfilled, but she did service to the community and she endured— whether in quiet desperation or not is unknown.

The industrial revolution significantly altered the woman's general life style in the nineteenth century. With the tremendous increase in machine production, in the creation of factories, and in the growth of urban, industrial centers, many skilled tasks formerly performed in the home were moved to factories, bringing the labor (women) with them. More important, perhaps, than women's working in factories (most of them were young, unmarried girls), was the creation of an enlarged, leisured middle and upper class. The stage was being set for the emergence of the middle-class model of what an American woman should be: educated, but not too educated; a dabbler in society's affairs through participation in charitable and cultural organizations; and a dutiful wife and mother who still defined wifehood and motherhood as her primary reasons for being, although many of her traditional chores had been relegated to the school and other social institutions.

The freedom afforded by industrialization enabled a small portion of the female middle class, its most energetic and moralistic portion, to become reformers. Abolitionism attracted them in the pre-Civil War decades, as did prison and educational reform. Temperance and suffrage, after 1865, also consumed the energies of women crusaders. As a result of their reforming activities, the role of women in American society became a much-talked-about and discussed subject—both by women participants and by wary nonparticipants. The more involved women became in society's affairs, the more they witnessed major injustices against themselves as women, as well as against various other deprived groups. Women reformers defied the traditional definition of woman, and by their actions they brought into question society's long-standing view of woman's role.

Thus a whole way of life, centuries old, was challenged seriously and vigorously for the first time in human history. Many nineteenth-century feminists, of course, did not fully realize the drastic importance of industrialization; they did not envision the tremendous possibilities resulting therefrom. The most venturesome did, and talked about collective living arrangements, birth control, women being given equal opportunity with men, and so on. But these women were considered visionaries, eccentrics, and radicals—hardly desirable labels for ladies. Although the term "cultural lag" was not invented until the 1920's, America in the nineteenth century was experiencing a cultural lag that would deepen, broaden, and be accentuated in the twentieth. For cultural attitudes did not change to accommodate, or even take cognizance of, the new reality. Thus a mammoth paradox resulted: the material conditions for women's equality came into being and the egalitarian rhetoric already existed, but the rhetoric failed to materialize into desirable reality. This gap became even more apparent—in fact, dramatic—by the mid-twentieth century, but it had been established early in the nineteenth.

Women shared the traditional attitudes with men; that is,

the majority did. There were, however, a minority of women, like the minority of men, who believed that society's provisions were unjust, inadequate, and improper for their sex. They tried to broaden the definition of woman's role, but with little success. The growing number of women who joined women's clubs in the last third of the nineteenth century more nearly typified the paradoxical status of American women: they had more freedom, but they used it in culturally approved and limited ways. Ostensibly, they were spending more time away from home, they were more aware of the greater world around them, and they displayed a greater independence than their ancestors had. But they were not feminists. They took advantage of their newfound leisure to improve their minds and to socialize with like-minded women. They did not deign to enter any profession in great numbers, to extend their formal education, or to alter their basic life style. They simply wanted to enlarge, in a modest way, their horizons and their understanding of the world in which they lived. They wanted "culture," a trait always attributed to women, the civilizers and domesticators of mankind. The women's desire to read and write romantic fiction, to hear an interesting lecture, and to become informed—in a genteel fashion, of course—about world problems was considered respectable and proper; in fact, it was a sign of distinction, of having achieved the desired status of middle or upper class.

Thus the emancipation gained from industrialization was an illusory one. Harmless and useless, but time-consuming, activities replaced the socially constructive and useful chores women had traditionally performed in the home. Instead of making their families' clothes, women attended lectures on the latest piece of romantic fiction. This pastime occupied the mainstream of middle-class women at the turn of the century. There were, however, at least two groups of middle-class women who used their free time in other ways: one group were the "organization" women, and the smaller group were the "feminists."

There were three major women's organizations that interested the organization women: the National American Women's Suffrage Association, the Women's Christian Temperance Union, and the amalgam of women's clubs known as the General Federation of Women's Clubs. None of these organizations were feminist in philosophy or program. None wanted to redefine the role of woman; none argued that woman was first a human being and second a member of the female sex capable of many things, including motherhood and wifehood. The first two of these women's groups had specific goals in mind: suffrage and temperance. Recent historians, such as Anne Scott, have argued quite convincingly that the WCTU, for example, had comprehensive goals and did a great deal to create social consciousness among women. In the early twentieth century, however, the goals had narrowed; each believed that the fulfillment of its goal would lead to the millennium. Each considered that the successful completion of its program would mean the material improvement of the human species.

If women could vote, argued the suffragists, the quality of politics would be elevated considerably; poverty and social evils would disappear; good men would become our representatives in government; and peace would prevail on earth. If the evil of drink were eliminated, contended the temperance workers, goodness and virtue would reign supreme; workingmen would respect their wives; children would not be neglected; and all would be well. None of the basic institutions needed revision, according to most suffragists and temperance workers. Neither did the role of woman have to be changed. Although some suffragists did believe that women's suffrage would lead inevitably to women's legal, educational, and economic equality, they did not examine the full import of this possibility. Some temperance workers, most notably the early and forceful leader Frances Willard, were socialists, but by the twentieth century conservatism had taken over the WCTU. The General Federation of Women's Clubs, on the other hand, was a loose amalgam of women's groups, many of which were devoted solely to providing women with a degree of sociability.

Although these organizations were exclusively the domain

of the female sex, they did not pursue feminist goals. They subscribed to the culture's dominant view that women, as the perpetuators of life and culture, should exercise a high moral tone and should work for temperance, cultural uplift, and spiritual goals. Within this same frame of reference, the suffragists argued that voting women would raise the level of politics and guarantee truly representative democracy. They never believed that the family structure needed alteration or that marriage should be questioned as a desirable mode of living for all men and women. They never discussed the indiscreet subject of female sexuality or questioned openly the seeming lack of control women had over the number of children they produced. God's, and man's, will prevailed.

The suffragists often found themselves in a most difficult position: if they claimed too much for their cause—that is, if they said that voting women would reform humanity—they had a mighty task to accomplish; on the other hand, if they said that voting women would not materially change the body politic, then why all the fuss and bother? The suffragist never effectively resolved this dilemma. Perhaps many of them did not know precisely why women should vote; some, of course, argued simply and forcefully that adult women should vote because they had the same natural rights as adult men. Ultimately, this was the most logical and truthful position to take, but it was hard to convince men of the validity of the argument, so suffragists found themselves making other claims that were more difficult to fulfill and verify.[1]

The minority category, made up of the few women who were feminists, considered the larger issues. But they were the minority of a minority; they were the few women, inside or outside women's organizations (some feminists were also organization women, although most organization women were not feminists), who challenged the established truths and in so doing were often censured and ostracized. For example, the great nineteenth-century feminist leader, Elizabeth Cady Stanton, found women willing to work with her to obtain suffrage, but not to discuss, let alone work for, reforming divorce laws or to question the institution of marriage. The feminists, therefore, then and now, remained the smallest group, the most radical, and the most comprehensive in their criticism of America's behavior toward women. However, as the following chapters will demonstrate, there was a wide spectrum of opinion within the feminist minority. There were radical feminists who saw the woman's problem from the point of view of the class struggle and class analysis; others who took a sexist viewpoint and considered all women similarly oppressed; still others were pragmatists who worked for women's rights within women's organizations. All the feminists, however, differed from the dominant women's groups, as well as the mainstream of American women, in their basic questioning of the culture's definition of them. While the traditional clubwomen accepted their wifely and motherly roles as eminently valid, the feminists criticized the constricting quality of these roles.

Indeed, at the turn of the century, a growing number of middle-class young ladies who graduated from college wrestled with the question, "What was the purpose of my advanced education?" And it was largely from this group that the next generation of feminists emerged. The elite of women's colleges—Bryn Mawr, Vassar, Wellesley, and Smith—produced the bulk of women who worked in the Henry Street Settlement House in New York and other similar institutions in New England.[2] The newly emerging group of college-educated women in the early 1900's wanted to do something with their advanced education, and the answer from their elders that a classical education would make them better mothers sounded hollow and unconvincing. Diapering and cooing to a baby did not require a proficiency in Latin. So many of these women came to New York City and found enough social causes to occupy a lifetime. Lillian Wald found immigrant mothers who knew nothing of child care. Grace Abbott discovered in Chicago that newly arrived immigrants were vulnerable to every shrewd manipulator. Jane Addams found that collecting garbage in slum neighborhoods required a mammoth political effort. Unconsciously in many cases, these women plunged into reform movements, organized votes, wrote propaganda pamphlets, and tried to use their advanced education and privileged economic position to help those less fortunate than themselves. They were moralists and idealists who believed literally in their responsibility to help their fellow human beings improve their earthly lot.

In pursuing their specific causes, they often found that one obstacle was insurmountable: their sex. Being a woman, much to their amazement, was cause for suspicion, if not hostility, from both exploiters and exploited. Immigrant men were not accustomed to listening to women's advice; establishment bosses surely did not defer to their wives in business matters and saw no reason to change their habits. Thus some of these crusading women came to consider, question, and discuss the role of women in social affairs. They found that this issue had to be settled before they could get on with their particular crusading projects. They became, therefore, feminists in spite of themselves. They had unconsciously accepted their right to participate in all human affairs. When they found that this right was not naturally accepted by many men, *and* women, they had to fight for it, justify it, and defend it. And so they did. Jane Addams discussed and advocated suffrage and female equality after she saw, through her experience at Hull-House, how women were treated and the potential power that voting women could have in the political arena. So a whole group of reform-minded, college-educated women became feminists out of pragmatic necessity. They saw their efforts discounted because they were women; they saw women being badly mistreated; and they viewed the men's handling of all matters as shoddy and immoral. Active and equal women became, then, an imperative if the quality of life in twentieth-century America was to be improved.

Often feminists were drawn from among the educated middle-class young women who personally experienced discrimination in their quest for professional opportunities. Some of them—though not all, of course—developed a heightened awareness of, and sensitivity to, woman's potentialities once they had realized their own potential. Women writers such as Fannie Hurst and Pearl Buck, for example, did not experience discrimination simply because they were women. Their writings were judged by literary standards; perhaps because theirs was a profession that had long occupied women, they did not encounter prejudice. But be that as it may, their success made them contemplate the plight of their sisters. Were all women being given equal opportunity? Were women being admitted to the medical profession as readily as to the literary guilds? How were women in general treated in this country? Misses Hurst and Buck asked and answered these questions in some of their writings. They continued to pursue their professional careers while devoting some attention to the larger woman problem. Many professional women, no doubt, followed this model; they continued to practice their careers while giving time, attention, and energy to the women's movement.

In the early years of this century, the few women who considered themselves feminists found that some urban communities in America harbored like-minded people. Greenwich Village, the bohemian center of New York City, and the Hull-House neighborhood in Chicago, for example, offered communities of men and women (in the case of Greenwich Village) and a community of women (in the case of Hull-House) that espoused and/or sympathized with feminist goals. Max Eastman, a self-proclaimed male feminist living in the Village during the 1910's, marched in suffrage parades and advocated women's equality in every domain, such as economic independence, birth control, and a single moral standard. Jane Addams, for many young college-educated women, was a living example of what a woman could do. To some young girls who aspired to a life other than wifehood and motherhood, Greenwich Village and Chicago were utopias. Writer Susan Glaspell left Des Moines, Iowa, and Neith Boyce left California for the Village because for them the myth of freedom for women and of an experimental, exciting life style was compelling and infinitely alluring. The uniqueness of Greenwich Village for feminism was that it provided not only a community of philosophically sympathetic people but also a group of practicing feminists. Here the middle-class, educated young woman could live according to her own lights. She could share an abode with a young man without benefit of marriage, if she so chose; she could go to law school (in the early years of this century) without having a college degree or encountering highly restrictive admission policies; she could act, dance, paint, sculpt, work as a sales clerk or in a factory or office—in short, her life options seemed to be many. The companionship was congenial, the city offered multiple possibilities of diversion and employment, and the Village was beyond the reach of parental supervision.

At the turn of the century, the "new woman" became a frequently used term in contemporary magazines to describe the leisured, educated upper- and middle-class woman as well as the organization woman. It was a broad term, encompassing many different kinds of women—the essential point in the definition being the changed life style of the American woman, especially the younger middle-class woman. She had more schooling, was economically and socially independent, was more aware of the world's opportunities and problems, and, if she was single, was living in the growing apartment houses of the big cities. This freedom, as already suggested, was more apparent than real; most of the better educated young women assumed the culture's values and returned to the home after college. The fact that more women were working was heralded as a sign of progress, but a close examination of the records might have shown that more women were working for less money in a discriminating business world. But as one sympathetic magazine writer of the day pointed out, the younger generation of suffragists (another label often used interchangeably for the "new" or "emancipated" woman), wanted to make life more attractive and reasonable for women. They were not bent upon dragging women down to the men's level, but rather wanted to make life equitable, moral, and interesting to both sexes. The younger suffragists, the author continued, were often feminists; they saw the vote as the means to a larger end, "that end being a complete social revolution."[3] Typically, the writer did not elaborate on

how or when the revolution would occur; rather she hoped
that sympathetic readers would work toward its success.

"I wanted all the freedom, all the opportunity, all the equality there was in the world. I wanted to belong to the human
race, not to a ladies' aid society to the human race."[4] So
stated Rheta Childe Dorr, a newspaperwoman, magazine
writer, suffragist, and trade union sympathizer. Miss Dorr
typified the "new woman"-feminist of this century. She came
from a small town in Nebraska, read Ibsen's *Doll's House*,
heard Elizabeth Cady Stanton and Susan B. Anthony speak
when she was twelve years old, and became convinced that a
woman's life in America had serious drawbacks. After an
ill-fated marriage, she went to New York with her young
son in 1898 to begin anew. Years of struggle followed; the
newspaper business did not admit women as eagerly and
openly as they greeted young men. Good qualifications and
merit were superfluous. City editors reminded her that men
had to work all their lives while she was just biding her time
until she married again. Indeed, this attitude prevailed among
most young men and women. Miss Dorr experienced great
frustration when she saw young immigrant girls move from
job to job without becoming members of the Women's Trade
Union League. "What's the difference?" each girl said. "I'm
going to get married anyhow."[5] The lack of a common unity
among all women, which Miss Dorr witnessed, became one
of the major blocks in the feminist effort. How could the few
self-conscious feminists change men's minds when most wom-
en agreed with the men? How could working-class girls be
made aware of their common link with middle-class, educated
women? The new feminists of the middle class spoke about
women's needs and goals as if all women had a conscious perception of their shared problem. But all women did not intuit,
read, or see the problem as the same one. Miss Dorr and the
leadership of the Women's Trade Union League found the
factory girls uneasy and unpredictable allies.

The restless quest for freedom, felt in the hearts and minds
of a growing number of middle-class young women, was not
shared by all members of their sex. The "new woman" phe-

nomenon was a class, not a sex, characteristic. Further, not even all female members of the emerging middle class shared a world-view. As the opening pages of this introduction suggest, many organization women had limited goals for their work; many had private aims, not social ones. Many defined the problem of women as easily solvable: the vote became the key to true equality. Most of them never thought in terms of a social revolution, contrary to the popular magazine writer quoted earlier. Most believed that marriage, a home, and children were natural life goals for all women, but that economic and educational opportunities should be available to those women interested in pursuing them. How the problem of combining marriage and a full-time career would be effectively solved, with everyone benefiting and no one suffering, was not considered by the majority of women. Only the minority, the feminists, confronted this problem head on and offered solutions.

The preservers of the status quo, in 1900 as in 1970, of course saw every secretary, every clubwoman, and every professional woman as a vital destroyer of the home and family. The growing number of working women was immediately correlated with the growing divorce rate. The earlier traditionalists decried the activities of the suffragists, lamented the increase in women lawyers and doctors, and generally shook their heads in dismay when they read newspaper advertisements describing time-saving devices for the home that would free women from drudgery and household chores. The increasing number of typists and factory girls frightened the moralists. Staunch males, they believed, would be tempted by their pretty secretaries into illicit relationships and their husbands' fidelity would wither away.

Anti-suffrage organizations (with both male and female members prior to 1919) worked feverishly to prevent women from receiving the vote. Conservative newspapers, including the respected *New York Times* in the early years of this century, printed stories about the most radical feminists, only to have irate women readers write letters of rebuttal, stinging with indignation. "Who wants to leave the home?" cried

Mrs. Average Woman. "I am content to be in my comfortable house, away from the hurly-burly world of business." Thus, while activist women claimed that victory for their particular cause would lead to the millennium, the conservatives warned that the success of feminism would end Western civilization. Ultimately, of course, both groups were wrong. The acquisition of women's political, legal, and economic rights did not materially alter the society; neither did it lower the quality of life.

How have feminists, that small number of self-conscious culture critics, analyzed the woman problem in the twentieth century? What solutions have they proposed? Before considering these weighty questions, it is necessary to reflect upon the larger philosophical problem of discussing the woman problem as if the female sex were a monolithic group with common characteristics, thoughts, and behavior patterns. Feminists recognized the difficulty of dealing with such a generalization, but proceeded to speak in abstract terms (as did their antagonists) because not to have done so would have resulted in a total breakdown of their argument. Once you grant that women can be categorized according to class, religion, and social background, just like men, you destroy the whole sexist basis of the claim. The power and force of the feminist argument rests upon the fact that the entire female sex is affected by the cultural patterns devised for it; all classes of women are expected to behave in socially approved ways. The roles defined for women by the American culture, with little deviation, apply equally to Mrs. Vanderbilt and the black cleaning lady.

Further, the feminists rest their philosophy upon another crucial and classic foundation: the "natural rights" school of thinking. Just as eighteenth-century philosophers argued that all men have natural and inalienable rights, so feminists have extended the argument by saying that the same theory applies to women. Natural-rights theory transcends all cultural restraints; man-made values imposed upon one sex cannot contradict or interfere with fundamental human rights.

The feminists insist that when a culture develops living patterns, set roles and social expectations that inhibit, contradict, or violate the natural rights granted to all members of the species *homo sapiens,* the culture's artificial impositions must be removed. This has become the persistent theme in all feminist writings. While pointing out the fallibility of cultural values, the feminists emphasize the infallibility of natural rights. Cultures can change, adapt, and accommodate themselves to changing realities. Thus, the feminists argue, the new urban, industrial America that emerged in the nineteenth century and was fully developed in the twentieth requires a complete reexamination and revamping of traditional behavior patterns and values that are no longer relevant to the new material world that now exists.

The feminist viewpoint, resting upon this basic foundation, has not changed significantly during our century. Feminists of the 1910's defined the problem in much the same terms as did feminists of the 1960's. There has been a difference in emphasis as well as range and language, but the perspectives are more often similar than different. Another common approach to feminist thought can be described in the dualistic terms in which many social issues are debated: nature versus nurture. That is, there were (and are) feminists who believed that women's nature is more like men's than not and that it is man-made culture (nurture) that has been the determining factor. Woman's biology, according to the "feminist-nurturist" view, does not inherently prevent her from becoming a doctor, an engineer, or a steamfitter. Woman's biology does not preempt her right to vote, make business decisions, and play tennis or handball. Rather, it is the culture's values, man-made values, that have restricted woman's freedom of expression. According to this analysis, the male-dominated culture has chosen, consciously or unconsciously, to limit woman's societal role to wifehood and motherhood, and the laws and customs of the society have been designed to guarantee her fulfillment of these roles and no others.

The feminists who adhere to this school of thought, however, often also assign unique qualities to women. It is not uncommon to hear members of the current generation of women liberationists talk about woman's special gift for bringing peace to the world, harmony to humankind, and disarmament to the world powers. Woman's nature, combined with her particular nurture, makes her especially well suited to solve problems of race, militarism, and violence. Woman's training in the home, her patience, her ability to cooperate and compromise enables her to deal with complex worldly problems. Roxanne Dunbar, whose article "Female Liberation as the Basis for Social Revolution" (1970) is a key statement of women liberationists, argues that community is a female institution, unknown to men. In her survey of early human history, she explains how the male hunters had little experience in political governing. "The experience of the hunter had led him to value dominance; he had become unsuited for living as equals in the community, because he knew only how to overpower and conquer the prey." With Marx, Lenin, and Engels providing the framework for her remarks, Miss Dunbar went on to develop the thesis that women—conscious, liberated women—are best equipped to lead the socialist revolution. Hence the feminists who share her view of the male-dominated, capitalistic culture may deride the corrupt culture men have created, but they still accept the idea of woman's "differentness." The fundamental distinction, of course, between their view and the traditional "nature" school of thinking is in the interpretation of what precisely woman is best equipped for; motherhood, answers the traditionalist, while the new feminists cry revolution.

Given the fact that women, too, are products of the culture, it does make eminently good sense to assume that they have been taught specific behavioral traits that prepare them for their life in the home. A mother must be patient, long suffering, and a good arbitrator. A wife must learn to defer to her husband's and children's will on many occasions. Because she is a creator of life (and this is an argument long made by feminists), woman respects life and abhors violence. "I Didn't Raise My Son to Be a Soldier" was a popular First World War song. Thus many members of the current generation of feminists hold that woman's personality and training make her best able to deal with modern society's problems.

The antifeminists, in contrast, have been generally committed to the "nature" view of woman. They have described, in both prose and poetry, woman's ephemeral nature, her mystical temperament, and her soft characteristics. Even when they have glorified and romanticized her traits, they have restricted her range of options. Freud, a late nineteenth-century contributor to the "nature" school of thought, contended that anatomy determined destiny. Therefore, women were naturally equipped to be mothers and those who strove for worldly activities were guilty of penis envy and were frustrated in their natural role definition. Prior to Freud, of course, there had been a long, respected tradition of viewing motherhood as the primal experience of a woman's life and her major reason for being. Woman, after all, has always been the producer of life, and this essential fact became the central definition of her social role.

Until well into the nineteenth century, knowledge about birth control was quite primitive; women were pregnant often and the maternal role consumed most of their daily lives. Thus there was adequate reason for men and women to assume that women's biological and cultural role was one and the same. The "nature" view of woman, of course, has continued to have adherents well into the twentieth century, when birth-control knowledge and technology have altered woman's life possibilities considerably.

In the early years of this century, two women, Ida Tarbell, the famous muckraker, and Charlotte Perkins Gilman, the feminist philosopher, epitomized the polar opposite points of view. Miss Tarbell, although herself a reporter and vigorous investigator of social ills for the popular magazines of the day, supported the traditional "nature" view of women. "To bear and to rear, to feel the dependence of man and child . . .," she contended, were the meaningful womanly roles. Women who had "bachelors' souls," as she put it, have always existed, "but they are not the women upon whom society depends; they are not the ones who build the nation."[6] Ostensibly, Miss

Tarbell considered herself an anomaly, a woman with a bachelor soul, who did not follow the natural rhythms of the female life. The exceptional woman existed in every age, but she was not the one upon whom society depended.

Mrs. Gilman, on the other hand, who wrote prolifically from the 1890's well into the 1920's, developed the first systematic analysis of the feminist position. She reviewed human cultures in a sweeping fashion, and concluded that in androcentric—that is male-centered—cultures women were always relegated to the domestic chores. Men had discovered, quite early in the human game, that they could dominate women; and women, in turn, had learned that their sexual attractiveness would secure for them a mate. "Wealth, power, social distinction, fame—not only these, but home and happiness, reputation, ease and pleasure, her bread and butter,— all must come to her through a small gold ring."[7] Woman was economically dependent, intellectually dependent, dependent in every way. "Her backward condition is not due to any deficiency in race quality, either of mind or body; neither is it in any way connected with what used to be called 'the disabilities of sex,' but which we are beginning to recognized (sic) as abilities not dis-abilities."[8]

Although Mrs. Gilman shared with Miss Tarbell a belief in the differentness of women in many ways and in the importance of the traditional womanly roles, she stressed the similarities between the sexes rather than the differences. Women may be more constructive and creative than men, the feminist philosopher contended, but in human qualities and power they are essentially like men. The contemporary feminists would share the essence of Mrs. Gilman's thought. They too condemn the male-determined culture and argue for women's equality. They agree that the woman's unique biology has been overemphasized at the same time that they join hands with their sisters of fifty years ago in believing that women do, in fact, have distinctive traits. To Mrs. Gilman it was a question of emphasis. But the feminists in all generations have found themselves vulnerable once they concede any worth to the "nature" argument. If women are different from men, in essential and significant ways, then society's institutional provisions to deal with these differences are proper. Of course, at this point in the argument, the feminists argue that the culture's arrangements are based *not* on real distinctions between the sexes but on artificial ones. Restricting women's admission to graduate and professional schools, the feminists note, goes beyond meaningful differences between the sexes. No, retorts the antifeminist; women Ph.D.'s and lawyers would neglect their wifely and motherly roles and in so doing thwart their natural roles. And so the argument goes.

The feminists who lived in Greenwich Village in 1910, as well as those who live there in the 1970's, recognized that basic institutions in society would require changing to accommodate their philosophy. Henrietta Rodman, a high school teacher of English and an early feminist leader, advocated as early as 1914 a new kind of living arrangement that would speak to the needs of professional working women. She suggested the construction of an apartment house that would be totally mechanized: an efficient kitchen serving the whole building would be located in the basement, and a rooftop schoolroom would provide schooling for preschool youngsters. Utilizing only professionals in each specialized capacity, the house would meet the needs of the professional woman who wanted a home, children, and a career. Although the apartment house was never built, Miss Rodman found sympathetic supporters in her Greenwich Village community. Of course many New Yorkers found her ideas ludicrous and her comments, quoted in *The New York Times,* outrageous; but this early feminist's ideas prophesied one crucial ingredient of the feminist philosophy: the need to rearrange the institution of the home to allow women greater opportunity for self-expression.

Miss Rodman contended, in one interview, that feminism's weak point was management of the preschool years of a child's life, when the mother was confined to the home. Middle-class career-minded mothers could not afford nurses, so some collective child-care arrangement was necessary to lib-

erate them from the home. Readers of the *Times* considered
Miss Rodman guilty of "monstrous egotism," but the few
feminists of the city shook their heads knowingly.[9] Feminists
in the 1960's and 1970's looked to Israel and Sweden for
models for new family institutions. To them the kibbutz,
symbol of the communal life style, and the sexually emancipated Swedish mode of living typified the direction the United
States and other Western cultures should take in freeing
themselves according to feminist precepts. The evidence is
not yet in as to the general success of these alternative institutions; however, the feminist perspective remains the same:
women cannot realize their human potential when their total
time and energy are devoted to motherhood and wifehood.

Many twentieth-century feminists also accepted the
Marxist-Leninist view of the woman problem. That is, they
followed the explanation first suggested by Marx, and then
promulgated by Lenin and Engels, on the origin of the family
and the role of women in capitalistic society. According to
this view, as soon as man, in the mythic past, acquired pos-
sessions, he wanted to be sure of his patrimony so that his
legitimate heirs would carry on his empire. Thus he attached
himself to one woman, insured his offsprings' legitimacy, and
established monogamy to protect his private property. While
many of the feminists of the 1910 generation did not hold this
doctrinaire position, they did argue that only in a socialist
state would women be treated equally. Using both the platform of the Socialist Party of America and the example of
the Bolshevik Revolution, they claimed that in a cooperative
state, where human beings were respected and cherished for
their innate worth, women would be treated equally.

The Socialist Party was the first political party in this
country to include suffrage as a plank in its platform. The
Bolshevik Revolution of 1917 proclaimed, among its significant changes, the emancipation of women. One socialist woman writer in 1919, who did accept the total thesis of Marxism,
noted that American women should be for suffrage but socialist women should not work for it. "The struggle today is a

class struggle. The reforms that might be procured by use of the ballot are insignificant and could only serve to patch up existing society. We Socialists don't want it patched."[10] While the less absolute feminists worked within the American system to pass desirable laws—suffrage, the freedom to distribute birth control information, and the end of legal and educational discrimination—the doctrinaire socialist-feminists wanted to work for the eventual revolution in America.

"Bearing in mind that it is the economic relations that determine the social relations . . .,"[11] the same writer observed, the solution to woman's servitude was economic liberation; Charlotte Perkins Gilman, although not a Marxist, agreed that economics was at the base of the issue. In contrast to the Marxist-feminists, however, Mrs. Gilman believed that the needed transformations could be accomplished within the capitalistic mold. Industrial efficiency, in fact, was one of her goals for the home. She viewed the factory, with its mass-production techniques, as being the desirable model for the revolutionized home. "The home, as now existing, costs three times what is necessary to meet the same needs. It involves the further waste of nearly half the world's labor. It maintains a low grade of womanhood, overworked or lazy."[12] If women were to be economically liberated, the home had to be reorganized according to mass-production methods. She envisioned collective kitchens, laundry areas, and nurseries to do each specialized task in the home more efficiently and expertly. Henrietta Rodman's idea for a feminist apartment house, in fact, was based upon Mrs. Gilman's views. Only in a collective home, the feminist philosopher argued, could women free themselves from inefficient, time-consuming domestic chores; only in this way could they become productive human beings.

To the Marxists, capitalism could not be reformed or modified. Only through a total revolution could the profit system, the capitalists, and private property be removed and replaced with a community of equals, of collective ownership, of work according to ability and merit, and of reward according to need. Day nurseries to care for children, communal living arrangements, birth-control methods easily available, and all adults fulfilling useful and socially constructive jobs became the Marxist-feminist solution to the woman problem. Women in the home, who are actually exploited labor, would no longer exist. All women would work according to their talents and predilections. Everyone would serve herself and society to the fullest. Life roles would not be based upon sex but rather upon the country's needs and the citizen's talents. This was the utopia envisioned by many twentieth-century feminists.

Margaret Benston, a contemporary feminist writer, has outlined the causes of women's oppression within the Marxist framework.[13] Her underlying premise is that women work outside the money economy in a culture where money is the major determiner of value. Work within the home, she continues, although socially significant, is not valued because it is not paid for. Women are unrespected, unpaid workers. They are severely exploited and enter the labor market only in marginal ways. They do not occupy positions of power and influence and will not be freed until they can do so. However, the present capitalistic structure would not pay women who perform domestic services, do not need them in the labor force, and do not want to alter the basic institutions of society.

Miss Benston concludes that the transition from the present profit motive system of production to a collective one will require a revolution; "our task is to make sure that revolutionary changes in the society do in fact end women's oppression."[14] Collectivizing the functions of the home is an essential part of her view of what the feminist revolution must include. Her 1969 article does not present views that differ significantly from Mrs. Gilman's and Miss Rodman's, published in the 1910's. With or without the Marxist vocabulary, feminists of this century have envisioned collective home arrangements as a necessary precondition for woman's emancipation. The feminists, contrary to the comments of their critics, never believed in choosing *between* marriage and a career; they believed in both and they argued that both could be accomplished in a society that cooperated rather than competed.

In the Marxist analysis of the woman problem, class, rather than sex, is emphasized. That is, the proletarian class, the working class, is seen as the exploited group; while the middle class, obtaining some rewards, acts as the middleman, keeping the lower class in line and accruing profits for the handful of rich at the top. Women, according to this view, are an exploited class—not only the working-class woman but also the economically dependent and unequally treated middle- and upper-class woman. Using their sexual charm to snare men, since it is their only weapon in a discriminatory, capitalistic society, women are used and misused constantly. In this way the Marxist argument attempts to embrace both the "nature" and the "nurture" positions. Woman's physical nature prevents her from asserting herself with men; and her sexual nature becomes her only tool in a repressive culture that is based upon selfish male values. The "nurture," that is, the capitalistic culture, is the culprit that must be transformed into a more humane, ethical culture, one based upon egalitarianism and liberty, in order to achieve the communist society.

This point of view assumes that human culture can be transformed into something radically different from what it is at present. Further, it assumes that the same human beings who built a superstructure of greed, discrimination, and injustice are capable of producing a just, ethical society, one based upon positive, cooperative values. How the dramatic and radical change of attitudes will be performed is not described. How men and women, conditioned by a male-dominated value system, will shake off their cultural shackles and adopt a more perfect perspective is not predicted. Moreover, from the evidence gathered so far about the behavior of socialist states, as opposed to capitalistic ones, it is not at all clear that female exploitation is the monopoly of capitalistic societies. Discrimination against women, by placing them in subservient positions and upholding male, militaristic virtues, seems to characterize all societies. Thus the seeming connection between capitalism and female oppression is not borne out by the evidence.

Cooperation, in fact, does not seem to be the unique personality and character trait of either sex. Greed, similarly, does not seem to be entirely the attribute of men. Hence the feminists who assign key virtues to women and major evils to men are describing a desired ideal rather than reality. On the level of economic organization, the same charge can be made. Collective societies, where the means of production and distribution have been centralized and communalized, may in theory eliminate hierarchy, privilege, and discrimination; but, in practice, status differences, class differences, and sex differences often still prevail.[15] This is a fact that many contemporary feminists, including Margaret Benston, have come to realize. Socialist states may become a haven for feminists, if they live up to their own ideals, but it is not inevitable that socialism will produce sexual equality. Idealists in every age focus upon human goodness, diversity, and imagination. They emphasize the human potential for positive achievements rather than the negative traits of man. The radical feminists see sexual exploitation as an inevitable product of capitalism; because the private-enterprise profit system emphasizes individual accumulation and achievement, at the expense of social values, the majority are repressed and manipulated. Women, being a naturally vulnerable group, become the major objects of repression. Thus, according to logic and faith (but not necessarily empirical reality), a cooperative economic order *should* eliminate the restrictions imposed upon the defenseless majority.

Before the culture as a whole can operate along feminist lines, however, all shades of feminism have to unite to pursue the common goal. Often the class analysts and the sex analysts have clashed, and in-fighting has considerably weakened the woman movement. Charlotte Perkins Gilman, in a 1912 poem entitled "The Socialist and the Suffragist," captured the internal dispute within feminism and offered a solution:

The Socialist and the Suffragist

Said the Socialist to the Suffragist:
  "My cause is greater than yours!
  You only work for a Special Class.
  We for the gain of the General Mass.
  Which every good ensures!"

Said the Suffragist to the Socialist:
  "You underrate my Cause!
  While women remain a Subject Class.
  You never can move the General Mass.
  With your Economic Laws!"

Said the Socialist to the Suffragist:
  "You misinterpret facts!
  There is no room for doubt or schism
  In Economic Determinism—
  It governs all our acts!"

Said the Suffragist to the Socialist:
  "You men will always find
  That this old world will never move
  More swiftly in its ancient groove
  While women stay behind!"

"A lifted world lifts women up,"
  The Socialist explained.
  "You cannot lift the world at all
  While half of it is kept so small,"
  The Suffragist maintained.

The world awoke, and tartly spoke:
  "Your work is all the same:
  Work together or work apart,
  Work, each of you, with all your heart—
  Just get into the game!"[16]

"The root of the discontent in American women is that they are too well educated."[17] So wrote Pearl Buck in 1938 in a very perceptive essay on women. Miss Buck's views offer another interesting way of organizing and analyzing the woman problem in the twentieth century. Sensitive to the power of each culture to shape its attitudes toward people, Miss Buck found, upon comparing the American culture with the Japanese, that America was as backward in its treatment of women as was the Japanese. Contrary to the popular American view of individualism and egalitarianism, women were relegated to a second-class status and deprived of equal opportunity in every area of life. However, in Japan women were trained from childhood on to be content with their inferior status. Thus there were no discontented Japanese women, while American women, raised on the rhetoric of equality, felt frustration as adults because the reality was one of inequality.

"Of one thing I am sure," the famous novelist said.

> There will be no real content among American women unless they are made and kept more ignorant or unless they are given equal opportunity with men to use what they have been taught. And American men will not be really happy until their women are.[18]

Either American culture should train its girl children from infancy on to be subservient, she continued, and to recognize the place males establish for them, or the culture should train its girl children to be equal to boys, offer them the same life goals, and give them the opportunity to fulfill their human potential. American society suffers from equivocation. Peace and contentment can come to both sexes if honesty replaces hypocrisy.

Miss Buck's beliefs, of course, showed an awareness of the culture-boundedness of our view of women and shared with the feminists the conviction that human beings can indeed change the values and roles they have believed in and practiced. During the twentieth century, America has increased its commitment to women in numerous ways: more women are going to school, more are working, and more are participating in civic and cultural affairs than ever before. These facts would seem to suggest a narrowing of the gap between the rhetoric of equality and its practice. However, a look at statistics demonstrates the equivocal nature of the American commitment. In the opening years of this century, of every one hundred girls who lived to be twenty-five, eighty-seven married. Wifehood and motherhood was the major lifework of most women. It still is; in 1963, over 90 percent of all women in their thirties had been married.

Marriage, of course, has not prevented many young women from working before they marry or in the early years of their marriage before children arrive. Further, many women return to the labor force after their children have grown up. Twenty percent of all women worked in 1910; the figure in 1970 was 43 percent. In 1910, women were present in the factories of America, in the offices, and in the schools. The average woman worker in 1920 was single and twenty-eight years old; in 1970, she was married and thirty-nine years old. Women professionals, then and now, were mainly schoolteachers. However—and this is one significant fact that has changed in a *negative* way—in 1910, 8.6 percent of the physicians in this country were women; today, the statistic is 7 percent. Similarly, women lawyers had already gained 3 percent of the profession's membership in the early years of the century, and they have not increased their percentage at all. Over 15 percent of all Ph.D.'s granted in 1920 were given to women; never before, nor since, have women matched this record. Rather than making steady progress during the century, women have lost ground in most of the professions.

The opening years of the twentieth century, therefore, seemed to portend all kinds of exciting possibilities for the American woman. She worked outside the home in growing numbers, entered professions, participated in the cultural life of the community, and seemed to be earning the term "new woman." Other social changes went hand in hand with the emerging woman; while only one marriage in fifteen ended in divorce in 1900, the figure was one in seven by 1920.

To the alarmists, of course, this signified the inevitable result of allowing women to abandon their traditional and sacred roles in society. Clearly, there was some kind of connection: women who became economically independent, or at least somewhat more independent, might well assert their right to independence. Men, too, especially in the growing middle class, found themselves more able to afford divorce. Thus divorce became more likely as the number of women wage earners increased. But other factors, not related to "woman's emancipation," also must be cited. The relaxing of religious bonds and customs and the movement to the cities, where social pressure is less stringent, have surely contributed to the divorce statistics.

Throughout this century, more young women have gone to school and increased their education. While only 20 out of every 100 girls were graduated from high school in 1920, 78 out of 100 were graduated in 1970. But the increase in education has *not* led concomitantly to an increase in occupational and professional opportunities. The recent outcries of many college-graduate feminists for equal opportunity are tied to the fact of their having been educated in a society that does not want or know how to use the educated talent it has created. As Pearl Buck suggested, if you educate women, you must accept the consequences. If a society does not want thoughtful or restless women, it should not teach them to read, write, or think. In 1900 and in 1970, women who work were and are treated as temporary workers; the comment made by a newspaper editor to Rheta Dorr, quoted earlier, continues to be made. Women will eventually marry and therefore should not be given responsible positions; they are taking the jobs that belong to men. Women have been paid less for the same jobs throughout the century and have been discriminated against in promotions. All these practices have continued because the cultural view of women has not changed significantly in seventy years. The material changes, the technological changes in our society have not resulted in changes of values and attitudes.

In 1900, knowledge about sex and birth control was very inadequate. Doctors rarely examined women, knew little about the reproductive system, and less about controlling conception. The Victorian moral code forbade women from discussing sex with anyone. The double standard of morality prevailed, and manly experience was desired and admired while feminine chastity was insisted upon. Medical technology has advanced greatly in seventy years. Birth-control methods are now known and proven effective. Women's anatomy and physiology are better understood. Yet many of the same attitudes still predominate. The so-called sexual revolution of the sixties, reminiscent of that of the twenties, has been more rhetorical than real. Popular views change slowly. Premarital sexual experience may be increasing among young women, but these very same girls usually choose marriage and a conventional life structure after their premarital affairs. It is still rare to see young people abandon the traditional modes of behavior. The hippie life style and communes received much popular coverage in the early 1970's, but it is not at all clear whether these phenomena have enough endurance to stand the test of time.

The classic feminist argument, as well as its utopian scenario, has not changed substantially in seventy years. The justness of the cause, the power of the claim, the urgency of the need—all remain. In this age of space trips, drug trips, cloning, the Pill, and female longevity, the feminist view appears more pressing and more pertinent than ever before. The following discussion will deal with selected women intellectuals in this century who have asked and answered some of the feminist questions touched upon in this introduction. The focus will be upon self-conscious American feminists whose world-view has been largely humanist in its outlook but has depended, in an essential and complete way, on the liberation of women. The few American women, the movers and shakers, who found their purpose in life less than satisfactory and defined the problem as a woman problem, rather than a personal one, are the subjects of the following pages.

Notes

1. For a detailed discussion of the suffrage movement, see Aileen Kraditor's *The Ideas of the Woman's Suffrage Movement, 1890-1920* (New York, Columbia University Press, 1965) and Eleanor Flexner's *Century of Struggle: The Woman's Rights Movement in the United States* (Cambridge, Mass., Harvard University Press, 1959).

2. See John Rousmaniere's "Cultural Hybrid in the Slums: The College Woman and the Settlement House, 1889-1894," *American Quarterly*, Spring 1970.

3. Winnifred Harper Cooley, "The Younger Suffragists," *Harper's Weekly*, 58 (September 27, 1913), 7-8.

4. Rheta Childe Dorr, *A Woman of Fifty*, 2nd ed. (New York, Funk and Wagnalls, 1924), p. 101.

5. *Ibid.*, p. 111.

6. Ida M. Tarbell, *The Business of Being a Woman* (New York, Macmillan, 1912), pp. 19, 242.

7. Charlotte Perkins Gilman, *Women and Economics* (New York, Harper and Row, 1966), pp. 71-72.

8. Gilman, *The Forerunner*, 2 (May 1911), 126.

9. For a further discussion of Henrietta Rodman, see Chapter Two.

10. Olive M. Johnson, *Woman and the Socialist Movement* (New York, Socialist Labor Party, 1919), p. 36.

11. *Ibid.*, p. 18.

12. Charlotte Perkins Gilman, *The Home, Its Work and Influence* (New York, Charlton Company, 1910), p. 320.

13. Margaret Benston, "The Political Economy of Women's Liberation," *Monthly Review*, September 1969, pp. 13-27.

14. *Ibid.*, p. 24.

15. See Kate Millett's discussion in *Sexual Politics* (New York, Doubleday, 1970), Chapter Four.

16. *Survey*, 27 (March 9, 1912), 1915.

17. Pearl S. Buck, "America's Medieval Women," *Harper's Magazine*, 177 (August 1938), 229.

18. *Ibid.*, p. 232.

2

Feminism in the Early Years, 1900-1920

FEMINISM, LIKE BOSTON, IS A STATE OF MIND. IT IS
THE STATE OF MIND OF WOMEN WHO REALIZE THAT
THEIR WHOLE POSITION IN THE SOCIAL ORDER IS AN-
TIQUATED, AS A WOMAN COOKING OVER AN OPEN FIRE
WITH HEAVY IRON POTS WOULD KNOW THAT HER EN-
TIRE HOUSEKEEPING WAS OUT OF DATE.

Rheta Childe Dorr, *A Woman of Fifty,* 1924

IF THE FEMINIST PROGRAM GOES TO PIECES ON THE
ARRIVAL OF THE FIRST BABY, IT IS FALSE AND USELESS.

—Crystal Eastman, 1920

Many young girls growing up in the opening years of this
century shared Mrs. Dorr's state of mind; they too felt that
feminism was the new, the appropriate, and the meaningful
point of view for their lives in this exciting time. They may
not have been sure what the precise ingredients of feminism
were or what specific or different life experiences were on
the horizon, but they knew, they *felt,* that life was going to
be different for them. All the signs, in fact, confirmed the
optimism of these young women: more were going to high
school and college, more were moving into the growing cities
of Chicago and New York, and more believed that the new
machinery, the products of industrialization, ordained a
freer, fuller life for women. The sewing machine, the type-

31

writer, the improved stove and washing machine all portended exciting opportunities for previously home-bound
women. In 1904, the newly elected president of the General
Federation of Woman's Clubs, Sarah Platt Decker of Denver,
effectively sounded the new tone in her acceptance speech:

> Ladies, you have chosen me your leader. Well, I
> have an important piece of news to give you. Dante
> is dead. He has been dead for several centuries, and
> I think it is time that we dropped the study of the
> Inferno and turned our attention to our own.[1]

Optimism reigned generally in the first fourteen years of
this century before a world war jarred everyone's consciousness. The reality of war indicated that infinite and inevitable
progress was not to be the future of the twentieth century.
The scenario of continued and continuous freedom for more
and more people in this best of all possible worlds was replaced with a vision of blood, constant turmoil, deception,
and struggle. But to American women—indeed to all people
prior to the Great War, as it came to be called—it seemed
certain that poverty could be eliminated, equal rights for all
minorities, including women, would be granted, and the
world would settle its disputes peaceably. Hopefulness was
the dominant tone in all the writings of women reformers.

Margaret Drier Robins, president of the National Women's
Trade Union League during part of this period, captured
the spirit of hope and of faith in progress; in a report describing the working conditions of women and children in
1911 she said: "The right arm for this work is union organization and the left arm is social and industrial legislation.
The two combined can abolish every industrial evil that
exists today. . . ."[2] The implicit assumption underlying this
statement is the possibility, if not the probability, that both
effective unionization (in a period when unions were being
cruelly suppressed) and social legislation could be realized
in the near future. By patient and continued effort, by sheer
perseverance, and by wholehearted dedication, women reformers believed all social evils could be eliminated.

A few enthusiastic males, who welcomed the new freedom

for women, shared their optimism and their belief that measurable progress had already been made and would continue to be made. Floyd Dell, a well-known Greenwich Village writer of the period, wrote a book in 1913 entitled *Woman as World Builders: Studies in Modern Feminism* that described the feminist movement as a *fait accompli*. *The Marriage Revolt* by William E. Carson (1915) was a sociological study of women's changing roles over the previous fifty years. According to Carson, the census reports on women working on jobs and in professions, the novels of the day, the divorce statistics, and the number of women in school— all confirmed the fact that a radical change had occurred in woman's status. Indeed, many critics pointed to the same evidence in lamenting the dramatic changes in woman's life style. In either case, however, they acknowledged that a change had occurred, and their view prevailed. Books with such titles as *The Awakening of Women* (1915) and *The Unrest of Women* (1913) became quite common. The twentieth century—or so thought social commentators as well as reformers in its early years—would see the complete emancipation of the American woman.

During these exciting and hopeful years, years in which everything seemed possible, a number of impressive women rose to leadership positions in the woman movement. Young women who wanted to participate in creating the new, egalitarian order joined a variety of women's organizations, each devoted to redressing a specific grievance suffered by women. Some became active members of the women's suffrage organization, others worked in settlement houses, and still others became active in the labor movement. There seemed to be so many choices, so many worthwhile groups to join, and so much good work to be done. And these young women, coming of age in the opening years of this century, wanted to be part of the woman movement. Some had become feminists like writer Rheta Childe Dorr, who, as a young girl, rebelled against the limited freedom accorded to women. Others had benefited from the educational opportunities open to women and then had to answer the question, "What was I educated for?"

If they were unfortunate enough not to marry early, they found themselves searching for an ideologically stimulating work experience. Jane Addams and many of her settlement house colleagues came to their work by this route. Still others were immigrant girls who came to America believing all the rhetoric they had heard and read about this country—only to find sweatshops, crowded slums, and a high infant mortality rate. Mary Anderson from Sweden and Emma Goldman from Russia are only two outstanding examples of this type; both came to this country at the age of sixteen and saw at first hand what labor conditions were like for the poor immigrants. As a result, they and many like them became union organizers, feminists, and sometimes Socialists.*

The women who signed suffrage petitions, hounded their Congressmen, and urged their sisters and neighbors to join their particular cause are far too many to be discussed individually—as indeed, are the articulate leaders of all the women's groups in America. Rather, I have chosen a few feminists—representing three categories: *general, radical,* and *pragmatic*—to demonstrate the kinds of women they were as well as the kinds of activities they carried on. Each feminist described in these pages had her unique view of feminism, although she shared a basic philosophy with others. Each, with her own particular expression and contribution, shaped the growing consciousness of American women.

GENERAL FEMINISTS

General feminists were few, but they were the precious few who set the tone, provided the total vision, and inspired the ranks. They were the women who saw the whole female sex as subjugated to the values imposed upon them by the

---

*This is not to say that some middle-class native American women did not join the labor movement. Margaret Dreier Robins came from a respectable, solidly American family, and Mary Heaton Vorse, whom I will describe later, fit into this latter category.

male culture. The general feminists adopted a sex-based analysis of the woman problem in America. In contrast to the radical feminists (to be discussed later), the general feminists saw poor and rich women, as well as black and white women, as the oppressed. Some portions of womankind might suffer more than others because of additional burdens placed upon them, but they all shared the common burden of womanhood. Charlotte Perkins Gilman, as historian Carl Degler has said, was the first comprehensive feminist philosopher in this country. As suggested in the first chapter, she contributed a significant foundation to feminist thought, as did one of her most ardent followers, Henrietta Rodman.[3]

Miss Rodman used the intellectual rationale of Mrs. Gilman as the basis for her propaganda work for feminism in New York City in the 1910's. A natural leader, dynamic and charming, Henrietta Rodman bobbed her hair, smoked in public, wore smocks and sandals in the decade prior to the roaring twenties, and generally lived an emancipated life— a life defined by her own wishes and needs, not dictated by society's conventions. Born in New York City in 1878 and educated at Columbia Teachers College, she taught high school English for many years. In addition to her teaching career and her free life style, which could easily be lived and enjoyed in the cozy environment of Greenwich Village, Miss Rodman was a reformer; she wanted to do something to improve the lot of womankind, especially of professional middle-class women like herself who desired a home, a husband, children, *and* a career. **1758925**

Having married in 1913,[4] she retained her teaching career, her separate identity, and her interests. She displayed a zestful energy and became involved in many specific causes, each related to the larger feminist issue. One factor, more than any other, marked her as a general feminist: her larger vision of a feminist society coupled with her active involvement in specifically feminist causes. Henrietta Rodman lectured frequently to mixed audiences about the need to remove all discriminatory laws against women and to reeducate the sexes to live equally. Her chief goal as a feminist was to make life fuller for women and, in so doing, to improve the quality of life for men and for their families as well. That is why she could also be called humanist. Her solutions were not based on hostility toward men or on destroying the male-female relationship. Rather, she strove for the fulfillment of womens' human potential by altering traditional American institutions.

In April 1914, Henrietta Rodman organized the Feminist Alliance to articulate and carry out the feminist program. The Alliance proclaimed:

> Feminism is a movement, which demands the re-moval of all social, political, economic, and other dis-criminations which are based upon sex, and the award of all rights and duties in all fields on the basis of individual capacity alone.[5]

Pragmatically translating the theories of Mrs. Gilman into action, Henrietta Rodman focused the efforts of the Alliance upon removing discrimination in specific areas. A prejudicial admissions policy, for example, prevented many women from attending universities, graduate schools, and professional schools. If the Alliance wanted to produce new women, she reasoned, they would have to provide higher educational and professional opportunities for them. Thus, under Miss Rodman's leadership, the Alliance told its membership to stop donating money to men's universities, and to write letters to the Yale and Harvard medical schools protesting their discriminatory policies toward women.

Supported by rich women, such as Mrs. O. H. P. Belmont, Mrs. Max Heidelberg, and attorney Jessie Ashley, the Alliance investigated conditions affecting women and urged President Wilson to pass on amendment saying that "no civil or political right shall be denied to any person on account of sex."[6] They protested the fact that American women who married foreigners lost their citizenship, and they lobbied for the passage of the Thompson Immigration Bill, then before the Senate, to correct this injustice. Remedial legislation, they hoped, would rectify much of the existing discrimination against women.

But it was in her proposal for a new type of housing structure, especially suited for professional middle-class working women, that Miss Rodman developed her most radical conception about releasing women from society's traditional chains. Once again relying upon the theories of Mrs. Gilman, Miss Rodman hoped to show the world that the feminist ideology was not mere fantasy. Her utopia was to be an apartment house equipped with a fully mechanized basement utilizing the latest industrial products and principles, in which meals for the entire building were prepared by professionals. The twelve-story building would provide an electric service elevator for the food to be delivered to each apartment. The apartments would have dull-surface walls to minimize the cleaning chores. Teachers trained in the Montessori method of education would provide schooling for the children in a rooftop schoolroom. Thus mothers would be freed from what Miss Rodman called the "four primitive home industries." No longer would they have to be responsible for the "care of the children, preparation of food, care of the house, and of clothing."[7] The professional mother would be able to work during the day in the profession she was trained for and be a companion to her husband in the evening. "For a man doesn't love a woman any more because she does his washing," argued Miss Rodman, "nor does it make a mother love her child any better to have to wash its face a dozen times a day."[8]

To Miss Rodman, this apartment house was the necessary basis of feminine equality. True feminism required it. In an interview with a *New York Times* columnist who was interested in knowing more about this radical scheme, she explained:

> At the present time the care of the baby is the weak point in feminism. The care of children, particularly those under four or five years of age, is the point at which feminism is most open to attack. We must

have this apartment house before we can be honest
feminists.[9]

Although she appreciated the importance of raising a child,
Miss Rodman contended that "intelligent mothering" meant
"an intimate spiritual relation between mother and child
which enables the mother to give to the child all that she has
gained from life, so that the new generation is started in
advance of the old." A career mother, living a productive
life in the world, could offer her child greater knowledge,
insight, and love than a mother who had abandoned her
profession and sullenly performed her motherly duties. Miss
Rodman explained that

> feminism is the attempt of women to grow up, to
> accept the responsibilities of life, to outgrow those
> characteristics of childhood—selfishness and cow-
> ardliness—that we require our boys to outgrow, but
> that we permit and by our social system encourage
> our girls to retain.[10]

To Henrietta Rodman, the woman who stayed in the home
and knew nothing of the outside world was a "child-woman."
She could not teach her children any more than she had
learned from her mother and would therefore perpetuate her
ignorance. Participating in the world by holding down a
job would make the wife-mother a vital human being. This
concept applied equally to nonprofessional women. Henrietta
Rodman spoke for the Women's Trade Union League as well
as her feminist apartment house. She wanted to see unskilled
working women better their lives as much as professional,
middle-class women. She hoped to see a society that would
offer women opportunities to discover and to express their
unique talents. Thus she tried to refute the antifeminist
females as well as the male opponents to her scheme. The goal,
as Charlotte Perkins Gilman also stressed, was humanness, not maleness. Working in the marketplace did not con-
taminate the married woman; rather it acquainted her with a
broader range of life's experiences.

Although the practical details of Miss Rodman's plan for a feminist apartment house made it sound like a cold, scientific laboratory where the necessary but unpleasant job of child raising occurred, it had many significant features. The building was designed for professional women, women who had already trained for a career and wanted an opportunity to practice their profession while raising a family. How could both be accomplished simultaneously? This was the dilemma and what Miss Rodman called the weak point in feminism. If women should have the right to vote, if women should be given higher education, if women should be able to secure professional jobs, then how could they accept these new opportunities if they were tied to child raising? In a real sense, Henrietta Rodman was trying to answer the question that must inevitably arise after women gained equal rights. Having convinced society that women should function outside the home, she had to explain *how* they could do so.

The feminist apartment house was two steps ahead of its time. Most people in the early 1900's had not yet accepted equal rights for women in principle, let alone ways of accomplishing them in practice. The tightness of the mortgage market was given as the reason why the feminist house was not built in 1915, although an architect, Max Heidelberg, had been hired and a site in Washington Square agreed upon. Probably there were other reasons more fundamental than the economic one. Henrietta Rodman's solution to an admittedly difficult question was too drastic and too antithetical to the culture's values regarding home and family to be successfully accepted.

Typical of the feminists of her day, Miss Rodman perceived the woman problem as twofold: economic and cultural. If a woman was self-supporting, she could achieve the independence she deserved. If she was able to free herself from the male-dominated culture in which she lived, she could fully explore her capabilities. Only if male-oriented values were replaced by equal values for both sexes could a truly free society be created. This single standard should apply to all areas. Women should not pay for sexual blunders any more than men should. Whatever was right or wrong for men should be right or wrong for women. Hence a revolution in both values and economics was needed to achieve the feminist utopia. As Miss Rodman's mentor, Charlotte Perkins Gilman, stated:

> Masculine ethics, colored by masculine instincts, always dominated by sex, has at once recognized the value of chastity in the woman, which is right; punished its absence unfairly, which is wrong; and then reversed the whole matter when applied to men, which is ridiculous.[11]

Henrietta Rodman's whole set of feminist provisions rested on sound rational premises. However, Americans often did not use reason when they thought about the home, the family, and the wife. Their views on woman and her role were all of a piece. Sexual standards gave men privileges not allowed women, and motherhood was deemed one of women's most essential needs and privileges. Miss Rodman conceded that "the bringing up of a child is the greatest creative work of the average man or woman."[12] Perhaps the word "average" revealed her particular bias. Having no children of her own (although she and her husband raised two teen-aged girls whom they "all but adopted"[13]), Henrietta Rodman did not consider the business of raising children a suitable lifework for exceptional women. Rather, high school graduates trained in the domestic sciences should take charge of the children of intelligent, educated parents.

This aristocratic concept of child raising, which she admitted modeling after the English royalty's system,[14] was incompatible with most Americans' cultural views of the family. Most women, college graduates or no, believed that child raising was a primary responsibility of both mother and father. Indignant traditionalists called Miss Rodman's plan egotistical and one which "would chain women to the oar to make money, that with that money they may buy immunity from all that is disagreeable drudgery."[15] Most women, Henrietta Rodman discovered, enjoyed being at home, considered it a minor triumph to be there and not have to grub for a living, and shrilly criticized any woman who tried to pull them out of their comfortable domicile. Further, Miss Rodman's undiplomatic statement to the effect that the time-consuming and heart-rending task of child raising should be, and could be, effectively done by a high school domestic science graduate was not designed to win friends and influence people. But her view of collective nurseries and collective homes anticipated by many years the feminist suggestions of the sixties. Henrietta Rodman may have sounded a chord which the majority of women in her time ignored, but it was a chord which would reach attentive ears in the future.

Simultaneously with planning for a feminist apartment house, Henrietta Rodman worked to eliminate discrimination against married women in the schools of New York City. In the year 1914, there were only three large city school systems in this country which granted leaves of absence for maternity.[16] New York City was not one of them. In fact, as noted earlier, the practice was not to hire married women unless they had been separated from their husbands for at least three years or were widowed. If a woman married while teaching and became pregnant, that ended her teaching career. This policy prompted *The Masses,* a radical Greenwich Village magazine, to editorialize:

> The impulse of life to reproduce itself will probably not be entirely annihilated by the New York Board of Education, but we are glad to see that institution doing what it can to suppress this craze. Women teachers at least shall not be allowed leave of absence to have children.
>
> Maybe it does not come within the province of "education" to prevent babies from being born, but at least it makes their education unnecessary.[17]

The consensus was that only single women could make good teachers; married women, and especially mothers, were

too burdened with their domestic and family chores to provide effective teaching in the classroom. Pregnancy and the
absence following the birth of her baby would take the
married teacher away from the classroom for a prolonged
period of time and thereby upset the continuity of the class.
The feminists and radicals, of course, countered this argument by saying that married women made better teachers
because they understood and practiced child psychology,
while unmarried women were inexperienced in dealing with
children. Also, and more essentially, the feminists argued
that no law should prevent any woman from pursuing any
career. Teaching, which had always been accepted as one
of the few proper professions for women, should not be
denied to married women with children.

To Henrietta Rodman, who had married while teaching
in the New York City school system but who had kept it a
secret, this discrimination against teacher-mothers, as they
came to be called, was a clear and burning example of the
limits society placed upon the development of the woman.
Not being a mother herself placed her crusade upon a philosophical level, above the reproach of mere self-interest.

Miss Rodman's fight against the Board of Education became good press material. Knowing Henrietta Rodman as a
radical feminist and having reported many of her activities
with the Feminist Alliance, the newspapers were pleased to
report her fight with the Board. This particular campaign
was more concretely based than the plan for the apartment
home of the future; and newspaper readers could identify
more closely and sympathetically with the battle for equality
for teacher-mothers.

By the fall of 1914, there were a number of test cases pend-
ing before the New York Commissioner of Education. The
following procedure led to this action: A pregnant teacher
requested a leave of absence for a year; because of the
Board's policy, this was never granted. Thus, when the
teacher did not report for work, she was suspended for
neglect of duty. Henrietta Rodman organized meetings to
rally support for the suspended teachers and used the offices

of the Feminist Alliance to publicize their plight. Charlotte Perkins Gilman participated in the protest meetings and accompanied Miss Rodman when she appealed to Mayor Mitchel on behalf of the teachers.[18]

The mayor, who was anxious to see the publicity end, urged compromise. One Board member took the suggestion and offered a plan by which a teacher would leave teaching during the fifth month of pregnancy and return eighteen months after the child was born, providing she passed a physical examination.[19] Although the radical feminists considered the time-off period too long, this marked the first time that the New York Board of Education acknowledged that it employed married women who could become mothers; it was also the first time provision was made to reinstate teacher-mothers to their former positions.

The drama moved to a new level of interest when Henrietta Rodman was suspended from her teaching position. During the heat of the controversy, she had written a letter to the sports columnist of the *New York Tribune* in which she suggested that there was a new game called "mother baiting"; the object was "to kick the mothers out of their positions in the public schools." The Board of Education decided the rules, and although "The game is rather rough, . . . like wifebeating, which used to be so popular, it's always played for the good of the women."[20] The already sensitive Board considered this the last straw and suspended Miss Rodman for gross misconduct and insubordination. This became fresh fuel for the feminist fire. Free speech, civil liberties, and basic American freedom now became additional issues for which to fight. And Miss Rodman, loving a good battle and freed from daily teaching, devoted the next six months to speechifying, declaiming, and propagandizing for her cause. After a hearing, the Board transferred her to a different high school for the next academic year and refused to reduce the suspension period. But because of Henrietta Rodman's work, the New York Board of Education became the fourth big city school system to grant maternity leaves.

Henrietta Rodman seemed indefatigable. She went from one reform effort to another. She supported Margaret Sanger's birth-control campaign; worked for Morris Hillquit, a Socialist political candidate who considered women's rights a major issue; and became an active pacifist during the First World War. After the war, she helped to organize a teachers' union and criticized the red-scare hysteria that overcame the country. She died prematurely in 1923 at the age of forty-five. Her work symbolized the best of feminism. She continually spoke to the larger issue of women's status in our society at the same time that she engaged in concrete, limited reforms intended to redress specific grievances suffered by women. Henrietta Rodman understood the power of cultural values to harness human action; she appreciated the influence of attitudes and tradition. However, this awareness did not stop her from propagandizing and lecturing on the need to redefine roles. In other words, she attempted to "raise consciousness," a term frequently used in the sixties and seventies to describe the feminists' efforts to educate both sexes to a new point of view. Also, she exhibited enormous energy in working for the elimination of sex discrimination. Allowing women equal entry into the universities, for example, was one of the Feminist Alliance's goals, because Miss Rodman knew that the educated people in a society are its respected leaders, and if women never received educational opportunities, they would never leave the home.

Henrietta Rodman's multifaceted, or rather comprehensive, understanding of feminism, led her to advocate new child-raising techniques and new educational programs for children. For it is the children who are the next generation of adults, and if they are raised and educated in the same fashion as their parents were, no meaningful improvement can occur. Miss Rodman advocated the Montessori method of education because it seemed to be free of sexual stereotypes; each child developed at his or her own pace, and no predetermined view of what a girl or a boy should be or learn prevailed. Further, Henrietta Rodman advocated that both boys and girls learn cooking, sewing, and baseball. Finally, like many Greenwich Village feminist friends of hers, she wanted men to join the crusade for women's rights; she believed that both sexes would be freed when women were freed. Along with her fundamental moral belief in human equality, she understood the latest ideas of anthropology and psychology and displayed a keen awareness of the new possibilities open to women in an industrial, urban world. She devoted her life to teaching, writing, and acting out her feminist beliefs, and in so doing fulfilled her human potential.

". . . Wherever she moved she carried with her the breath of courage and a contagious belief in the coming triumph of freedom and decent human relations."[21] So wrote Freda Kirchwey in an obituary editorial for *Nation* on Crystal Eastman. Fully deserving of the title of feminist, Crystal Eastman, in her life and work during the first twenty years of this century, expressed the full meaning of feminism. Born in Marlboro, Massachusetts, in 1881, Crystal Eastman was raised in upper New York State, where both her parents were Congregational ministers. She lived and worked in New York City from 1904, when she came to study law at N.Y.U. at the age of twenty-two, until the early 1920's when she left to live in England with her husband and children. A skilled speaker, writer, and organizer, Crystal Eastman participated in every significant woman's rights activity during the period. She worked in the suffrage movement, helped organize the militant wing of that movement with Alice Paul, supported the Feminist Alliance, the women's trade union movement, the birth-control drive, and, when war came, led the New York Woman's Peace Party, the most radical chapter of Jane Addams' respectable Woman's Peace Party. A long-standing socialist, Miss Eastman synthesized her beliefs in peace, in socialism, and in feminism into an integrated, wholly consistent philosophy. To quote again from her old friend and co-worker, Freda Kirchwey:

> As a feminist, Crystal Eastman was more than an ardent, militant advocate of votes for her sex. She

was to thousands of young women and young men a symbol of what the free woman might be. Unlike some of her contemporaries, embittered by the long and unreasoning struggle, she never lost her sense of balance or her friendly sympathy with men. She fought not for a sterile victory for her sex but for her religion—the triumph of freedom and decent human relations.

When she divorced her first husband in 1915, she refused alimony because, she said,

> No self-respecting feminist would accept alimony. It would be her own confession that she could not take care of herself. Alimony has nothing to do with the support of children, which, of course, must always be the mother's and father's joint responsibility whether they live together or not.[22]

The subject of women intrigued Crystal Eastman all her life; in unpublished essays, many of which were autobiographical, she explored her own private reactions to being an intelligent, sensitive woman who upheld many of the traditional values about womanhood but who also strove for additional reasons for being. "When I was about twenty-six years old," she wrote in one undated essay, "I began to wonder if I would get married in time to have children."

> I was in the midst of a busy professional career which was not without its fun and fame. I had enough romantic affairs going to keep my evenings and Sundays from being dull, and six or seven men had actually wanted to marry me.[23]

But she was plagued with the thought that she was unfulfilled in the basic and eternal way that fulfillment had been defined for a woman in Western culture: she did not have children. The maternal drive, she believed, was central to woman's nature. As a child, she was a "tomboy and a feminist," but one who had seriously announced to her family that she wanted "to be the head of an orphan asylum so as to be sure to have enough children."[24] Could a society be created which would permit women to have children without permanent husbands in their lives? Miss Eastman recognized the multiple difficulties inherent in this type of situation, but she thought seriously about it nevertheless. In her personal life, she decided upon a novel solution. If she did not marry before the age of twenty-nine, she would go to Italy, have a child, and return with an "adopted baby." Since she did not believe in wasting away with anxiety, she thought it essential to have a plan of action. It never became necessary for her to carry out her idea, however, for seventeen days before her twenty-ninth birthday she married.

In another essay, she explored the possibility that a married couple with children might maintain two households. Ignoring the economic burden involved, "Marriage Under Two Roofs" suggested the ideal combination: the man would have his privacy in his separate domicile while the wife and children would maintain another household. The man would telephone his wife every day, arrange a dinner meeting, which had the appeal of a rendezvous, and see his children in the evening under relaxed circumstances. Since the woman always cared for the children anyway, they would suffer no loss of attention. The advantages would be greater peace and tension-free times for the parents when together.[25]

The woman, under this arrangement, would be forced to be more independent because she would make many more decisions. Although the tone of this unpublished essay was jesting, it was indicative of Miss Eastman's perpetual search for new ways for two people to live together happily. In her own commentary upon this hypothetical situation, she noted that her interest was in eliminating the tension that characterized modern living. The impulse for togetherness, which was so important to American culture, had its unhappy aspects. Perhaps a little healthy separateness, she mused, might solve the problem.

Besides her fanciful explorations into innovative human relationships, Crystal Eastman concerned herself with the concrete changes needed to improve the woman's lot. Being an attorney, she was especially sensitive to discriminations in the legal system. According to the common law still prevalent in the twentieth century, women were dependent upon their husbands and not entitled to joint ownership of the husband's estate. The law, of course, reflected the culture's view of the woman. Miss Eastman anticipated later generations of feminists by suggesting that the marriage laws be rewritten to read:

> You are partners (the Husband and Wife) embarked on the joint enterprise of making a home and raising a family. You have agreed that one shall go out and get the income and the other shall do the work of the home and raise the children. Whatever surplus there is at any time, over and above the cost of maintaining the home, belongs to both of you.[26]

Crystal Eastman argued that a redefinition of the marriage contract was essential to the emancipation of women. Also anticipating later studies in psychology, Miss Eastman intuitively and empirically observed that women had low self-esteem because of their unpaid, inferior position in the home. In a money economy, only those with financially rewarding jobs are respected. A housewife working forty, sixty, or eighty hours a week is not honored for her work and must often ask her husband for money to run the household as well as to buy a new dress. Her position of dependency and inferiority is accentuated in this way. If keeping a home and raising children are significant social accomplishments, Crystal Eastman suggested, then society (with the husband being its agent) must recognize the importance of the work and reward it. Energetically and persistently, Crystal Eastman scrutinized all American society's institutions and provisions for women and found most of them wanting. But she had no audience for her views; the un-

published nature of her writing attests the fact that the
publishers did not consider her concerns worthy of print.
The comment is a cultural one and highlights the lack of
sensitivity toward the woman's dilemma, the utter lack of
credibility of the feminist cause, that characterized society's
verdict.

In addition to her basic feminist perspective, Crystal
Eastman was a socialist who expressed her views often in
terms of the class and the sex struggle. She tried to synthe-
size both views without taking a doctrinaire Marxist position. "As a feminist," she once wrote, the woman "knows
that the whole of woman's slavery is not summed up in the
profit system, nor her complete emancipation assured by the
downfall of capitalism."[27] But the struggle for woman's
rights was harmonious and compatible with the worker's
quest for equal rights. Crystal Eastman believed that the
likelihood of a feminist victory was greater in a socialistic
state than in a capitalistic one. The feminist knows, she said,
"that the vast majority of women as well as men are without
property, and are of necessity bread and butter slaves under
a system of society which allows the very sources of life to
be privately owned by a few."[28] Thus the commonality of
interests. But the feminist, although participating in the
class struggle as a socialist, must engage in the separate sex
struggle for her rights. She could, and should, count "herself
a loyal soldier in the working class army that is marching
to overthrow that system,"[29] but she must also remember
that she is a woman whose struggle for emancipation is not
guaranteed under any socioeconomic system.

Crystal Eastman envisioned both a woman's movement
and a communist movement. She hoped that industrial capitalism could better itself and move toward the communist
ideal. She hoped and worked for a humanistic culture in
which all people's rights would be respected. The reeducation
of children, she believed, was an essential need, so "it must
be manly as well as womanly to know how to cook and sew
and clean and take care of yourself in the ordinary exigencies
of life."[30] Role changes were demanded in order to achieve

the new society. Tasks should not be differentiated along sex lines. No sex had an exclusive right or inclination toward household chores.

True to the feminist party line, Crystal Eastman argued that the culture decided which sex would perform which duties. Cultural anthropology had taught her that each culture inculcates its citizens with a set of roles and spells out the demands of each role. There are very few roles determined solely by biology. Although women are child-bearers in every culture, men can, and in some cultures do, participate in the raising of the child. By highlighting this fact, Crystal Eastman hoped to create the awareness needed to expand the roles of women. Recognize your possibilities and be freed by them, she advised women. Along with a reeducation of children, Miss Eastman considered birth control as "elementary and essential in our propaganda as 'equal pay.' "[31]

Economic independence for the woman must also be guaranteed for women whose primary task was child raising as well as for working women. The government, through federal legislation, should provide "motherhood endowment" for mothers without income. Mothers who were raising children were contributing to the welfare of society along with professional mothers; therefore, society should pay them for their efforts.[32] Women could then stay home and be full-time mothers without financial risk or sacrifice. This solution spoke to the need of working mothers who had to take jobs from economic necessity, and not desire; but it did not deal with professional women who wanted to be both mothers and workers. Henrietta Rodman's plan appealed to educated woman, while Crystal Eastman's would satisfy the unprofessional working mother.

From another perspective, Crystal Eastman wrote about, and identified with, the emotional strains of the modern woman. She realized that American culture had provided women with time-saving devices but not the knowledge, tools, or opportunity to utilize their newfound leisure. She wanted to see society reward the position of mother, but she appreciated the limitations of the motherly role. A woman might want to be a mother, but she also wanted to be a human being with interests and accomplishments in other areas. The modern woman Crystal Eastman defined as being

> not altogether satisfied with love, marriage and a purely domestic career. She wants money of her own, she wants work of her own, she wants some means of self-expression, perhaps, some way of satisfying her personal ambitions. But she wants husband, home, and children, too. How to reconcile these two desires in real life, that is the question.[33]

Crystal Eastman did not find a satisfactory answer to her question. She did not create a feminist alliance that would build a home of the future; she did not think that one change in legislation would solve all of women's problems. Although she thought and wrote about the perplexing life of the modern woman, her professional life was devoted to law reform before the war and then pacifism during the war. As head of the New York Woman's Peace Party, Crystal Eastman propagandized against the war and argued that feminists (those in New York especially, since they had received the vote in 1917) should organize and vote only for peace candidates and peacemaking bills. As executive secretary of the American Union Against Militarism, she encouraged all men and women to work for peace. She did not believe that either sex had a monopoly on peaceful or aggressive traits; she thought, however, that tactically a woman's peace party could draw upon the newly enfranchised women to work effectively for peace.

Thus, in her concrete actions during the war, Crystal Eastman combined her long-standing interest in women with her interest in peace. If women used their new political power to bring about peace, they could use their newly acquired power, after the war, to effect feminism. This hope was not realized. By the end of 1917, she had become discouraged about the value of peace work during wartime and retired from the propaganda arena to write. Crystal Eastman succeeded, in her own life, in reconciling the roles of wife, mother, attorney, publicist, and social reformer. She also became an inspiring model to her colleagues in the two peace organizations.

At the end of the war, with woman's suffrage won, Crystal Eastman expected millions of voting women to begin a new feminist campaign, one dedicated to removing all legal barriers to women's rights: a program that included more liberal divorce laws, the right of women to have access to birth-control information, and the right to educational and job equality. But the organized suffrage movement became the League of Women Voters, committed to educating women to use the vote intelligently; the Women's Peace Party became a permanent peace propaganda organization as part of the Women's International League for Peace and Freedom; and the National Women's Party concentrated on an equal rights amendment fight (to which it was still committed fifty years later) and would not consider any of the specific feminist causes suggested by Crystal Eastman. Nineteen-twenty did not begin a new era for women's freedom, it ended one; and the women workers who had devoted long hours and years to the suffrage struggle as well as other struggles, had no more time or energy to give. The younger generation considered the battle won, and Crystal Eastman found herself without organizations or workers willing to continue the fight.

Although she moved to England shortly after 1920, she still kept in touch with the feminist struggle in the United States and worked for women's freedom in England as well. In a letter to the editor of the *Nation* in November 1924, she displayed her still fervent and eloquent commitment to feminism. She rebutted the *Nation*'s refusal to support the National Women's Party's position of supporting all women political candidates despite their party or ideology. She agreed with the National Women's Party's work for the equal rights amendment in order to

> blot out of every law book in the land, to sweep out of every dusty court-room, to erase from every judge's mind that centuries-old precedent as to

women's inferiority and dependence and need for protection; to substitute for it at one blow the simple new precedent of equality, that is a fight worth making if it takes ten years.[34]

The equal rights amendment did not win passage during the next decade. When Crystal Eastman returned to this country in 1927, women's equality had not been achieved; her unfortunate and untimely death the following year at the age of forty-seven silenced one of the most courageous and dogged workers for women's rights.*

Both Crystal Eastman and Henrietta Rodman shared a concern for the destiny of woman after she had received the vote as well as educational and job opportunities. Both asked, What then? Both tried to envision what the culture of the future, with its enlightened view of woman, would be like. Vigorous governmental aid to dependent mothers, collective apartment houses for professional middle-class mothers, a humanly equal view of the marriage contract, and collective child raising without stereotyping of roles were all part of their plan and their hope for a feminist future. Neither woman lived long enough to see the problem she articulated become increasingly important as the century progressed. Neither lived long enough to remind the next generation of the unfinished social revolution; their articulate and dynamic presence was absent from the consciousness of the young flapper of the twenties. But their contribution to feminism, through their writings and their personal actions, provided a lasting foundation for future generations.

RADICAL FEMINISTS

Among the minority of feminists in America in the opening years of this century were some radical feminists, women who perceived that revolution was necessary to bring

*For a more detailed description of both Henrietta Rodman's and Crystal Eastman's feminist activities, see the author's *The New Woman: Feminism in Greenwich Village, 1910-1920* (New York, Quadrangle Books, 1972).

about the desired feminist conditions. They differed from the general feminists primarily in their means of fulfilling the feminist goals. Henrietta Rodman and Crystal Eastman, for example, were socialists, and there is some evidence to suggest that Miss Eastman accepted communism after 1917 as the most viable governmental structure conducive to feminism; but neither of them spoke in the rhetoric of revolution or adopted an exclusive class analysis of the woman's problem. Both Henrietta Rodman and Crystal Eastman advocated only legal, educational, and legislative means to obtain their desired ends. Crystal Eastman was instrumental in forming the American Civil Liberties Union during the First World War because she believed that the legal system would protect conscientious objectors to the war; both women worked for Socialist candidates and, in so doing, showed their commitment to the electoral process. They remained methodologically committed (and implicitly philosophically committed) to legal, rational, and nonviolent means of achieving their ends. But both the general and the radical feminists were direct-action oriented and were effective propagandists for their particular cause.

The radical feminists rejected the American capitalistic system and did not believe that piecemeal change could bring about the desired ends. They believed that women could neve receive equal opportunity and treatment in a capitalistic America. Those who became devout Marxists—such as Elizabeth Gurley Flynn, Kate Richards O'Hare, and Rose Pastor Stokes—propagandized for a socialist revolution, a radical redistribution of wealth, and an end to private property. This is not to suggest that they advocated violence; in fact, Elizabeth Gurley Flynn eschewed violent methods and always told workers (during her days as an organizer for the "Wobblies," the Industrial Workers of the World) to use such methods as slow-downs and strikes to gain their demands.

Radical feminists differed from the general feminists in methodology, temperament, and rhetoric. Although they had the same vision, their emphasis and tactics were different. The radical feminists continuously allied themselves with the socialists and avoided strictly women's organizations. Most important, they identified closely with the working class rather than the middle class, considered their class identification rather than their sex identification as primary, and saw the class struggle as central, with the feminist struggle subsumed under it. As Kate Richards O'Hare, a fiery speaker and writer, wrote in her magazine, *Social Revolution*:

> I, as a Socialist, most emphatically state that I demand Equal Suffrage, not merely as a *Sex Right* but also as a *Class Right*. I demand not only better laws for MY SEX, but more particularly, for MY CLASS.[35]

According to Mrs. O'Hare, women must fight for economic equality alongside their menfolk. Because industry had been taken out of the home, women followed, became cheap labor, and suffered the same exploitation as their fathers, husbands, and brothers. Hence their need to vote, to organize into unions, and to resist war, which profited the industrialists and victimized the working class.

All four of the radical feminists described here—Elizabeth Gurley Flynn, Kate Richards O'Hare, Emma Goldman, and Rose Pastor Stokes—were dynamic, effective speakers and charismatic personalities. All worked energetically for many years to see the end of oppression of the working class.

At fifteen years of age, beautiful, dark-haired Elizabeth Gurley Flynn attracted audiences on the street corners of New York. One reporter in 1906 heard her tell a street crowd that

> the state should provide for the maintenance of every child, so that the individual woman shall not be compelled to depend for support upon the individual man while bearing children. The barter and sale that go under the name of love are highly obnoxious.[36]

The reporter may have wondered how such a young girl had arrived at such conclusions. Had he asked her, Elizabeth Gurley Flynn would have proudly told him about her Irish revolutionary grandfather, who was known as "Paddy the Rebel," and her parents' devotion to the laboring class. Her speeches, as well as her participation in some twenty strikes in the twenty-year period 1906-26, always included consideration of the woman and child issue, for union men could provide a living wage for their families and thus eliminate the need for working-class women to take jobs. Birth-control information, if properly understood, could bring a measure of control to women, so that their burden could be lightened and they could then develop their human potential.

At eighteen, Elizabeth Gurley Flynn had married a man sixteen years older than she; the birth of her son did not interfere with her mission—organizing workers for the Wobblies. She decided then that her public life must take precedence over her personal life. As she later recalled:

> A domestic life and possibly a large family had no attraction for me. My mother's aversion to both had undoubtedly affected me profoundly. She was strong for her girls "being somebody" and "having a life of their own." I wanted to speak and write, to travel, to meet people, to see places, to organize for the I.W.W. I saw no reason why I, as a woman, should give up my work for his [her husband's]. I knew by now I could make more of a contribution to the labor movement than he could. I would not give up.[37]

The workers' cause became her cause. From Seattle to New York, from the coal mines of Colorado to the textile mills of Massachusetts, Elizabeth Gurley Flynn traveled, spoke, and worked for the Wobblies. As one Italian woman said, "Women and children, and any man that lika mother and sister, lika Miss Flynn and listen."[38] During the First World War, she split with the leadership of the I.W.W. but never gave up her interest in union organization. Arrested fifteen times in different parts of the country during the first twenty years of this century, she was never convicted of a crime. Federal imprisonment came later to Elizabeth Flynn; she lived long enough to become a victim of the anti-Communist hysteria of the early fifties. But from 1905 to 1920, she represented the radical woman—the woman whose active public life set her apart from the majority of women.

Indeed, deciding between a career and a family was one of the difficult but necessary choices activist women had to make. A woman could not maintain a home at the same time that she traveled around the country; she could not care for her own children while raising money for striking workers. While men could always have careers and families, women most often had to choose one or the other. True, Elizabeth Gurley Flynn had an understanding mother who cared for her son; and Kate Richards O'Hare had a helpful husband, Frank, who played a significant role in caring for their four children and their home, and in managing Kate's speaking tours.

Kate Richards O'Hare was an active and important member of the Socialist Party, becoming a member of the National Executive Committee in 1912. Along with Eugene Debs, who contributed to her magazine, the *National Rip Saw* (later called *Social Revolution*), she toured the country speaking before Socialist groups. To her, as to Elizabeth Gurley Flynn, the woman issue was contained in the larger issue of social- ism. In one debate on woman's suffrage, she explained her belief in the traditional roles for men and women:

> We cannot expect men to usurp women's natural place in the scheme of things and do the work of women in caring for and protecting the family. Man's concerns are the masculine ones in the direc- tion of harnessing the elements, conquering nature and creating and directing the machinery of pro- duction and distribution. Our prehistoric ancestors

settled the question of man's and woman's place in
life back in the far past when instinctively the man
went out to hunt the game and left the women and
children to tend the fires, prepare the food and dress
the skins.[39]

Mrs. O'Hare's main reason for not practicing this traditional division of roles, which had once existed, and should
continue to exist, was the misery suffered by the working
class. Women had to participate in the struggle for freedom;
ostensibly, when that was won, they could return home.

I am not asking for better laws for women, I am
asking for no special privilege; I am whining for no
privilege without responsibility. I demand better
laws for the working class and the power to convert
the whole human race into useful workers and to
eliminate the parasitical idlers. I want no special
privilege for myself, for my sex, or for my class. I
merely demand equal opportunity for all. I want to
shoulder my own responsibility and I ask for the
ballot to strengthen my arm for its task.[40]

In 1910, she ran for Congress on the Socialist party ticket
from the second Congressional District in Kansas City. In a
brief statement describing her reasons for running, Mrs.
O'Hare said: "I long for domestic life, home and children
with every fiber of my being. . . . The home is becoming
archaic. Socialism is needed to restore the home."[41] Thus,
Kate Richards O'Hare's list of priorities demanded her
active participation in the outside world so that the home
could be secured and improved.

All the feminists described so far, of both the general and
the radical variety, opposed the First World War. Henrietta
Rodman and Crystal Eastman spoke against conscription and
military preparedness. Crystal Eastman led the New York
branch of the Women's Peace Party, an organization which
propagandized against the war, and after April 1917, when

the United States entered the war, worked for legal aid to conscientious objectors and for a speedy negotiation of the peace treaty. When Europe went to war in 1914, Mrs. O'Hare, writing in her regular column in *Social Revolution,* reminded her readers that

> It is the women of Europe who pay the price while war rages, and it will be the women who will pay again when war has run its bloody course and Europe sinks down into the slough of poverty like a harried beast too spent to wage the fight. It will be the sonless mothers who will bend their shoulders to the plow and wield in age-palsied hands the reap-hook.[42]

A month before President Wilson led America into the war, she declared that men had women's permission to fight for their selfish purposes if they wished, "BUT SO HELP US, GOD, YOU SHALL NOT SEND OUR SONS TO DO THE FIGHTING."[43] As a result of this stand, as well as of specific antiwar speeches she made, Kate Richards O'Hare was sentenced to five years in the Jefferson City, Missouri, penitentiary in April 1919. She was released thirteen months later after a presidential pardon.

Elizabeth Gurley Flynn had been indicted in September 1917 for her Wobblies activities, which the Justice Department said obstructed the war effort, but her case was eventually dropped. The two additional radical feminists yet to be discussed here, Emma Goldman and Rose Pastor Stokes, also suffered prosecution under the Espionage Act of 1917—an act specifically designed to inhibit what the government considered unpatriotic behavior during wartime. With a zealous Attorney General in office, A. Mitchell Palmer, as well as a diligent Postmaster General, Albert S. Burleson, antiwar socialists found themselves unable to publish their newspapers and to continue speaking in public.

Rose Pastor Stokes was a poor Jewish immigrant girl who attracted newspaper headlines in 1905 when she married millionaire socialist J. G. Phelps Stokes. She shared the militant Socialist position of Kate Richards O'Hare. Well known for her effective speaking style, she campaigned, with her husband, for better working conditions for laborers, for strikes, and for socialism. When the First World War broke out, she supported it, arguing that the Hohenzollerns were a great threat to the world's future. When President Wilson declared that it was a war to end all wars and one which would spread democracy throughout the world, she praised his position.[44] Since the Socialist Party of America had renounced the war in 1917, both Mr. and Mrs. Stokes resigned from the party and supported the war effort. However, early in 1918 Rose Pastor Stokes broke with her husband, departed from her previous stand, and rejoined the party. In a speech at Kansas City in March 1918, she explained why she had returned to the Socialist party position:

> Surely there is not a capitalist or well-informed person in this world today who believes that this war is being fought to make the world safe for democracy. It is being fought to make the world safe for capital.[45]

This speech, as well as others like it, got her into trouble with governmental authorities. At her trial, she summarized her feelings against the government and the industrial order:

> For ten years I have worked and produced things necessary and useful for the people of this country and for all those years I was half-starved. . . . I worked at doing useful work and never had enough. But the moment I left the useful producing class, and did not have to do any productive work in order to exist—I had all the vacations I wanted, all the clothes I wanted. I had all the leisure I wanted— everything I wanted was mine without my having to do any labor in return for all I had received.[46]

Although she still claimed that she had not changed her position and still supported the original reason President Wilson gave for American entry into the war, Mrs. Stokes was found guilty of sedition and trying to impede the war effort, and was sentenced in May 1918 to ten years in federal prison. In March 1920 an appeals court overruled her sentence and conviction, and in November 1921 President Wilson ordered her case dismissed.

The Socialist Party of America, as a result of the successful Bolshevik Revolution in Russia, had to come to terms with the existence of a socialist state. A serious split occurred between those who wanted the American party to retain its autonomy and those who wanted to identify with the new Bolshevik state. Rose Pastor Stokes sided with the Moscow supporters and helped organize the Communist Party in September 1919. She remained a loyal party member until her death in the early 1930's.

In a play she wrote in 1916, called *The Woman Who Wouldn't,* Rose Pastor Stokes envisioned a time when the working class would be free of oppression and women particularly would be allowed to live independent lives. The heroine, Mary Lucey, the daughter of a mill worker, had a child out of wedlock, overcame adversity to become a famous labor organizer, and looked forward to the day when "The woman of tomorrow will approve what many people of today frown upon, and my little girl is going to be one of those women of tomorrow."[48]

The last radical feminist to be discussed here was not a member of any political party or labor organization. She was an anarchist who spent her life explaining the principles of her philosophy to anyone who would listen to her or read her writings. Emma Goldman, perhaps the most famous anarchist of the century, believed in women's freedom as part of her total belief in human freedom. Each individual, regardless of sex, had the fundamental right, according to Emma Goldman, to express himself or herself freely and fully. Born in Russia in 1869, she left her parents at age sixteen to come

to this country. The following years were hard and Emma
Goldman learned, from firsthand experience, what factory
life was like, how poor immigrants live in slum conditions,
and the oppression suffered by workers, especially women
workers. Trained as a nurse and by inclination quite motherly, Emma Goldman helped mothers with their children but
decided against having children of her own. Her personal experience convinced her that immigrant lower class women
were doubly discriminated against: first by producing large
numbers of unwanted children, and then by working for poor
wages under unspeakably insanitary conditions. True individualism, true anarchy would free women as it would free
men. The woman's independence, she wrote,

> must come from and through herself. First, by as-
> serting herself as a personality and not as a sex
> commodity. Second, by refusing the right to anyone
> over her body; by refusing to bear children, unless
> she wants them; by refusing to be a servant to God,
> the state, society, the husband, the family, etc.; by
> making her life simpler, but deeper and richer.[49]

In addition to her numerous writings, Emma Goldman became a very popular lecturer on anarchism. Because of her
open advocacy of free love, and her long alliance with Alexander Berkman (a well-known anarchist who spent many
years in jail for his aborted effort to assassinate industrial-
ist Henry Frick), her public appearances were always well
attended and accompanied by police and press coverage. Her
immigrant status eventually resulted in her deportation
after the First World War, but before that she displayed an
extreme alternative, a radical side of feminism rarely seen.
Emma Goldman's feminism was unique, revolutionary, and
inimitable. Her personal magnetism and determination convinced all who heard her that they were in the presence of a
completely authentic individual, that here was a woman who
had freed herself of society's restrictions and lived according
to her own lights.

Emma Goldman's feminism was integrated into her philosophy of anarchism. Although she frequently spoke and wrote about woman's problems in an industrial society, her larger concern was opening up people's minds to the possibilities of freedom. Personally abhorring violence, she understood why sabotage, assassinations, and bombings characterized the behavior of some of her anarchist friends; but to Emma Goldman, educating people to their human potential was her primary task. Propagandizing and lecturing, therefore, were her major activities, although sometimes she engaged in activities for specific causes, such as open distribution of birth-control pamphlets, which resulted in her arrest in New York City in 1916.

In her writings on women and how they could achieve anarchic freedom, Emma Goldman criticized the existing women's emancipation movement. She believed that they imitated men and were willing to give up their uniquely feminine qualities to achieve external and superficial equality with men. "The problem that confronts us today," she wrote,

> and which the nearest future is to solve, is how to be one's self and yet in oneness with others, to feel deeply with all human beings and still retain one's own characteristic qualities. This seems to me to be the basis upon which the mass and the individual, the true democrat and the true individuality, man and woman, can meet without antagonism and opposition. The motto should not be: Forgive one another; rather, Understand one another.[50]

To Emma Goldman, the attainment of political and economic equality, which she thought had come in a sense, robbed women of their essential roles as sweethearts and mothers.[51] In a free atmosphere, free, individual women could express their womanly characteristics. Working-class women were at present bound to exploitation in the factory and at home, while middle- and upper-class women were narrowly confined to the home. The few middle-class women who had become professionals had given up their womanly natures and had become pale imitations of men. Thus the achievements of the woman's movement, she thought, were more apparent than real. Extending the vote to women had not raised the level of politics and businessmen had not been purified by the presence of women in their offices. "A so-called independence which leads only to earning the merest subsistence is not so enticing, not so ideal, that one could expect women to sacrifice everything for it. Our highly praised independence is, after all, but a slow process of dulling and stifling woman's nature, her love instinct, and her mother instinct."[52]

Emma Goldman's supreme goal was to liberate all human beings to be themselves; she wanted each person to experience an infinite variety of sensory, intellectual, and emotional possibilities. She saw all cultures as inhibitory and restrictive. Laws prevented people from learning about themselves and about others. Emma Goldman wanted to see intellect, soul, and heart unite. In the case of women, this meant that the loving quality of the woman should not be snuffed out by the intellectual part. A woman was different, by nature, from a man. A whole woman would be one who harmonized all her womanly and human traits.

Because of her deep commitment to anarchism, Emma Goldman stood alone in this country. She did not ally herself with the Socialist-Feminists, the Feminist Alliance, or anyone else. Despite her occasional support of specific causes, she stood essentially alone, speaking and writing in her magazine, *Mother Earth,* and living the life she preached.

The radical feminists shared many themes and personality characteristics. They all envisioned a revolutionary time in which the customary relationships and values would be overthrown and women would receive their respectful and equal position alongside men. They wished for the end of social and economic classes and of sex discrimination. Their strong pacifistic views made them vulnerable targets for the sensitive government during and after the First World War. Because they were well-known speakers, the government feared that their implacable antiwar stance would negatively influence the masses and took steps to avert this. All these women knew, therefore, what jails were like, what the deprivation of basic human rights meant, and how oppression felt. They knew, in a personal and direct way, what happens when you challenge the established truths of your society. To advocate the distribution of birth-control information in New York City when it was illegal to so do; to advocate free love, as Emma Goldman was wont to do; to discuss redistributing the wealth in a country that loved private property; and, finally, to be against war when your country was at war—all this marked these women as dangerous radicals in the eyes and minds of the majority. The egalitarian society that the radical feminists hoped for portended such dramatic changes that the overwhelming majority of Americans feared it. To a culture that never discussed people in class terms and never acknowledged the absolute power that stereotyped sex roles played in their thinking, Elizabeth Gurley Flynn, Rose Pastor Stokes, Kate Richards O'Hare, and Emma Goldman were unnatural witches, crazy women who defied the natural order.

PRAGMATIC FEMINISTS

The third group of feminists, the pragmatists, was larger than both the general feminists and the radicals. It consisted of women who were committed to specific educational and propagandizing functions and who joined primarily middle-class women's organizations. The National American Women's Suffrage Association and the Women's Christian Temperance Union were the largest organizations in this category until after the First World War, when the Federation of Business and Professional Women became another large group. These organization women were pragmatic in their world-view and their orientation. They tried to identify specific grievances suffered by women and to solve them in traditional ways. They focused on the concrete and the discreet and did not undertake campaigns to revamp the culture's value system or to revolutionize its way of educating the sexes.

Indeed, these women, for the most part, did not see the woman problem in the same way as did the sex-conscious feminists or the class-conscious radicals. The pragmatists did not believe the situation was as grave as these other groups did; they did not want to upset the traditional sex roles; and most of them believed that motherhood and homemaking were the true and essential occupations of women. They believed that reasonable men would allow women to obtain a professional education, the right to vote, and equal job opportunities. Their rhetoric was respectable and conciliatory; their tone reasonable. They did not want to end private property or to collectivize the home. They tried to avoid discussions of birth control and would not consider studying the problem of abortion.

Because the pragmatic feminists did not define the problem in the class or sex terms used by the other feminists, they got along better with the established powers, although they did not win easy or quick victories either. Both the suffrage and the temperance groups spent the first twenty years of this century working for their cause, and only in 1920 did they experience the sweet taste of success with the passage of the Eighteenth and Nineteenth Amendments. During this period, then, they continued their lobbying, their pressuring, and their propagandizing. In the next twenty years it would be their difficult task to evaluate their success, to determine whether the long years of toil were worth the effort. But while engaged in the struggle, they had high hopes.

Studies have already been made of both these organizations[53]—the National American Women's Suffrage Association and the Women's Christian Temperance Union—and their leadership is well known. Thus attention here will be focused on less known pragmatic feminists and their organizations. The Women's Trade Union League, for example, enlisted the energies and talents of many working women.

The WTUL had much in common with the other women's organizations already mentioned: for example, its members were solely women, in this case working-class women with some middle-class support; they concentrated on only one issue—organizing women into labor unions; and they believed that union organization would lead to the kind of life everyone desired. In other words, they exhibited the same mode of thinking as the suffrage and the temperance organizations. Just as the vote and the elimination of liquor would elevate the standard of living, and of politicking, for all, so union women, in league with union men, would experience an improved quality of living. Such thinking seems, in fact, to be a natural process that all reform organizations go through; while focusing upon one aspect of a social problem, they generalize from their experience and predict the complete improvement of all society as a result of their actions.

These union women did not adopt a Marxist perspective, but operated within the political and economic structures of America. They believed that persistent organization could lead to effective unionization. Mary Anderson and Agnes Nestor are two notable examples of union women who displayed the pragmatic American orientation to a social problem. Optimism, hard work, tremendous dedication, and a belief in the power of education characterized their approach and their philosophy. Mary Anderson had come to the United States in 1889 from Sweden at the age of sixteen. After living in Michigan and Wisconsin with a sister for a few years, she came to Chicago and went to work in a shoe factory. Working ten hours a day, she saw what factory conditions were like and quickly became convinced that a union was essential to the workers.

By the age of twenty-three, she was president of the Stitchers Local 94 of the International Boot and Shoe Workers Union.[54] Organizing women was particularly hard work, since most working women thought they would soon get married and no longer need to work. However, as Mary Anderson later recalled, the underpaid workingmen whom these women married could not afford to support wives and children. So the women often returned to work, receiving less pay for the same work that the men performed. The cycle did not end but rather worsened.

> I thought, as a young girl, that I would get married too, but somewhere I lost myself in my work and never felt that marriage would give me the security I wanted. I thought that through the trade union movement we working women could get better conditions and security of mind.[55]

Mary Anderson never married, and spent her evenings attending meetings and lectures. By 1913, she had become an important organizer for the Women's Trade Union League and an active member of her own local union. She eventually became the only woman on the executive board of the International Boot and Shoe Workers Union. Thus union organization became her all-consuming lifework. Each time one factory granted the workers a contract, each time a strike ended in success, all her unsuccessful efforts were forgotten. In 1910, Hart, Schaffner, and Marx, a big clothing firm in Chicago, reached a collective bargaining agreement with the United Garment Workers Union, and Mary Anderson acted as the go-between for the union and the company. She learned the value of negotiation and the role that patient, dedicated women could play in securing effective union contracts.

Because her major work entailed convincing young women to join a union, Mary Anderson thought about and occasionally wrote propaganda on the importance of labor organization to women. In one article, she reminded women that the union movement "means better wages and shorter hours. Better wages mean a home—a real home—and shorter hours mean family life, a life where father, mother and the children have time to be with one another and learn together and play together."[56] Convincing girls of the union's worth, however, was a difficult, uphill battle. Young women did not understand the meaning of arbitration and did not know when or why they should strike. Many of the girls in the Chicago factories were young immigrants from sixteen to twenty years old who had difficulty with the language and were afraid of the repercussions they would suffer from management if they joined a union. Further, union women found union men unwilling to help and cooperate with them; the American Federation of Labor gave them only token approval, no money to hire organizers and no voice in running the A. F. of L. They found themselves alone in their effort to convince working women to unionize.

Agnes Nestor's career paralleled Mary Anderson's. Born in Grand Rapids, Michigan, in 1880, she came to Chicago at the age of seventeen and went to work for the Eisendrath Glove Company as a glove-maker. She stayed with that company for many years, joined her local union, and eventually became a vice-president of the International Glove Workers Union of America. At the same time she became involved in the work of the Women's Trade Union League. The League was not a union in its own right, but rather an organization that tried to get women into unions in their respective trades, and then have them affiliate with the A. F. of L. Agnes Nestor became president of the Chicago branch of the WTUL in 1913 and worked closely with Mary Anderson. Both women were good speakers and tireless organizers. In 1909, Agnes Nestor lobbied in Springfield for the ten-hour day for working women and for women's suffrage. She was small in size but a spunky lobbyist who attracted the attention of the Illinois legislature when she spoke. In 1909, establishment of the ten-hour workday for women in Illinois was considered a major victory for working and union women.

During the First World War, both women served on presidential committees to help coordinate women workers for the war effort. Agnes Nestor was on the Woman's Committee of the Council of National Defense, and Mary Anderson worked in Washington for the Woman in Industry Service. In 1920, Miss Anderson became the head of the Women's

Bureau in the Department of Labor where she remained for the next twenty-five years. Agnes Nestor returned to Chicago and her union work after the war.

Throughout this period, the Women's Trade Union League worked for an eight-hour day for working women, equal pay for equal work, and a minimum wage scale. Also included in its platform was the goal of full citizenship for women.[57] Mrs. Raymond Robins, national president of the WTUL during most of the period, wrote about the need to give both boys and girls the same education. Since women may continue to be workers after marriage, she reasoned, they had to be given vocational and academic education to the same degree that men received it. Further, men had to learn to be good fathers, while women had to learn to be good mothers. After the war, the WTUL broadened its platform to include advocacy of the League of Nations, Wilson's Fourteen Points, support for Bolshevik Russia, and the public ownership and worker control of all public utilities, including mines, stockyards, and grain elevators.[58] Although these concerns demonstrate a broader perspective than previously noted, the primary aim of the League, as of all union groups, was to organize the workers; after 1920, this aim became increasingly difficult to accomplish.

While Mrs. Robins came from a wealthy background, both Agnes Nestor and Mary Anderson were working-class women; both had worked in factories and had joined unions because this seemed to be the only practical way to improve their economic lot. All these pragmatic women realized that as women they were viewed differently from men; that women workers were discriminated against precisely because they were women; and that the job of organizing women had its special difficulties because of women's fear of being assertive. Coupled with this, the average woman's belief that she was working temporarily, not permanently, militated against developing effective women's unions.

While all three women understood that birth control, the educational system, and the whole production and distribution system were interrelated, their major concern was union organization. The modest successes in the garment, textile, and cigar-making industries before 1920 encouraged them to continue their activities doggedly. The eight-hour day did not come to Illinois until 1937, and the women's clothing industry did not win union recognition until the New Deal thirties, but these women lived to see such victories and to take satisfaction in knowing that they had participated in the early struggles that had led to success.

Women reformers also staffed many important social agencies in the early years of this century. Jane Addams' Hull-House, Mary McDowell's University Settlement, and Lillian Wald's Henry Street Settlement House are only a few of the many examples of settlement houses established by women leaders. Another organization, important to the social service work of this period and typical of pragmatic feminism, was the Immigrants Protective League in Chicago, headed from 1908 to 1917 by Grace Abbott.

Born in Grand Island, Nebraska, in 1878, Grace Abbott came to Chicago in 1907 to do graduate work in political science at the University of Chicago. Her sister Edith, already associated with the School of Social Work at the university, provided her with an easy entry into the academic and social-worker world. Grace Abbott lived at Hull-House for a while and came to know the living conditions of the neighborhood immigrants. Her master's essay at the University of Chicago was on the legal position of married women in the United States. She began with this statement: "Under common law upon marriage a woman lost her rights, responsibilities and even her identity." She concluded the study by saying: "Apparently what is most needed to complete the revolution which is already well-started is to give her political responsibility for the laws under which she lives and works."[59]

Grace Abbott came from a family that was committed to social justice and sex equality. Her Quaker mother, Elizabeth Griffin Abbott, actively supported the Nebraska Women's

Suffrage Society and told her children that "the rights of women belonged with the rights of the Indian and the Negro. Everyone must be free and equal and everyone should be dealt with on the basis of equality and justice."[60] Mr. and Mrs. Abbott read John Stuart Mill's *Subjection of Women*, exchanged comments on it, and presented it to their daughters. In an early diary, Grace Abbott pondered the role of women and wondered what occupations a married woman could have in our society.[61]

Grace Abbott came to Chicago at the age of twenty-nine. Her graduate studies at the university and her life at Hull-House kept her very busy. A natural researcher, she became very interested in the immigrants she observed in the Hull-House area, and undertook a comprehensive study of immigration law as well as an analysis of who they were and what their problems were. In 1908, Grace Abbott, with the support of Jane Addams, proposed that an immigrant protective society be formed under the auspices of Hull-House. Grace Abbott zealously undertook the responsibility for the Immigrants Protective League, and devoted the next nine years to this work. She met thousands of immigrant girls upon their arrival at Chicago railroad stations, aided them in gaining employment, and helped immigrant families in their struggles with the schools and the courts. The IPL acted as a middleman, a negotiator, trying to bridge the gap between the immigrants and the established authorities. Cooperating with the WTUL, the IPL tried to ease the adjustment of immigrant workers to Chicago labor conditions.

In addition to her organizational tasks, Grace Abbott wrote frequently about the need to treat newly arrived immigrants with respect and equality. "No assertion of the superiority of Americans will make us superior, but such claims will make it more difficult for us to deal with other national groups."[63] Miss Abbott insisted that League workers speak at least one foreign language so that they could communicate effectively with the new arrivals. They tried to protect young immigrant girls from unscrupulous men who pretended to offer them legitimate jobs, only to consign them to houses of prostitution. Many of the girls were illiterate and were especially vulnerable to this approach. Grace Abbott became personally committed to the immigrants' causes; she took part in the garment workers' strike of 1910, for example, addressed their meetings, and collected food for the strikers.[64] She gathered information regarding crime, illiteracy, working conditions, and the ethnic backgrounds of the immigrants in her neighborhood. The more she and the IPL investigators searched, the more problems they uncovered. Immigrant parents sent their children to work rather than to school, knew little or nothing about prenatal care, and had their babies delivered by untrained midwives. The police department arrested immigrants indiscriminately and made no effort to understand their language or culture.[65] The IPL worked to publicize the social ills they saw and to educate both the immigrants and the public.

As a result of her testimony before a House Committee regarding an immigration law in 1912, a Bureau of Immigration and a Bureau on Naturalization were formed in the U.S. Department of Labor. Grace Abbott's testimony also contributed a few years later to the passage of a child labor law. When the First World War began, Miss Abbott hoped that this country could remain uninvolved. A convinced pacifist, in 1915 she attended a peace conference with Jane Addams in Belgium. The next year she organized a Conference for Oppressed or Dependent Nationalities. Since immigration was virtually halted during the war, the IPL concentrated on helping those immigrants who were already here. Their troubles were many and varied; non-naturalized men often received draft notices from their countries of origin; communication between relatives abroad and those here was disrupted, and money sent back to pay for the passage of relatives was lost. Grace Abbott believed that "our countrymen are all mankind," and described her pacifism as Garrisonian in origin.[66] She hoped that this nation of immigrants would see the natural links between all peoples and respect cultural differences.[67]

The Immigrants Protective League did not fare well during or after the war. Suspicion of immigrants in wartime and concern for winning the war prevented the League's prewar supporters and workers from continuing their work; the 1917 Comprehensive Immigration Act became the first of many restrictive immigration laws. At its height, in 1912, the IPL had serviced some fifteen thousand immigrants; by 1919, funds had nearly run out, and the League moved back to Hull-House as an economy measure. After the war, Grace Abbott moved to Washington to serve as director of the Children's Bureau in the Department of Labor. Like her friend Mary Anderson, who now headed the Women's Bureau, she spent the next fifteen years in Washington as a career government official. Grace Abbott's involvement with the problems of immigrants now took a different turn; she focused upon children, immigrants' children as well as natives' children, and worked in the tangles of the Washington bureaucracy rather than the more intimate and direct environment of the Chicago streets. But her years in Chicago as head of the Immigrants Protective League put her in the ranks of pragmatic feminists—side by side with Jane Addams, Agnes Nestor, Mary Anderson, and many other women who did social work, nursing, union organizing, and teaching among the city's poor and needy.

All these pragmatic feminists worked with men and did not display any hostility to the male sex. In fact, all the feminists described in this chapter cooperated with men and worked together with them to achieve their version of the good society. The pragmatists learned the names of the city politicians, the newspaper reporters, and the prosperous businessmen so that they could enlist their aid in their particular crusades. They displayed continued devotion, cautious optimism, and a steadfastness difficult to match. They also gave many years to their causes, never slacking or relenting. The union women lived to see unions win respectability and recognition; they also saw child labor and minimum wage laws enacted. In one way at least, the pragmatic feminists were similar to the radical feminists: they too addressed themselves to one class, the working class, and worked for the betterment of its members. The special problem of vulnerable immigrant girls was only one aspect of the larger immigrant dilemma; and since union women wanted the same rights as union men, their mode of action was consciously modeled on that of the men's unions. Thus these particular pragmatists dealt with the social problems of the lower class, not problems common to one sex or to all humanity. They differed significantly from both the general and radical feminists in their narrow focus, their practical methods, their conciliatory rhetoric, and their devotion to the basic worth of the existing culture.

FEMINIST WRITERS

Although all the feminists already described did a good deal of writing, there is a separate group of women, the professional writers, who explored, both in fact and fiction, the role of woman in American society. (Writing has always been an acceptable womanly occupation.) Two feminist writers during the early 1900's were rather well known to contemporary readers but have been virtually forgotten by later generations—Susan Glaspell and Neith Boyce. Both lived in Greenwich Village in the prewar years, both espoused the latest views of feminism, and both knew Henrietta Rodman, Crystal Eastman, and Emma Goldman. Their fiction, printed in the popular magazines of the day, dealt with the problems and challenges of modern American women. Most of their heroines revealed an uneasiness about, and a questioning of, their life's work; they did not complacently accept marriage and a family as the only desirable alternative. In fact, a restless search for life's purpose characterized much of the fiction.

Susan Glaspell wrote short stories, novels, and plays, and was best known for her plays performed by the Provincetown Players. Her heroines were of two kinds: either the romantic yearner who eventually settled for a premarital relationship followed by marriage, or the destroyer who could never come

to terms with herself. In either case, the woman expressed
dissatisfaction with the traditional definition of her life, and
rebelled against the society's definition of her future. The
heroine of her novel *Fidelity* had a "diffused longing for an
enlarged experience."[68] Once she discovered her true love, the
same heroine declared:

> "All my life I've wanted to do something with my-
> self, something exciting. And this is one thing I *can*
> do. I can"—she hesitated—"I can help create a new
> breed of fierce and athletic girls, new artists, musi-
> cians, and singers...."[69]

But this reconciliation to her life's work did not come until
late in the novel. Another woman in *Fidelity* possessed a
burning, insatiable desire for knowledge; she read every book
she could find, and although her newly acquired knowledge
never brought her economic rewards or personal fame, it en-
riched her life. Another one of Susan Glaspell's heroines believed that obeying the rules of life "took life from you," and
"was that not enough to say against it?"[70]

What happens to the truly desperate woman who cannot
face the drudgery, the anonymity, and the sterility of her
life? What happens to the ultrasensitive woman who has
interests and ambitions beyond the home and cannot fulfill
them? One Glaspell heroine had an unquenchable urge to
create new plant forms; she had a compulsive need to break
every established form in nature and continually develop
new ones. This urge finally led her to suicide.[71] Another
woman committed suicide to free her husband and give him
the self-confidence he lacked while she lived.[72] In yet another
play, a woman killed her husband because of his insensitive
treatment of her.[73] All women, Susan Glaspell seemed to in-
dicate, were unsuited to modern living. The mysterious mal-
ady struck a simple farm wife as well as an intellectually
sophisticated woman. In addition, a natural bond of sympathy connected all women. As one woman said about every
woman: "We all go through the same things—it's all just a
different kind of the same thing!"[74]

Susan Glaspell's maladjusted women could not cope with their lives, and those few who committed suicide suggested that the woman's problem was a profound one that could worsen if conditions did not change. Prophetically, Susan Glaspell described the psychological hell experienced, but never articulated, by extremely sensitive women who found the restrictions of their lives unbearable. To the audiences of 1910, suicide was a horrible and idiosyncratic solution to a problem; it signified the illness of the individual, not the society. However, from the perspective of the 1970's, the ceaseless anxiety and restlessness of Susan Glaspell's heroines appear not only tragic but heroic; the guilt appears to be society's, not theirs.

Neith Boyce, also a Village resident and friend of all the Village bohemians, shared the feminist philosophy. In one unpublished dialogue between an artist and his girl friend, the artist says:

> "Neither of us wants that—domestic atmosphere, home and all that, . . . I should hate a woman who wanted to take care of me and make me comfortable and depend on me. Of course she has her work, and I have mine, and we can go independently of one another."[75]

In most of her published fiction, however, Neith Boyce's heroines displayed the typical womanly traits of long suffering, discipline, and steadfast devotion to their husbands. In each case, the caddishness of the men is so clear that the reader cannot help questioning the injustice of the woman's role. In one piece, a woman celebrating her golden wedding anniversary described how she had always obeyed the indomitable will of her husband.[76] Another heroine supported her undiscovered artist-husband by painting miniatures. She never sought pity for the heavy responsibility of earning a living but worked diligently to allow her husband the freedom to create. When his talents were discovered, she smiled happily and noted that the world simply acknowledged what she already knew.[77] A third heroine, who had been abandoned by her husband, grimly accepted her destiny; she became a seamstress to support her two small children and "could bury her grief and her hurt pride in a proud silence that repelled pity."[78]

Neith Boyce's women were always chained to an existence not of their own making. They heroically persevered and endured in an almost Christlike way, but they shared with Susan Glaspell's heroines a profound unhappiness, a deep discontent with a destiny they had not carved for themselves. These two women writers displayed, in fictional form, one symbol of the modern American woman. They captured the uncertainty of her mind, although they did not propose any solutions. As writers, they expressed the new psychological reality as they viewed it and, in so doing, provided an important dimension to feminism. The realism and sympathy of their fiction destroyed the image of the complacent and eternally happy heroine. Yet although the well-known magazines of the day published their stories and large audiences saw the performances of Susan Glaspell's plays, the larger implications of their writing were not appreciated. The particular truths portrayed did not seem to relate to real-life women; the psychological and social validity of their fiction remained unnoticed.

Both Neith Boyce and Susan Glaspell were married to men who were interested in the subject of feminism. Hutchins Hapgood, Neith Boyce's husband, was a well-known Greenwich Village personality and an occasional writer; he recalled in his memoirs how he, his wife, and all their friends were preoccupied with the problems and possibilities of the man-woman relationship.

> Neith and I, like many another couple who on the whole were good fathers and mothers, were conscious of the latent feminism urging men to give up the ascendency which women thought they had, and women to demand from men that which they didn't really want, namely so-called freedom from the ideal of monogamy.

But, he continued, during that period "there was still healthy vigor and moral idealism underlying the effort. So that the total result was a working-out of the situation into a more conscious companionship, greater self-knowledge, and a broader understanding of the relations between the sexes."[79]

In a debate between Hutchins Hapgood and Lincoln Steffens, the muckraking journalist, at Mabel Dodge's famous Fifth Avenue salon, Hapgood playfully presented the anti-feminist point of view while Steffens defended feminism. Hutchins Hapgood satirized women for their claim that sex antagonism caused hostility between men and women. Because there is no such thing, Hapgood reasoned, there should be no such thing as feminism. Steffens, however, accepted the validity of women's claims for emancipation and excused their belligerent natures by saying that "women are in the transition stage, that is why she is sex antagonistic. But that feeling does not exist within her."[80]

Neith Boyce seemed to accomplish her goals as wife, mother, and writer successfully, as she gave birth to four children within a seven-year period and continued to write a number of stories and novels at the same time. She worked "a little every day," her husband related in his memoirs, "with that quiet inevitable persistency, which either by habit or by nature, is the characteristic of the artist."[81] In plays for the Provincetown Players as well as in her correspondence with her good friend Mabel Dodge, Neith Boyce devoted a lot of attention to the subject of love and marriage in the modern world. She expressed an emancipated attitude toward love, and once told Mabel Dodge that "Both Hutch and I feel that we are free to love other people—but that nothing can break or even touch the deep vital passionate bond between *us* that exists now as it always has."[82] In another letter, she answered Mrs. Dodge's question: "Why do we want men to be monogamous?" with "Do we?—so long as they won't be, why should we want them to be? Why want anybody to be what they are not?"[83]

Together, the Hapgoods typified the strivings of a married couple who attempted to combine bohemian life patterns with the traditional mode of living. They tried to respect each other's individuality but found the going difficult. In what sounded like a session in a psychiatrist's office, their jointly written play, *Enemies,* narrated a conversational quarrel between a husband and a wife who considered themselves modern and emancipated; each had accepted the other's love affairs as an integral part of the marriage arrangement. But it did not work out. The wife called her husband a romantic mystic whose concept of love was outmoded. She claimed that

> "Men and women are natural enemies, like cat and dog, only more so. They are forced to live together for a time, or this wonderful race couldn't go on. In addition, in order to have the best children, men and women of totally opposed temperaments must live together."[84]

An armed truce was effected at the end of the play, but it did not resolve the difficult human problem presented. Freedom in or out of marriage carries with it responsibilities. The Hapgoods appreciated this, and in both their work and their lives they tried to come to terms with it.

Susan Glaspell and her husband, George Cram Cook, also shared an active interest in redefining man-woman relationships. Cook, who was the manager of the Provincetown Players during the 1910's, collaborated with his wife on a one-act play called *Suppressed Desires* that became quite popular in its day. It was a spoof on Freudianism, with a heroine who seemed to resemble feminist Henrietta Rodman. Testing the new theories of psychoanalysis on her husband, the heroine, Henrietta Brewster, eventually discovered that her infatuation with the new science threatened her marriage; she quickly suppressed her desire to pursue it.[85] In memoirs that Susan Glaspell compiled from her husband's notes after his death in 1924, she revealed his preoccupation with love and with having a woman be his equal. "He did not want to be her master," related Susan Glaspell. "Her love as a free and equal soul was what he craved."[86] Cook saw the union with

a woman as one source of emotional and intellectual fulfillment. "The Christian spirit is like an unmated woman; the
pagan spirit an unmated man. Creative fruitfulness of mind
and body lies in their rightful union."[87] In another passage,
Cook, whose love of love seemed endless, proclaimed, "if a
woman loved me, it would be forever her gift and not my
right."[88]

Susan Glaspell also had mystical and romantic qualities.
Although not an experimenter in her own life, she believed
in the right of each individual to fulfill himself or herself in
love as well as in living. She was not a participator in the
Feminist Alliance or any of the other Village causes. "She
never, so far as I know," wrote her biographer, "refused to
adopt her married name, never had extra-marital affairs,
never, to be sure, took to nude-bathing nor advocated wear-
ing short haircuts and smocks."[89] However, she did write
professionally under her maiden name as did most feminists.
Her professional identity was separate from her identity as
a wife and mother, and the name difference accentuated this
separation of roles. Susan Glaspell's stepdaughter (Cook had
two children from an earlier marriage) has related how
strict a parent she was. She forbade Nilla Cook, at age fourteen, from walking on the beach with a young man. When
Nilla reminded her that all her heroines did just that, she retorted that that was for love. Since Nilla did not love the
boy, she could not go walking with him![90]

As stepmother to George Cram Cook's two children, Susan
Glaspell wanted to practice enlightened motherhood as well as
to fulfill her career aspirations. Because of a heart lesion, she
never had children of her own; this caused her great pain and
disappointment. "Women say to one, 'You have your work.
Your books are your children, aren't they?' And you look at
the diapers airing by the fire, and wonder if they really think
you are like that."[91] A career never substituted for marriage
and a family. Susan Glaspell wanted what Neith Boyce
seemed to have: the best of both worlds. She expressed in her
writings the belief that the new woman was protesting the
limitations and restraints placed upon her; the young woman

of the twentieth century, she said, did not want to abandon the traditional roles; she merely wanted to enlarge them. This interpretation of the new woman, of course, was shared by many of the feminists described. Emma Goldman, Kate Richards O'Hare, and Crystal Eastman all respected motherhood and believed in its fundamental importance to a woman's life. Labor leaders Mary Anderson and Agnes Nestor acknowledged the importance of the family and the need to elevate the stature of working mothers.

Unlike the activist feminists, Susan Glaspell did not participate in feminist causes but confined her sympathies to literary expressions. Her heroes were usually socialists and her heroines strove for a fuller life. From 1916 to 1920, she and her husband "were too busy with their theater to participate in many of the other pursuits" of the Village.[92] Although the Cooks sympathized with the social causes of their Village friends, their support was strictly moral and literary. While Crystal Eastman and Henrietta Rodman became vocal pacifists, George Cram Cook showed his sympathy by writing a play called *Athenian Women* which presented the evils of war and the ways in which women try to prevent war. Crystal Eastman's Women's Peace Party of New York City sponsored presentations of *Athenian Women* and appreciated the support of their playwright friends. But when the war mood was accelerated in this country, the literary pacifists were not in the forefront among the vigorous defenders of peace.

Neither Susan Glaspell nor Neith Boyce wrote very much after the war. Susan Glaspell went to Greece with her husband in the early twenties only to return in 1924 after his sudden death. She took up novel writing again, but her fiction, in quality and content, had lost its earlier verve. Her heroines and her prose lacked vitality. One play, written in 1930, however, did gain wide public notice and won her the Pulitzer Prize for that year. *Alison's House* was a sensitive study, based upon the life of Emily Dickinson, about a family's profound memory of one of its members, a maiden aunt whose posthumously published poetry received great acclaim. During the New Deal days, under the Works Progress Administration, Susan Glaspell became the director of the Midwest Play Bureau for the Federal Theatre Project. She died in 1948. Neith Boyce suffered a terrible personal loss in 1919 when her eldest son, seventeen-year-old Boyce, died. She never recovered fully from this loss, which virtually ended her writing career. From then on, she lived a private life and died in 1951.

Mary Heaton Vorse also qualifies as an important literary feminist. A resident of Greenwich Village in the early years of this century, Mrs. Vorse wrote fiction that fitted into the new-woman genre. She also became a first-rate journalist whose specialty was reporting labor's efforts to organize. She combined her interest in studying the woman problem with a lifelong devotion to the working class. Born in Amherst, Massachusetts, in 1882, she had a very pleasant upbringing in a middle-class academic household. She was headed, she later recalled, "for an agreeable existence with a number of pleasant tastes and interests and that peculiar American un-awareness of conditions."[93] However, she was widowed young and had the difficult task of raising two children herself; writing became a financial necessity. She had to face the difficulties and frustrations of being a writer and a bread-winner. She met and subsequently married Joe O'Brien, a labor reporter, who showed her what working-class life was all about.

In 1912, Mrs. Vorse accompanied O'Brien to the Lawrence, Massachusetts, textile strike. This experience was "a point of intersection." She now realized

> the human cost of our industrial life. Something transforming had happened to both of us. We knew now where we belonged—on the side of the workers and not with the comfortable people among whom we were born.[94]

Mary Heaton Vorse, from then on, wrote fictional stories

about women as well as human-interest stories about workers. As she said in one story, "To have a place in anyone's life one must be something oneself."[95] Raising three children (she had another son by Joe O'Brien in 1913), writing, and reporting on labor strikes often became an impossibly demanding life. In a letter to a friend, Mary Heaton Vorse admitted:

> I have lately felt very strongly the need of the bachelor existence and wish I could go off and live in a furnished room. That doesn't mean that I wish to escape from Joe. I wouldn't mind at all his having a corner of my furnished room, but it is the domestic system, with its attendant huge expenses, that I wish to "can."

One of her children had been very ill with diphtheria, so that "writing anything with much continuity under such circumstances is difficult."[96] But she did endure and continue to do all the things required of mothers and writers. A letter from her friend Elizabeth Gurley Flynn in 1916 reminded her of the importance of her sympathetic articles on labor's struggle to organize: "Mary, dear, there never was a time when we needed our writer friends to get busy more than right now if Carlo, Joe Schmidt and a few of our best men are to be saved from the Penitentiary."[97] Creating favorable publicity about union leaders was an essential part of the crusade.

Mary Heaton Vorse's magazine articles on labor strikes often took the form of a personal interview with a striker's family. The reader was introduced to another human family, with a loving, concerned mother; normal, outgoing children; and a worried father. Often the bright son of the family had quit school at age eight or ten to help support his brothers and sisters. The local priest, who sometimes accompanied Mrs. Vorse on her trips, lamented the loss of a brilliant student who could have had a university education had he been born into a wealthy family.[98]

Mrs. Vorse's articles often described the children of the strikers:

> A society that allowed children to die because their parents didn't make enough money seemed senseless and vicious. I couldn't bear it. I couldn't bear it that children should die needlessly.[99]

When reporting the steel strike of 1920 from Braddock, Ohio, she wrote:

> It might be supposed that the chief product of Braddock and the other steel towns is steel.
> This is not true.
> Their principal product is children.[100]

At Lawrence and later at Ludlow, Colorado, at the Mesaba Range in Minnesota, and at the Braddock, Ohio, location, she stayed in the homes of the strikers and described their lives and their aspirations. "We knew what unemployment meant in human terms."[101] Often the strikers were immigrants from eastern or southern Europe who had come to this country to obtain a better life. At Lawrence, more than thirty-three dialects were spoken by Syrians, Italians, Slovaks, Germans, and Jews living side by side in their respective ghettos.[102] The discriminatory treatment shown these immigrant workers was often directly related to the fact that they were not native-born Americans. Mary Heaton Vorse (she always wrote under this name) reported virtually every major strike for the next two decades.

While reporting on the strikes and the plight of the unemployed, she lived in the midst of the labor struggle. But in the summertime she took her family to Provincetown, Massachusetts, where they lived the life of comfortable resorters. The disparity between her personal life and the life of deprivation which she saw when living with the workers disturbed her greatly. Mrs. Vorse marveled "that either our world of Provincetown, where everyone lived in a comfortable house, where the children were rugged and rosy, was not real, or Bayonne and the troubled locations of the Mesaba Range were not real."[103] But both worlds *were* real, and she hoped that labor could achieve, through peaceful demonstrations and organization, the comfortable life she cherished for her children in Provincetown.

When the First World War began, Mrs. Vorse became interested in the women's peace movement and spent a good deal of time in Europe, first reporting the Women's Peace Conference in Amsterdam, then traveling throughout war-torn Europe. She revisited countries she had known as a teenager and became convinced that militant pacifism was as necessary to peace as militant labor was to unionization. She believed, as did many of her Village feminist friends, that women had a natural urge for peace, while men engaged in aggressive behavior. "The one small green leaf left on the withered tree of internationalism by the spring of 1915," she wrote, "was the woman's movement."[104] And in a report from France, in 1917, she quoted a Frenchwoman friend who said: "As long as men love war like that, there will be war, and when they hate it as we hate it, there will be no more war." Birth seemed to be woman's most intense experience, while men's "intensest moment is when they are called on by war to go out and destroy the lives for which we have risked our own."[105] Joe O'Brien, who shared his wife's pacifistic feelings, accused the male sex of being "the homicidal sex; he has the psychological need to kill which has been strengthened rather than diminished by centuries of conduct indefensible on any ground save force."[106] While the radical feminists saw the warlords and the peace-lovers in class terms, Mary Heaton Vorse defined the problem in sex terms. Although she knew that women did not universally seek peace, and that all men did not want war, she thought the maternal quality of women gave them a unique reason for desiring peace.

After the war, Mrs. Vorse became very impressed with Sidney Hillman and his efforts in behalf of a cooperative, industrial democracy. She started organizing workers for the Amalgamated Clothing Workers and reported, in glowing terms, the accomplishments of that union. She also did work for the War Labor Board in Washington and described the organization as a "traveling university of applied democracy."[107] Her reporting for labor continued for two more decades, and she lived to witness the great success of the unions.

What characteristics did all the feminists described in this chapter share? In what ways were they different? How did they collectively differ from the great majority of American women who were not sympathetic to, or knowledgeable about, feminism? In terms of class origins, all the radical feminists came from the working class; both Rose Pastor Stokes and Kate Richards O'Hare had worked in factories and knew from personal contact the wretched conditions experienced by workers. Similarly, two of the pragmatists viewed the union as the workable new structure that would give workers power and freedom within the American system. The feminist writers and general feminists were all middle-class, well-educated women. Neith Boyce, Susan Glaspell, Mary Heaton Vorse, Henrietta Rodman, and Crystal Eastman all came from comfortable families; Susan Glaspell, Crystal Eastman, and Henrietta Rodman received college educations. All the women, except for the three pragmatists, were married, and five out of the nine women had children. The four others, however, all raised children: Susan Glaspell and Rose Pastor Stokes had stepchildren whom they cared for, Henrietta Rodman adopted two teenage girls, and Emma Goldman, as a nurse, cared for many children.

Therefore, the only unmarried women in all the feminist categories (and the total number is twelve) were the three pragmatist-feminists: Agnes Nestor, Mary Anderson, and Grace Abbott. This point is important, as all the antifeminists hastened to remind their readers that women who worked would deprive themselves of husbands and families and that all career women were robbed of the traditional womanly roles of wife and mother. Yet these women defied the stereotype. Most feminists did not renounce the sacred value of motherhood. Even those who did not marry did not renounce marriage; they simply did not get the opportunity, so they filled their lives with other constructive work.

All these women were remarkable. Each had a high energy level, a deep commitment to her particular cause, and a great deal of personal security. Speaking in public, after all, was still considered in 1910 to be a very unwomanly activity. Traveling around the country was equally novel. To do both in the name of socialism and/or unionism further confirmed the majority's view that they were eccentrics and dangerous. Thus these women displayed a strong sense of identity and a sureness of purpose which were rare in those days. They defied the society's definition of woman's role because they held a larger view of themselves and of their society. They wanted something better for themselves, their families, and their communities.

Most of the dozen feminists described here were young women in 1900, eager to begin life, and it was in the first twenty years of this century that they came of age.

NAME	AGE IN 1900	AGE WHEN THEY DIED
Henrietta Rodman	22	45, in 1923
Crystal Eastman	19	47, in 1928
Kate Richards O'Hare	22	70, in 1948
Rose Pastor Stokes	21	53, in 1933
Emma Goldman	31	71, in 1940
Elizabeth Gurley Flynn	10	74, in 1964
Grace Abbott	22	61, in 1939
Mary Anderson	27	91, in 1964
Agnes Nestor	20	68, in 1948
Mary Heaton Vorse	26	92, in 1966
Susan Glaspell	18	66, in 1948
Neith Boyce	23	74, in 1951

Emma Goldman, the oldest woman of the group in 1900,

displayed enormous energy and stamina, but she did not possess the characteristics now assigned to the over-thirty generation. Of the dozen women described, two died rather young: Henrietta Rodman at forty-five and Crystal Eastman at forty-seven. Otherwise, these feminists lived long lives. Many of them, as subsequent chapters will suggest, lived productive lives after 1920 and continued their particular work.

Generalizations cannot be made from the biographies of these women regarding age, class origins, or family background. They represent an interesting cross section of middle- and lower-class America. Some middle-class women became (if these women are any indicators) general as well as pragmatic feminists, while some lower-class women became radicals as well as pragmatic reformers. The factor they all shared as feminists was not class or educational background but, rather, personal exceptionality.

It has already been suggested that they had strong individual personalities; they were self-confident. How did these few women achieve such a sense of security, as well as a sense of rebellion, when their sisters, the large majority of them at least, complacently and/or silently fitted into the traditional wife-mother mold? Some writers, in answering this question, would suggest that they were maladjusted, mentally incapable of accepting the status quo. This analysis is always offered in a pejorative tone—it assumes that social adjustment is the highest good and that those women (or men, for that matter) who are incapable of accepting the society's values are emotionally sick. In the post-Freudian world of the 1970's, some laymen and professional psychiatrists have come to appreciate the value of healthy and constructive rebellion; they have come to see expressions of discontent with existing conditions as signs of healthiness and perception, with complacent acceptance marking the sick members of society.

In this context, the feminists of the 1900's should be reevaluated. To their contemporaries, they may have appeared unnatural and maladjusted, but to a later generation their philosophy and posture appear eminently intelligent. Indeed, it is their unheeding audiences that seem obdurate and unstable. It seems to me that the energy and willingness to go on, which these women displayed continuously, arose from at least two sources. Committed people, with few exceptions, need nourishment and encouragement for their beliefs and actions, and these were supplied by their families and/or their small coteries of friends. Crystal Eastman's mother was the first woman minister in upper New York State; the parents of both Kate Richards O'Hare and Elizabeth Gurley Flynn had actively participated in labor's struggle to organize and therefore eagerly supported their respective daughters' activities. In the cases where the feminists did not have strong parental support, they had husbands or lovers who encouraged and aided them. Kate Richards O'Hare had support from both parents and her husband. It has already been noted that Rose Pastor Stokes, Susan Glaspell, Neith Boyce, and Mary Heaton Vorse had husbands committed to feminism. Similarly, Emma Goldman's lover Alexander Berkman and Elizabeth Gurley Flynn's Carlo Tresca were revolutionaries who accepted women's equality along with workers' equality.

Thus most of these women had either parental models whom they could emulate and/or life partners who shared their philosophy and helped them when they faltered. Their life style, therefore, did not receive censure from those they loved; it was encouraged. To the union women, their organization, with its many women colleagues, often provided the family backing they may have lacked. Similarly, the settlement houses became homes to Jane Addams, Grace and Edith Abbott, and many others. These women did not have to battle the society entirely on their own. They had emotional and intellectual supporters. Knowing the importance of desirable adult models, we realize it was no accident that feminists Crystal Eastman and Henrietta Rodman, for example, emphasized the training of both sexes, at an early age, for all human roles, and encouraged women professionals to be conspicuous so that their girl children could emulate them. Women hero-figures—and these women, consciously or unconsciously, qualified—were living examples of what all women could become or at least strive for.

To the image-makers of the society, however, the feminists were not desirable models. The extensive newspaper reporting on these women was done with tongue in cheek (in the case of Henrietta Rodman) or in reproving tones. The antiwar speeches of all the radical feminists indicated to the reporters of the day, once the United States had entered the war, that these women were revolutionaries and un-American. Crystal Eastman was booed off many speakers' platforms, as was Elizabeth Gurley Flynn. Thus feminism, pacifism, and socialism were joined in the minds of the public and connoted a highly dangerous, different, and undesirable image. The feminists may have had support in their personal lives for their conduct but not in the society at large. They remained a determined, although by 1920 a shaken minority. Their ranks were not enlarged; rather, the war depleted them. The staunch few continued to work for feminism during the flapper twenties but they remained few.

Notes

1. Quoted in Dorr, *A Woman of Fifty*, p. 119.
2. *Report on Condition of Women and Children Wage-Earners in the U.S.* (Chicago, National Women's Trade Union League, 1911), p. 5.
3. Floyd Dell credited Henrietta Rodman with starting Greenwich Village, while Albert Parry, in his study of the Village, called her "a protester, a leader of demonstrations and ever-new factions, a blazer of trails."
4. The New York Board of Education would not hire married women to teach; thus, many young teachers, when they married, simply kept the fact a secret until they became pregnant. At that time, of course, they were forced to reveal their marriage, were dismissed, and not allowed to return. This issue became one in which Miss Rodman fought the board and eventually won. (See pp. 41-43.)
5. *New York Times*, April 5, 1914, IV, p. 4.
6. *New York Times*, April 13, 1914, p. 6. This measure anticipated the long struggle begun in 1923 by the National Woman's Party to pass a constitutional amendment (the equal rights amendment) to remove all discriminatory laws against women.

7. *New York Times,* April 22, 1914, p. 12.

8. *Times,* April 5, 1914, IV, p. 4.

9. *Times,* January 24, 1915, V, p. 9.

10. *Ibid.*

11. Charlotte Perkins Gilman, "Charlotte Perkins Gilman's Dynamic Social Philosophy," *Current Literature,* 51 (July 1911), 69.

12. *New York Times,* January 24, 1915, V, p. 9.

13. *Times,* January 12, 1915, p. 1.

14. *Times,* January 24, 1915, V, p. 9.

15. *Times,* April 25, 1915, V, p. 21.

16. *Times,* December 31, 1914, p. 1.

17. Max Eastman, "An Oz. of Prevention," *The Masses,* IV (August 1913), 1.

18. *New York Times,* issues throughout October and November 1914.

19. *Times,* October 11, 1914, II, p. 15.

20. Henrietta Rodman, in the *New York Tribune,* November 10, 1914, p. 8.

21. Freda Kirchwey, "Crystal Eastman," *Nation,* 127 (August 8, 1928), 123.

22. *Ibid.,* p. 124.

23. Crystal Eastman, "Modern Adventures in Maternity," unpublished manuscript in possession of Max Eastman, p. 1.

24. *Ibid.*

25. Crystal Eastman, "Marriage Under Two Roofs," unpublished manuscript in possession of Max Eastman.

26. Crystal Eastman, "Are Wives Partners or Dependents?" unpublished manuscript in possession of Max Eastman, p. 3.

27. Crystal Eastman, "Now Let Us Begin," *The Liberator,* December 1920, p. 23.

28. *Ibid.*

29. *Ibid.*

30. *Ibid.,* p. 24.

31. *Ibid.*

32. *Ibid.*

33. Crystal Eastman, "Pandora's Box, or What Is Your Trouble?" unpublished manuscript in possession of Max Eastman, p. 1.

34. Crystal Eastman, "Feminists Must Fight," *Nation,* 119 (November 12, 1924), 523.

35. Kate Richards O'Hare, "Shall Women Vote?" *Social Revolution,* 11 (August 1914), 5.

36. Harbor Allen, "The Flynn," *American Mercury,* 9 (December 1926), 426.

37. E. G. Flynn, *I Speak My Own Piece—Autobiography of*

"The Rebel Girl" (New York, Masses and Mainstream, 1955), p. 103.

38. "Elizabeth Gurley Flynn: Labor Leader," *Outlook*, 111 (December 15, 1915), 905.

39. Kate Richards O'Hare, "Shall Women Vote?" *Social Revolution*, 11 (July 1914), 6.

40. *Ibid.* (August 1914), p. 7.

41. Kate Richards O'Hare, *The Progressive Woman* (August 1910), 2.

42. Kate Richards O'Hare, "The Wounded Who Do Not Fight," *Social Revolution*, 11 (October 1914), 7.

43. *Ibid.* (March 1917), p. 5.

44. Rose Pastor Stokes, "A Confession," *Century*, 95 (January 1918), 457-459.

45. Reported in the *New York Times*, March 18, 1918, p. 15.

46. Quoted in Martha Gruening, "Rose Pastor Stokes," *Dictionary of American Biography*, Vol. 18, p. 69.

47. Reports in the *New York Times*, June 1918, March 1920, etc.

48. Rose Pastor Stokes, *The Woman Who Wouldn't* (New York, Putnam's, 1916), p. 172.

49. Emma Goldman, "Woman's Suffrage," in *Anarchism and Other Essays*, 3d rev. ed. (New York, Mother Earth Publishing Association, 1917), p. 217.

50. Emma Goldman, "The Tragedy of Woman's Emancipation," in *Anarchism and Other Essays*, pp. 219-220.

51. *Ibid.*, p. 233.

52. *Ibid.*, pp. 222-223.

53. Eleanor Flexner's study as well as Aileen Kraditor's (see Chapter One, note 1) adequately describe the suffrage movement.

54. Mary Anderson's autobiography, *Woman at Work* (as told to Mary N. Winslow, Minneapolis, University of Minnesota Press, 1951), contains a description of her early life.

55. *Ibid.*, p. 65.

56. *Ibid.*, p. 46.

57. Margaret D. Robins, "Trade Unionism for Women," in *The Woman Citizen's Library*, Vol. 11 (Chicago, Civics Society, 1914), pp. 2908-2929.

58. Henrietta R. Walter, "Women as Workers and Citizens," *Survey*, 42 (June 21, 1919), 465-466.

59. Grace Abbott, "The Property Rights of Married Women in the United States," unpublished master's thesis, University of Chicago; in the Grace Abbott Collection, University of Chicago.

60. "Grace Abbott: Her Sister's Story," unpublished MS, Special Collections, University of Chicago, Chapter 6, p. 1.

61. Undated entry in the diary, which is also in the University of Chicago Collection.

62. Edith Abbott, ed., *Historical Perspectives of the Immigration Problem* (New York, Arno Press and the *New York Times,* 1969), pp. 54-56.

63. Grace Abbott, "The Immigrant as a Problem in Community Planning," *American Sociological Society,* (1917), 167.

64. "Grace Abbott: Her Sister's Story," pp. 34-41.

65. Grace Abbott, "The Treatment of Aliens in the Criminal Courts," *Journal of Criminal Law and Criminology,* May 1911-March 1912, pp. 554-567.

66. "Grace Abbott: Her Sister's Story," folder 22, p. 4.

67. Abbott, "The Immigrant as a Problem in Community Planning," p. 298.

68. Susan Glaspell, *Fidelity* (Boston, Small, Maynard, 1915), p. 41.

69. *Ibid.*

70. Susan Glaspell, "The Rules of the Institution," *Harper's Magazine,* 128 (January 1914), 208.

71. Susan Glaspell, *The Verge* (Boston, Small, Maynard, 1922).

72. Susan Glaspell, "Bernice," *Plays* (Boston, Small, Maynard, 1920).

73. Susan Glaspell, *A Jury of Her Peers* (London, Ernest Benn, 1927).

74. *Ibid.*

75. Neith Boyce, "Art and Women," unpublished manuscript in the Neith Boyce and Hutchins Hapgood Collection, Yale University, n.d., p. 8.

76. Neith Boyce, "The Golden Wedding," *Harper's Weekly,* 54 (December 26, 1914), 615-616.

77. Neith Boyce, "The Wife of a Genius," *Harper's Weekly,* 54 (December 12, 1914), 556-568.

78. Neith Boyce, "The Return," *Harper's Weekly,* 60 (January 9, 1915), 42.

79. Hutchins Hapgood, *A Victorian in the Modern World* (Seattle, University of Washington Press, 1972; reprint of 1939 edition), p. 395.

80. Lincoln Steffens and Hutchins Hapgood, "Sex Antagonism," MS in the Neith Boyce and Hutchins Hapgood Collection, pp. 3-4.

81. Hapgood, *A Victorian in the Modern World,* p. 233.

82. Neith Boyce to Mabel Dodge Luhan, undated letter, Neith Boyce and Hutchins Hapgood Collection, pp. 2-3.

83. Neith Boyce to Mabel Dodge Luhan, undated letter, p. 1.

84. Neith Boyce and Hutchins Hapgood, "Enemies," *The Provincetown Plays: Second Series* (New York, Frank Shay Publishers, 1916), pp. 105-106.

85. George Cram Cook and Susan Glaspell, "Suppressed Desires," *The Provincetown Plays, Second Series.*

86. Susan Glaspell, *The Road to the Temple* (New York, Frederick A. Stokes, 1927), p. 174.

87. *Ibid.*, p. 183.

88. *Ibid.*, p. 174.

89. Arthur E. Waterman, "A Critical Study of Susan Glaspell's Works and Her Contributions to Modern American Drama," unpublished Ph.D. dissertation, Department of English, University of Wisconsin, 1956, p. 116.

90. Nilla Cram Cook, *My Road to India* (New York, Lee Furman, 1939), p. 10.

91. Glaspell, *The Road to the Temple*, p. 239.

92. Waterman, "A Critical Study . . .," p. 106.

93. Mary Heaton Vorse, *A Footnote to Folly* (New York, Farrar and Rinehart, 1935), p. 27.

94. *Ibid.*, p. 14.

95. Mary Heaton Vorse, "The Woman Who Was," *Good Housekeeping* 59 (August 1914), 176.

96. Mary Heaton Vorse to Arthur————, February 7, 1913, in the Mary Heaton Vorse Collection, Archives of Labor History and Urban Affairs, Wayne State University Library; hereafter known as the MHV Collection.

97. Elizabeth Gurley Flynn to Mary Heaton Vorse, July 24, 1916, MHV Collection.

98. Mary Heaton Vorse, "Aliens," *Outlook*, 125 (May 5, 1920), 24-26, and "Derelicts of the Steel Strike," *Survey*, 45 (December 4, 1920), 355-357, are examples of her labor articles.

99. Vorse, *A Footnote to Folly*, p. 39.

100. Vorse, "Aliens," p. 24.

101. Vorse, *A Footnote to Folly*, p. 61.

102. Mary Heaton Vorse, "The Trouble at Lawrence," *Harper's Weekly*, 56 (March 16, 1912), 10.

103. Vorse, *A Footnote to Folly*, p. 150.

104. *Ibid.*, p. 79.

105. Mary Heaton Vorse, "The Sinistrèes of France," *Century Magazine*, 122 (January 1917), 450.

106. Joe O'Brien, "Men and Guns," *Harper's Weekly*, 60 (May 8, 1915), 441.

107. Mary Heaton Vorse, "Bridgeport and Democracy," *Harper's Magazine*, 138 (January 1919), 152.

3
The Hope Deferred,
1920-1940

I SAW HER IN A BROADWAY CAR
    THE WOMAN I MIGHT GROW TO BE;
I FELT MY LOVER LOOK AT HER
    AND THEN TURN SUDDENLY TO ME.

HER HAIR WAS DULL AND DREW NO LIGHT
    AND YET ITS COLOR WAS AS MINE;
HER EYES WERE STRANGELY LIKE MY EYES
    THO' LOVE HAD NEVER MADE THEM SHINE.

HER BODY WAS A THING GROWN THIN,
    HUNGRY FOR LOVE THAT NEVER CAME;
HER SOUL WAS FROZEN IN THE DARK
    UNWARMED FOREVER BY LOVE'S FLAME.

I FELT MY LOVER LOOK AT HER
    AND THEN TURN SUDDENLY TO ME,—
HIS EYES WERE MAGIC TO DEFY
    THE WOMAN I SHALL NEVER BE.
                —Sara Teasdale," The Old Maid"

NOW THIS PARTICULAR GIRL
DURING A CEREMONIOUS APRIL WALK
WITH HER LATEST SUITOR
FOUND HERSELF, OF A SUDDEN, INTOLERABLY STRUCK

BY THE BIRDS' IRREGULAR BABEL
AND THE LEAVES' LITTER.

BY THIS TUMULT AFFLICTED, SHE
OBSERVED HER LOVER'S GESTURES UNBALANCE THE AIR,
HIS GAIT STRAY UNEVEN
THROUGH A RANK WILDERNESS OF FERN AND FLOWER.
SHE JUDGED PETALS IN DISARRAY,
THE WHOLE SEASON, SLOVEN.

HOW SHE LONGED FOR WINTER THEN!—
SCRUPULOUSLY AUSTERE IN ITS ORDER
OF WHITE AND BLACK
ICE AND ROCK, EACH SENTIMENT WITHIN BORDER,
AND HEART'S FROSTY DISCIPLINE
EXACT AS A SNOWFLAKE.

BUT HERE—A BURGEONING
UNRULY ENOUGH TO PITCH HER FIVE QUEENLY WITS
INTO VULGAR MOTLEY—
A TREASON NOT TO BE BORNE. LET IDIOTS
REEL GIDDY IN BEDLAM SPRING:
SHE WITHDREW NEATLY.

AND ROUND HER HOUSE SHE SET
SUCH A BARRICADE OF BARB AND CHECK
AGAINST MUTINOUS WEATHER
AS NO MERE INSURGENT MAN COULD HOPE TO BREAK
WITH CURSE, FIST, THREAT
OR LOVE, EITHER.

                                        —Sylvia Plath, "Spinster"

The young girls of 1920, coming of age as flappers, never
wanted to be old maids, or spinsters either. They shared Sara
Teasdale's and Sylvia Plath's view that women who were rejected, or who rejected love, were the society's rejects. Sara
Teasdale's old maid is a pitiful and pitiable creature; no one
loves her, and she withers away as a result. Sylvia Plath's
spinster, on the other hand, consciously and coolly chooses
selfhood over love, boundaries rather than abandon. In either

case, the epithet "old maid" was vigorously avoided by all healthy, normal American girls. True, the flappers of the twenties did not want to be like their mothers; they rebelled against parental authority, as every generation has, and created their own picture, their own image, of what young women should be like.

They created the flapper. The young girl of the 1920's wanted the same things ultimately from life as her mother did (and as opposed to the old maid), but her style, *prior to* marriage, differed from her parents' behavior a generation before. Necking in open cars, unchaperoned dates, bold advances to the opposite sex, and the use of cosmetics all marked the flapper as different from her mother. Upon scrutiny, the flapper's attitude toward the value of a family and/or marriage appeared quite conventional, but she gave observers the impression that she departed radically from her parents' values. She openly declared that she loved her mother but did not admire her because she was "always watching what we did, but never doing anything we want to watch."[1] The new generation of young girls were proud of their ability to be self-supporting, and seemed to know how many children they were going to have and what their future spouses would be like.

They all dressed alike, looked alike, and enjoyed the same amusements. They talked of sex, of Freud, of birth control, of free expression; whether they practiced all their preachings cannot be fully determined; however, it is surely clear that they *appeared* freer and more willing to explore all life's possibilities. Mary Heaton Vorse, returning from Europe in 1928, observed many flappers aboard ship. Their open necking on deck and their defiance of their chaperones caused her to comment that it was her generation that had "willed freedom. Well, here it is. Look at them."[2] Her tone was reproving, not approving. Mrs. Vorse looked grimly upon their hedonism, their social apathy, and their total absorption with their personal lives. Her youth had been spent marching for social causes; the flappers' youth was spent dancing.

When Charlotte Perkins Gilman, the grand old lady of

feminism, surveyed the scene in the early 1920's, she reiterated her commitment to equality before the law for all wom-
en, but reminded her readers, "Yet wifehood and motherhood
are the normal status of women, and whatever is right in
woman's new position must not militate against these essen-
tials."3 Women needed equal opportunity in education and
before the law, she argued, so that they could build good
homes and raise responsible children. The sixty-three-year-
old feminist looked critically upon what she considered many
of the misguided excesses of women's freedom—most notably
the misuse of birth-control information and the bad influence
of Freud's work. Birth-control information, she observed,
was crucial in order to free poor women from excessive
childbearing, but it was not a license to sexual irresponsibil-
ity. The "solemn philosophical sex mania" of Freud, she believed, had given respectability to promiscuity in the name
of freedom from inhibition and disease. Mrs. Gilman advocated the legitimizing of all children and the opening of all
professions to women, but she concluded, "women are first,
last and always mothers, and will so continue."4

Thus one of the leading feminist philosophers shifted her
emphasis considerably in her old age. She still accepted equality before the law for women but no longer talked about the
economic system that tied women to the home, which perpetuated domestic inefficiency and ignorance, and that values
the preservation of the status quo. The image of the
flapper appalled Mrs. Gilman; if this was the fruit of feminist
work, then the movement's purpose had been sadly distorted.
Harking back to the opposition's view that motherhood is the
primal experience and *raison d'être* for women's lives, Mrs.
Gilman appeared to concede the argument. Feminists, of
course, had always said that they supported motherhood; it
was only their enemies who accused them of abandoning that
sacred role. They had only tried to overcome the either/or
nature of the argument. They tried to preserve both sides of
it; traditional women's roles were still important, but feminists wished to expand those roles. Mrs. Gilman seemed to
acknowledge, along with feminism's traditional critics, that

this was difficult to do. Readers of *Current History* who might have read Charlotte Perkins Gilman's 1899 *Women and Economics* or who remembered the activities of the Feminist Alliance probably concluded that the lady had mellowed with age.

Neither the feminists, however, nor the non-feminists over thirty applauded the behavior of the younger generation. To Mary Heaton Vorse, Crystal Eastman, and Kate Richards O'Hare, among other stalwarts, the mission of the 1910's had yet to be accomplished, and flappers seemed ill-equipped for the job. Mothers with traditional outlooks shook their heads wonderingly at their daughters' behavior, as did Mrs. Gilman. Consumerism and Freudianism had overtaken the minds of young women. The fruits of the industrial revolution had become available to the growing middle class, as well as to the lower class, in the form of mass-produced, cheaper goods. During the twenties, the sale of washing machines doubled; while only some two thousand vacuum cleaners had been sold in 1914, over 36,000 were sold in 1923. Installment buying, coupled with newspaper and magazine advertising, encouraged women to buy, buy, buy. Indeed, the role of women as consumers for the family became the dominant one. Advertisers recognized that the little lady bought her clothes, her children's clothes, and often her husband's clothes; she bought the furniture and all household products.

The young girls, more of them working a few years before marriage as well as a few years after, became a desirable target for the new cosmetics and clothing industries. The June 1919 *Ladies' Home Journal* advertised four rouge produts as "imperceptible if properly applied"; ten years later, its ads praised the virtues of a lipstick that would stay on forever and retain its color. Mass production democratized clothing and cosmetics. Working girls could buy Lux "French" toilet soap and wear dresses that imitated Paris styles. In 1917, two people in the beauty culture business paid income taxes; by 1927, 18,000 firms and individuals were listed as income-tax payers. Lipstick sold in one year would reach, if placed from end to end, from New York to Reno. The number of department stores, supermarkets, delicatessens, bakeries, and laundries also rose greatly during the twenties. Commercial laundries increased their business by 57 percent between 1914 and 1924.[5] Women now spent their days shopping, window shopping, attending luncheons in greater numbers, and engaging in harmless cultural affairs. Consumerism became a new time-consuming occupation. More and more women no longer scrubbed their clothes in a tub, made their own clothes, or cooked soup from scratch. The ready-made wear in the department stores, the washing machines, and the canned soups lightened their household chores. But rather than replacing them, as the feminists desired, with political work and/or propagandizing campaigns for women's rights, the majority of American middle-class women, the chief beneficiaries of the new consumerism, filled their time with frivolous and ineffective social activities.

Frederick Lewis Allen, the famous journalist-observer of the twenties, claimed that every young girl's conversation was sprinkled with Freudianisms. Confession and sex magazines proliferated and prospered. By 1926, *True Story,* which had started in 1919, had a circulation of 2,000,000 and an advertising revenue of $3,000,000.[6] Clara Bow, Hollywood's "it" girl, symbolized the free, flirtatious young girl of the period—uninhibited, exciting, and excited about life's romantic possibilities. The theater and popular books of the day contained dialogue unheard of prior to the twenties. Illicit love affairs became popular subjects of drama. Men and women freely discussed sublimation, inhibition, inferiority, castration, and the Oedipus complex. "Say what you think and do what you feel" seemed to be the popular slogan of the day. The divorce rate steadily rose; while only one marriage in fifteen ended in divorce in 1900, one in seven ended in divorce by 1928.[7] The flapper image seemed to apply to married women as well as to single girls. The dress and cosmetic style of youth were imitated by all who could afford it.

Women became slaves to changing fashions in clothes, cosmetics, and household gadgets. They bought with astonishing frequency and dutifully discarded still wearable clothes when

Paris dictated a change in style. Henry Ruggles, editor of the *Independent,* wrote that women's emancipation was false and illusory. True, he suggested, they could carry their own flasks and drive their own cars, but their slavish devotion to styles not of their own making bespoke a form of slavery. The flappers seemed to be saying, "I suffer cold and pinched feet, I spend hours with elaborate cosmetics, I am only an expensive and pampered parasite and ornament." Their self-image was:

> I am not a progressive person but a "jazz baby."
> I am not a free and equal partner but a gold digger.
> I am not a herald of a new age but a "red hot mamma."[8]

Ruggles perceived that the much praised (or feared) emancipation of women was superficial, artificial, and meaningless in terms of authentic human relationships. The mainstream of American women had misunderstood, or perhaps never listened to, the message of the feminists. They had marched to the tune of the advertisers and product pushers, not the feminists. They accepted Madison Avenue's view of women, not one of their own making. Thus the new woman of the twenties, the flapper, was not new at all; she was simply a caricature of what had always been the culture's view of women: as sex incarnate—as temptress and playgirl. The genius of the packagers of this image was their ability to combine it with that of the respectable young wife and mother. The flapper was naughty but not evil; she was a flirt but not a whore. The flapper retained society's approval and thus won over many adherents. Cuteness rather than sinfulness characterized her pose.

There were in the twenties few contributors or embellishers of the basic feminist view expressed a generation before by sex-conscious and class-conscious feminists. No collective apartment houses were proposed, à la Henrietta Rodman's; few open or searching discussions of the dependency-role wives and mothers play; and no new articulation of the socialist utopia in which women would march happily alongside their freed husbands in a classless society. Few young

women feminists emerged to occupy the position of a Henrietta Rodman or an Emma Goldman. Some of the specific demands of the feminists, however, were incorporated into the
pragmatic feminists' organizational work. Women interested
in women's rights joined the women's organizations; and the
National Women's Party devoted itself to the passage of an
equal rights amendment. But the general discussion of wom-
en, as a problem, did not receive much of a public hearing in
the twenties. The flapper image dominated; its force dissi-
pated all others.

The feminists of the prewar years continued their work into
the twenties. Many were blessed with long lives[9] and did not
slacken in their devotion to feminism during the flapper era.
The only new visionary feminist who emerged during the
decade was a woman who had actually begun her work in the
1910's—Margaret Sanger. In 1916, the first birth-control
clinic under her sponsorship was opened in New York City.[10]
In the twenties, the birth-control movement that Margaret
Sanger founded and led gained momentum. Her books,
Woman and the New Race (1920) and *The Pivot of Civilization* (1922), helped to popularize her cause. Margaret Sanger
had seen the results of a woman's having too many children
in too few years. She had seen poor immigrant mothers on
the Lower East Side of New York struggling to survive in
disease-ridden apartments crowded with too many sick and
screaming children. As a nurse, she had been asked to give
pleading mothers the secret of birth control. Because she did
not know the answer to that question, she became determined
to find it out. She went to England, Germany, and elsewhere
to learn about birth-control techniques, a subject that was
legally banned from public discussion in this country. Despite
arrests, harassment from officials, and continued financial
crises, the birth-control cause spread and the number of
birth-control clinics proliferated throughout the twenties and
thirties.

Woman's acceptance of her inferior status was more

real because it was unconscious. She had chained
herself to her place in society and the family
through the maternal functions of her nature, and
only the chains thus strong could have bound her to
her lot as a brood animal for the masculine civiliza-
tions of the world.[11]

Women, Margaret Sanger continually preached, had to
bring conscious knowledge and control to their sexual activities so that they could become the mistresses of their own
fates. "No woman can call herself free," she declared, "who
does not own and control her own body."[12] Although her
message was primarily directed to lower-class women, birth
control was the necessary precondition for meaningful freedom for all women. Middle- and upper-class women discreetly
practiced birth control, but the knowledge and the devices
were not available to poor women. Margaret Sanger believed
that poverty and economic oppression were tied to over-
population and that greedy employers encouraged large families so that the costs of labor would remain forever low. For
women "to approach their problems by the avenue of sex and
reproduction is to reveal at once their fundamental relations
to the whole economic and biological structure of society."[13]
Workers could only improve their standard of living, argued
socialist Sanger, if they limited their families and demanded
higher wages for themselves. The solution to the workers'
problems was not larger families to produce more workers,
but fewer children to raise the quality of life for the living.
Similarly, women as mothers, even middle-class mothers,
could not even hope to play an independent part in the world
without birth-control knowledge.

In her writings as well as her speeches on birth control,
Margaret Sanger provided statistics to show reasonable
people a number of crucial facts: that abortion and infant
mortality rates were high in New York, and that the meaning of this evidence was that women had found means, however drastic, to restrict the number of children they had. The
mortality among women who tried to abort themselves was

also high. Mothering, contrary to the middle-class myth of how glorious motherhood was for all women, was a nightmare for working-class mothers. Women did what they could, with the inadequate knowledge they had, to prevent conception, and when that failed, they tried more drastic measures. Margaret Sanger never forgot the faces of the tired, drained women she had seen during her few years as a nurse; these faces inspired her to preach the message of birth control and she never abandoned that fight.

RADICAL FEMINISTS

Elizabeth Gurley Flynn, Kate Richards O'Hare, and Rose Pastor Stokes continued their crusading after 1920. Emma Goldman was deported as an undesirable alien, and although she was granted permission occasionally to return and speak in this country, her effectiveness had ended with the war.[14] Elizabeth Gurley Flynn, thirty years old at the beginning of the twenties, was the youngest of the radical feminists. Although she had never served a jail sentence, she had been in and out of jails for the previous fifteen years. In contrast, both Mrs. O'Hare and Mrs. Stokes served prison terms as a result of their wartime speeches and writings. Elizabeth Gurley Flynn devoted a good part of the twenties to raising money for political prisoners still in jail after the war; she chaired the Workers Defense Union and its successor, the International Labor Defense. Since many of the jailed men were Wobblies, she felt a natural loyalty to them. The case of Sacco and Vanzetti also engaged her energy, and she traveled around the country speaking on their behalf. Her dynamic speaking manner had not left her, and she continued to attract attention for her propagandizing work. But a heart condition forced her, in the late twenties, to live quietly in Portland, Oregon. In a letter to her friend Mary Heaton Vorse, in May 1930, she commented that the whole radical labor movement "is a mess—torn by factionalism and scandal and led by self-seekers, with one or two exceptions. I am glad to be out of it."[15]

The inauguration of a new era with the administration of Franklin Delano Roosevelt and his sympathetic attitude toward unions made her take heart and hope for better things. The mood of the 1910's seemed to return. In another letter to Mrs. Vorse, dated January 15, 1934, Mrs. Flynn asked:

Are we revolting or not? What has happened to the comrades since recognition of U.S.S.R. is a fact? Many names seem very familiar in the roster of the various alphabetical arrangements. Restoration of citizenship; E. G. [Emma Goldman] "visiting" the country—it seems all that is lacking to be back twenty years is that poor Tom Mooney should be out of prison.[16]

And in 1937 she wrote, "We are living in great days—dreams come true—. I feel sorry for people like Joe Ettor and Carlo who are living in the past and cannot see the C.I.O. and what it means to American Labor."[17] But during that same year, she joined the Communist Party because, as she later reported, she "wanted to advance a political party of the working class."[18]

The struggle and excitement attached to Communist Party doings in the late 1930's excited her and reminded her of the old days when the Wobblies worked against enormous odds to organize coal miners and steelworkers. "Here I am, still at it," she wrote Mrs. Vorse,

barnstorming for the Communist Party and struggling for free speech, as ever. In three weeks I have had two meetings broken up, two disturbed violently and here [Virginia, Minnesota] the City Council refused the Auditorium, so I feel as if the pages are turning back and we are fast approaching 1917 again, but with a better outlook.[19]

And a few months later, she wrote Mrs. Vorse that her

"present activities are like turning back the hands of the clock twenty years! Palmer Days!"[20]

At the dawn of 1940, life had not ended in any way for Elizabeth Gurley Flynn. New and difficult episodes still lay ahead. At fifty, she still believed in labor's right to organize and the worker's right to determine his own destiny. While she had been apolitical during the early years of this century, she came to believe in the worth of the Communist Party as the only viable political party that could create the desired world. To both friends and enemies, she still was "a warm, vital person, all Irish, with crystal blue eyes, a clear white skin and shining black hair."[21] In her fiftieth year, her only child, her son Fred, died, and the American Civil Liberties Union, an organization she had been associated with since its beginnings during the First World War, expelled her; a prison term for her membership in the Communist Party was still ahead. Affected by all this, but not defeated because of it, she kept on working for the Communist Party during the Second World War.

Rose Pastor Stokes, another radical feminist of the 1910's generation, continued her work into the twenties. Her jail sentence under the Espionage Act, coupled with her antiwar Marxist position, convinced her that the traditional political parties in the United States—and that included the Socialist Party—were unsuited to deal with the needed socioeconomic revolution. Thus she became a founding member of the Communist Party in 1919 and supported its activities throughout the twenties. She marched in labor picket lines established by the party, demonstrated for causes the party advocated, and generally devoted herself to it. She was arrested a number of times for her actions and once, in 1922, surrendered to the police in Michigan, where she had been charged with attending the convention of the Communist Party, an illegal organization at the time.

In 1925, her millionaire socialist husband, J. G. Phelps Stokes, divorced her, naming another man as co-respondent in the suit. In an interview, Rose Pastor Stokes criticized New York State divorce law which recognized only adultery as legitimate grounds for divorce. A loveless marriage, she said, was far more of a sin.

> On the other hand, love is always justified, even when short-lived, even when mistaken, because during its existence it enlarges and ennobles the natures of the men and women experiencing the love.[22]

Commenting on the same subject the following year, in an article for *Collier's Magazine*, she wrote:

> Dominant in my struggle for the new society is the hope that once the complete factual basis is laid— once economic security becomes the heritage of every member of society—permanence in the love relation will become widely possible.[23]

Because Mrs. Stokes supported divorce in this article, the editors of *Collier's* warned their delicate readers not to read it if they didn't want to be exposed to unorthodox views.

To Rose Pastor Stokes, honest man-woman relations could come only in an economically secure environment. Thus the elevation of the woman's role in society was inextricably tied to the elevation of the man's role. Until workingmen were free, women could never be free. The woman problem was part of the class problem. To both Elizabeth Gurley Flynn and Rose Pastor Stokes, class and sex could not be separated. The dominance of the rich elite in a capitalistic society affected all women as well as all workingmen. Mrs. Stokes remained a loyal party worker until cancer robbed her of life. She died at the age of fifty-four in June 1933.

Kate Richards O'Hare, the last radical feminist of the group, walked out of prison in May 1920, after serving fourteen months of a five-year term. Emma Goldman was with her

in the penitentiary at Jefferson City, Missouri, and later recalled how they had become friends despite their philosophical differences. Miss Goldman considered Mrs. O'Hare's
socialism to be cold and unreal, while Mrs. O'Hare believed
that Emma's anarchism did not speak to the material problems facing America. Miss Goldman remembered the aid
Frank O'Hare gave his wife by his frequent visits and by his
circulation of Kate's letters to her many friends as well as to
the *St. Louis Post Dispatch*. Her descriptions of the atrocious
conditions in the prison led to visible improvements. As
Richard Drinnon, Emma Goldman's biographer, noted, "The
Missouri Welfare League later declared that the whole country owed her [Kate O'Hare] a debt of gratitude for her 'fear-
less disclosures of abuses and cruelties in the women's department of the prison . . . [they] were of great value and
helped end an intolerable situation there."[24] In fact, as a result of Mrs. O'Hare's prison experience, she wrote a book on
prison life and embarked on a career in prison reform. She
believed that "while we are building the machinery of the
new order,"[25] it was necessary to repair the existing institutions as far as possible.

In March 1922, Mrs. O'Hare attracted newspaper headlines with her announcement that she was going to lead a
group of children to Washington to ask President Harding to
release the 114 political prisoners still in jail. While famous
political prisoners such as Kate Richards O'Hare and Eugene
Debs had been freed by 1920, humbler antiwar Socialists and
Wobblies were still behind bars. Although the 1917 Espionage
Act, which had convicted these prisoners, had been repealed
shortly after the war, the victims of the law remained in jail.
Along with the American Civil Liberties Union and other
liberal organizations, Mrs. O'Hare publicized the fate of the
prisoners, dramatized it with the presence of children, and
tried repeatedly to see the President. The "Children's Crusade," as it came to be called, arrived in Washington in May
1922, and had trouble securing a meeting with the President.
Mrs. O'Hare was quoted as saying:

If we don't see the President today, we will come
here at the same time tomorrow and the next day
and the day after until some definite announcement
is made or our petitions are acted upon. I want to
make it clear that we are not going to picket. We
are merely making peaceful petition and we think
three years is time enough for these cases to be investigated and acted upon.[26]

Demonstrations continued, but to no avail. President Harding insisted that the Justice Department was the proper
agency to contact and that the Department would review the
cases individually. Although Mrs. O'Hare's part in this crusade seemed to end shortly thereafter, a committee made up
of interested groups was organized to continue the agitation.
Senator William E. Borah of Idaho was one of the articulate
supporters of this cause. Slowly, in piecemeal fashion, Harding commuted the sentences of a number of the prisoners so
that eleven months later fifty-three prisoners still remained
in jail, fifty-one having been released.[27]

The Socialist Party, which had meant so much to Kate
Richards O'Hare, was beset with enormous difficulties in the
twenties. Factionalism plagued it. Its left wing went over to
the newly formed Communist Party, and its right wing
fought with those in the middle. Eugene Debs, the well-
known leader of the party and a colleague of Mrs. O'Hare's
seemed out of touch with reality after 1920.[28] Although biographical information is fragmentary at this point, Mrs.
O'Hare moved to California in the early twenties, divorced
O'Hare in 1928, and immediately married a San Francisco
engineer named Charles C. Cunningham. In 1934, her name
appeared on a letterhead endorsing Upton Sinclair for
governor of California, and in 1939, in recognition of her
work on penal reform, she was appointed Assistant State
Director of Penology in California. One of her accomplishments was the development of San Quentin into a model
penitentiary.[29] When Kate Richards O'Hare Cunningham

died in January 1948, she was remembered for her pre-World
War One Socialist activity and her postwar prison administration work. Her work for prison reform suggested a
domestication of her spirit. In any case, her seventy years
on earth had been filled with purposeful work devoted to
improving the lives of the workers of America.

PRAGMATIC FEMINISTS

Women's organizations grew in size and number during
the twenties. They were, after all, the home of many pragmatic, hard-working feminists. This is not to say that all
women in women's organizations were feminists, but most of
them, whether they knew it or not, accepted the basic premise
of feminism. Organization women were acutely conscious of
the woman's role in our society and most especially her inferior status. Being practical and moderate, they believed
that the passage of a desired law or the publicizing of a particular issue would materially alter woman's status and lead
toward the desired society. The League of WomenVoters best
typifies this point of view. Formed after 1920 out of the old
suffrage organization, the League concentrated on educating
women to use their vote wisely and on lobbying for legislation it considered desirable. Strictly nonpartisan, it did not
organize women into a separate political party but rather
advised them to work through the party of their choice. Its
tone was moderate and its aims modest. As Maud Wood Park,
the national president during the early part of the twenties,
suggested,

> What women saw in women's suffrage was not a
> panacea, but a help, for women as a sex are content
> to advance a little at a time. Women believed that
> experience had given them something of value to
> contribute to the cause of good government but they
> had no idea that there was in them any instinctive
> wisdom which would enable them overnight to

straighten out tangles over which generations of
men had worked in vain.[30]

This judgment, made in 1924, appeared to many to be a
rationalization for the fact that women's suffrage had not
altered the quality of politics one iota. However, the League
has always been characterized, from its inception until the
present, by its "step-by-step progress." At its 1924 convention, for example, a proposal to endorse a constitutional
amendment to provide a uniform marriage and divorce law
was denied; similarly, a bill to offer birth control as a study
subject was rejected.[31] Besides its moderate vision, the
League of Women Voters, being a national group, could not
effectively control its state chapters—the result being that
each state could pick and choose from the national platform
whatever part appealed to them.

During the twenties, the National League of Women Voters
supported a wide range of legislation. Among the most significant measures were the Cable Act of 1922, which granted
women independent citizenship despite the status of their
husbands; the Sheppard-Towner Act of 1921, providing
modest funds to states that would establish programs for
instruction in the hygiene of maternity and infancy; the
Muscle Shoals project under government ownership; and a
package of liberal labor bills including collective bargaining,
wages-and-hours laws, and equal pay for equal work.[32] State
chapters were often not so ambitious in their legislative programs. The Pennsylvania branch was headed by a woman
who emphasized efficiency in government and little else, while
the Kansas League president enjoyed arranging patriotic
meetings. The Illinois chapter in 1927 had ten major items on
its legislative program for the year. The first three dealt with
improving the ballot, the direct primary system, and the
civil service; of the remaining seven, four dealt specifically
with women: a call for women to sit on juries, a proposal for
a state reformatory for women offenders, an eight-hour day
for women workers, and an educational program for infant
and maternal hygiene.[33]

Women were not forgotten in the programs of the League chapters, but they were not the sole or central concern either. During the 1920's, the League participated, along with many other women's organizations, in the Women's Joint Congressional Committee. The wjcc acted as a lobby in Washington for legislation affecting women. Working through various subcommittees, the wjcc kept close watch upon such bills as those dealing with child labor, reclassifying the civil service, creating a federal bureau of education, and a uniform marriage and divorce amendment. (The League of Women Voters did not send a representative to the particular subcommittee considering the amendment, as they did not endorse it.) Thus each women's organization retained its autonomy and participated only in the subcommittees that it approved of.[34] The strength and influence of the wjcc, then, was limited to the support it evoked from its member organizations, not to mention the support it gained in the halls of Congress. A subcommittee that most of the eighteen women's organizations approved of was the one *opposing* the National Women's Party's equal rights amendment. The League of Women Voters, the National Women's Trade Union League, the General Federation of Women's Clubs, and the National Federation of Business and Professional Women's Clubs all agreed that the National Women's Party amendment was detrimental to woman's rights. The amendment read: "Men and women shall have equal rights throughout the United States and every place subject to its jurisdiction. Congress shall have the power to enforce this article by appropriate legislation."[35] Simple and seemingly desirable as it sounded, the equal rights amendment provoked intense opposition from women's groups and consumed much of their time, energy, and talent. Indeed, they often had little time left over to pursue other social goals.

To women in the trade union movement, the equal rights amendment would erase all of their hard-won protective labor legislation for women. To League of Women Voters members and to professional women, the amendment seemed too vague and too difficult to interpret. They also agreed with

working women that all of women's privileges would be
wiped away with the passage of the amendment; women
could be drafted into the army, made to pay alimony, and
forced into undesirable working conditions. As Mary Anderson later recalled, no one was against equal rights for women;
but the National Women's Party, by adopting that term to
describe their amendment had cleverly preempted the work
of all of the other women's organizations. All were working
to provide women with equal rights, but the amendment,
Miss Anderson believed, would be meaningless for at least
three major reasons:

> In the first place it was unsound from the legal point
> of view. There was no definition of "rights." There
> was no definition of "equality." If a state law had
> different standards for men and women, would the
> amendment mean that the men should have the
> women's standards, or the women have the men's?
> No one knew the answer. In the second place it was
> unnecessary because most of the real discrimina-
> tions against women were a matter of custom and
> prejudice and would not be affected by a constitu-
> tional amendment. In the third place it was danger-
> ous because it might upset or nullify all the legal pro-
> tection for women workers that had been built up
> through the years, which really put them on a more
> nearly equal footing with men workers.[36]

Supporters of the amendment insisted that the National
Women's Party advocated "not the removal of protection,
but the removal of the sex basis in protective laws."[37] If a
labor law was good for human beings, advocates argued,
both sexes should benefit; if it kept women in a separate
status, it should be eliminated. The battle over this amendment has not yet ended. But in the 1920's, it split the women's
organizations so badly that they spent more time fighting
each other than uniting against common enemies. In the
1930's, some of the women's organizations that had opposed

the amendment, most notably the National Federation of Business and Professional Women's Clubs, changed their position because they had come to believe that women's professional opportunities for promotion and advancement were hindered by protective labor laws. But the women's trade union movement, the American Association of University Women, the National Council of Jewish Women, as well as others, continue to this day to oppose the amendment.

The National Women's Party, the original sponsor and supporter of the equal rights amendment, had begun as the militant wing of the suffrage organization during the 1910's. Led by Alice Paul, a fiery Quaker girl from New Jersey, a small coterie of suffragists decided to dramatize the suffrage struggle by demonstrating in the streets of Washington on the day of Woodrow Wilson's first inauguration in 1913. These impatient suffragists, known as the Congressional Union, believed that the state-by-state strategy of the National American Woman's Suffrage Association would not reap the desired results. In 1913, women had been agitating for the vote for over fifty years with little effect. Thus Alice Paul used direct-action tactics to publicize the suffrage crusade. When war came and especially after April 1917, when the United States entered the war, the militants continued their fight, never relenting. While the dominant Suffrage Association volunteered for patriotic service and its members folded bandages, Alice Paul and her group marched in front of the White House, were arrested for disturbing the peace, fasted in jail, and generally made a nuisance of themselves. When the suffrage amendment became the law of the land in 1920, the radicals claimed victory while the more "respectable" moderates believed that Alice Paul had almost lost the vote for women by her intimidation tactics.

In 1920, then, when the National American Woman's Suffrage Association disbanded, with approximately one-tenth of its membership going into the League of Women Voters, Alice Paul's group became known as the National Women's Party and dedicated itself to increasing "the power of American women."[38] At the party's convention in February 1921, the decision was made to focus solely upon a national equal rights amendment. It was at this meeting that Crystal Eastman proposed a broad feminist program; however, it was rejected by Alice Paul as being unnecessary if the equal rights amendment were passed. Another dissenting voice at that convention reported on the fact that black women in the South were being deprived of the vote—but Alice Paul did not want to deal with this issue either. She controlled the activities of the convention, a fact noted by both her admirers and enemies. She stood apart, as one observer said, "because she is a revolutionist in tactics, and has the revolutionist's singlemindedness and destructive insistence and disregard of persons."[39] "Her exasperating willfulness" dominated the course that the National Women's Party would take for the next fifty years. Alice Paul stepped down from the chairmanship of the party but remained active in the organization, later becoming vice-chairman. During the 1920's, she continued her formal education (she already had received a Ph.D. in 1912), and obtained three law degrees in a seven-year period: an LLB from Washington College of Law in 1922, an LLM in 1927, and a DCL in 1928 from the American University.

Alice Paul's ability as a leader was unquestioned. Her followers zealously defended the equal rights amendment against all critics; they claimed that this blanket amendment would elevate women and put them on a par with men. But all feminists and all organization women did not agree with this assessment. As a result, as Frances Kellor noted in 1923, "The American woman's movement, and her interest in great social and moral questions, is splintered into a hundred fragments under as many warring leaders."[40] Pragmatic feminists did not turn out to be too pragmatic after all. Although they shared the general goal of equal rights for women, they differed seriously as to the best method to attain that goal. Writer Frances Kellor also observed that if the suffrage leaders had become active political candidates, women would have played a more critical role in decision-making. American women should have realized, she argued, that welfare movements were no substitute for "responsible women in public office helping to administer all affairs that concern women as well as men."[41] But neither the National Women's Party nor the League of Women Voters put up women candidates: the NWP supported women candidates in particular elections, while the League remained nonpartisan after one effort, in 1920, to unseat Senator Wadsworth of New York (an antisuffragist and militarist) proved unsuccessful.

While the NWP focused solely on the equal rights amendment throughout the twenties, the League developed a far more comprehensive legislative program. But neither organization gained substantial adherents to their respective positions. Alice Paul's legal training aided her tremendously in investigating the many state laws that discriminated against women. Women could not sit on juries during the 1920's in most states; neither could married women have independent property, equal inheritance rights, or, in some states, the possession of their children after divorce. An equal rights amendment, Alice Paul reasoned, would remove each state's particular set of sex-discriminatory laws. When a woman became governor of the state of Texas in the mid-twenties, she needed her husband's written consent.[42] Wisconsin was the only state during this whole period that passed an equal rights amendment. One of the provisions in the 1921 Wisconsin law, however, stated that it should not be construed as "to deny to females the special protection which they now enjoy for the general welfare."[43]

The personal bitterness between Alice Paul and the women fighters for protective legislation never abated. Florence Kelley, the head of the Consumer's League, an organization that had worked for child labor and women's wages-and-hours laws, considered Alice Paul ". . . a Fiend come to destroy . . ."[44] her twenty years of hard work. Miss Paul, on the other hand, determinedly argued that she was not opposed to the eight-hour day or the prohibition of night work, for example, but that "protective legislation [should] be made to apply to everyone alike so that industrial conditions may be definitely

improved."[45] Each side never convinced the other of the validity of its claim. During the twenties, neither political
party endorsed the equal rights amendment, although Herbert Hoover in 1928 did not come out against it, as did Al
Smith. European women seemed more congenially disposed
toward Miss Paul's amendment than did American women.
Beatrice Webb of England expressed the same point of view,
and in Norway women "wanted security for the entire population."[46] The International Woman's Suffrage Alliance,
however, would not grant membership to the NWP in 1926
because the League of Women Voters was already a member.
"It was felt unwise to admit a second organization from a
country where instead of complementing each other the two
would be in continual opposition."[47]

During the 1930's, Alice Paul transferred her activities
and energies to the international sphere. Displaying the same
vigor at forty-five (in 1930) that she had shown in 1912, she
became chairman of the Nationality Committee of the Inter-
American Commission of Women. In this position, she
worked to get Latin-American nations to grant equal nationality rights to its women citizens. Both the 1922 and the
1930 Cable Act in the United States had legislated in favor of
American women retaining their basic citizenship rights
even if they married foreigners. Miss Paul wanted to see
other nations grant their women the same rights. Further,
as a member of the executive committee of the Equal Rights
International, with its headquarters in Geneva, she lobbied
for an equal rights treaty to be signed by all the nations
of the world.

By this time, Alice Paul was an expert on international
law regarding women's rights. She wrote exhaustive studies
describing each country's laws concerning women, and commented upon them. Through the Inter-American Commission, the Equal Rights International, and the Committee on
Nationality of the League of Nations, she worked for the
adoption of the equal rights treaty. "Women, whatever their
race," Miss Paul wrote, "are united in demanding that, when
a world code of law is made for all the world, it shall be a

law that is free from all discriminations based on sex."[48] In 1934, under direct instructions from President Roosevelt, the American delegation to the Pan-American Conference at Montevideo, Uruguay, signed an agreement to support a treaty granting equal nationality rights to women.

> With the fascist governments moving as fast as they can in the direction of reducing women to the ancient status of domestic servants and breeders of soldiers, liberal governments should reaffirm their faith and prove it by their works.[49]

In 1938, Alice Paul worked in the newly created World Woman's Party. She reasoned that "The world is now so closely knit that it is no longer possible for any movement which concerns women all over the world to be localized in any one country."[50] With its headquarters in Geneva and with a ten thousand dollar donation from the NWP, the WWP began its work. Alice Paul became the NWP representative in Geneva from 1939-1941. When she returned to this country in 1941, another world war had started and she noted:

> This world crisis came about without women having anything to do with it. If the women of the world had not been excluded from world affairs, things today might have been different. . . . What we want to do is to have some say in the movement of peace when it comes. Women had no voice in the making of the treaty of Versailles, and if we had had, things would have been different today.[51]

The preamble to the United Nations Charter at San Francisco in 1945 adopted the equal rights for women resolution. Alice Paul considered it a major victory. Still optimistic and active, she believed that the U.N. Assembly's acceptance of the women's suffrage resolution in December 1946 meant that "all member nations will bring their laws in regard to

Suffrage up to the standard of equality recommended by the Assembly."[52] The work of the World Woman's Party then turned to obtaining equality in every other area for all women in all the countries of the world. A large order, indeed. The gap between the U.N. resolution and the actions taken within each country in the world was greater than Miss Paul anticipated. A nation might accept the pledge of women's suffrage but would not act upon it.

While Alice Paul turned from the equal rights amendment fight in this country to a crusade for world recognition of women's rights, the other women leaders and organizations continued their slow but dogged work for removing discriminatory laws against women in this country, urging Congress to pass desirable legislation. Trade union women found the twenties a particularly difficult time for organizing women workers. The Women's Trade Union League lost membership during that decade and curtailed its organizing activities considerably. One of the WTUL's most energetic workers during these difficult years was Rose Schneiderman, who became its national president in 1928 and remained in that position for the next twenty years. Rose Schneiderman was a vivacious redhead who had started working in a department store for $2.75 a week in 1907. She later became a cap-maker and participated in the waist-maker's strike in 1909. In 1908, she became an organizer for the WTUL. Like Agnes Nestor and Mary Anderson, she had seen the evils of sweatshop conditions and the ways in which employers exploited women workers.

In 1920, Rose Schneiderman ran for the Senate on the Farmer-Labor Party ticket. She had hoped that voting women would support her as well as the platform of the WTUL. Agitation for the forty-eight-hour week as well as equal pay for equal work were among the planks in her platform. When asked what she thought of the voting record of women in 1924, Miss Schneiderman replied:

I am just as disappointed in women's suffrage as I

am in men's suffrage. . . . Women have done very
little in four years of voting, but men have done
tragically little in a hundred and fifty years. Why
suddenly demand that women do the outstanding
thing which we've given up expecting from men?

While the suffragists had virtually promised an uplift in
political matters when the women voted, pragmatic unionist
Rose Schneiderman knew that a great deal more than the
vote was needed to produce desirable changes. She knew from
her organizing experience that women were reluctant to do
anything that was untraditional and bold. "Women shirk the
responsibility for decisive action in public questions. And it
is not surprising. For so many hundreds of years they haven't
been held responsible for anything outside their own households."[53]

Rose Schneiderman's remarks demonstrated a crucial
awareness of the importance and power of cultural attitudes
toward women. Because women had been restricted to the
home, to domestic activities solely, for such a long time, they
could not make the transition to active political participation
easily. The fact that women worked outside the home, Rose
Schneiderman knew, did not mean that they were emancipated in any meaningful sense. Working women needed mas-
sive educational programs so that they would vote and vote
intelligently. Similarly, working women had to broaden their
horizons if they were to advance economically. Most women
worked out of economic necessity, took no pride in their
work, and stopped working as quickly as they possibly could.
Even if they worked the better part of their lives, they saw
their work as temporary and unimportant. The meaningful
part of their lives occurred in the home, not in the factory or
office. Only through a major educational campaign could
working women become aware of other possibilities for their
lives.

Under the New Deal administration of Franklin D. Roosevelt, Rose Schneiderman became the only woman member of
the National Recovery Administration's Labor Advisory

Board. Because of her knowledge and experience in labor matters, she participated in the NRA's task of setting work codes for industries and dealing with wage-and-hour issues. Although she was not a member of the Democratic Party (she was part of Sidney Hillman's American Labor Party), she was a close friend of the Roosevelts.[54] To William Albert Wirt, the Gary, Indiana, superintendent of schools and a watchful critic of the New Deal, Rose Schneiderman was "the Rose of Anarchy" and one of the President's brain-trusters.[55] In 1937, she became the secretary of the New York State Labor Department, a position she held until 1944. Effectively typifying the pragmatic feminist, she continuously worked to improve working conditions for women and, like Mary Anderson at the Women's Bureau of the Department of Labor, worked within the structure of government. She keenly believed in the need for working women to receive protective treatment. Like all the pragmatic feminists, she focused on one segment of womankind, one particular group of women who needed aid. She did not share the general sex analysis of the feminist who saw all women oppressed; neither did she believe that the Marxist class analysis applied to all women. Rose Schneiderman had faith in the democratic and capitalistic structures of America and thought that the system could, and would, adjust itself to accommodate working women.

FEMINIST WRITERS

The feminist writers of every generation are the literary spokeswomen and propagandists for the feminist cause. They give public expression to the ideas of the visionaries as well as the pragmatists in the movement. In 1920, the Pulitzer Prize for drama was given to Zona Gale, the author of *Miss Lulu Bett*. When it came out as a novel in the early part of the year, it was an immediate best-seller, with *Main Street* its only rival. Zona Gale had been writing fiction for a decade before *Miss Lulu Bett*, but with this novel she came into her own and received widespread public recognition.

Zona Gale's life typified the new woman of the early twentieth century. Born in 1874 in Portage, Wisconsin, an only child, she received a college degree at the University of Wisconsin in 1895. She then lived in Milwaukee and wrote for a newspaper there for six years, and in 1901 moved to New York City. Zona Gale had wanted to write since she was eight years old, and her determination finally paid off. Her early published works were modest, realistic stories about small towns. *Miss Lulu Bett,* however, had a depth of characterization and poignancy that her earlier work lacked. Further, it displayed in dramatic, literary terms one of the major dilemmas faced by American women. It is in this respect that the book is germane; it portrayed quite effectively what happens to a woman who does not marry—how she is treated and how she sees herself. The reader's introduction to Lulu Bett is a very telling one:

> There emerged from the fringe of things, where she perpetually hovered, Mrs. Deacon's older sister, Lulu Bett, who was "making her home with us." And that was precisely the case. *They* were not making her a home, goodness knows. Lulu was the family beast of burden.[56]

A spinster, the outcast of American society, she performed all the domestic chores of her sister's household but always remained dutifully in the background. Her brother-in-law, Mr. Deacon, a pompous dentist and justice of the peace, continually reminded her of her dependency status. The plot thickened when Ninian, Deacon's brother, came to visit.

> "Is it Miss Lulu Bett?" he abruptly inquired, "Or Mrs.?" Lulu flushed in anguish. "Miss," she said low, as one who confesses the extremity of failure. Then from unplumbed depths another Lulu abruptly spoke up. "From choice," she said.[57]

Ninian assured her that he never doubted it. During the

course of his visit, he showered more attention upon Lulu than she had ever received before. Suddenly someone spoke to her, cared about her, and catered to her. She found herself thinking and saying things she had never thought or said before. Indeed, she had never known before that she had thoughts or opinions.

Lulu married Ninian and left town with him, only to return shortly thereafter without him, having discovered that he had been married before and did not know whether his first wife was living or dead. Eventually, Lulu married another man and left her sister's home forever. But the focus of the play, its power and success, rested upon its effective characterization of a woman coming into selfhood, an inhibited thirty-four-year-old woman named Lulu, who had had no identity before a man courted her. *Miss Lulu Bett* shows implicitly how impossible the status of an unmarried grown woman is in our society. She owned nothing, had no sense of self, was a non-person. Only when a man paid attention to her, when she married, did she reach fulfillment. Ironically, the happy ending of the story dramatized the narrow vision of our society regarding women. The only hope for happiness for women, Zona Gale seemed to be saying, was marriage.

And yet in "real" life, Zona Gale knew about feminism and the urge to freedom that women were experiencing in greater numbers in the early 1900's. She herself was an economically and spiritually independent woman living alone in New York City. Although her mother often wrote to her warning her not to involve herself with woman's suffrage or any other radical cause ("I would let that mess of women alone!"[58]), Zona Gale sympathized with all of the feminist causes of the period. She believed in woman's natural right to determine her own future and did not accept as gospel the traditional view of only one future for all women. One of her women characters in *A Daughter of the Morning* questions whether motherhood is the destiny of all women:

> "And you must see—I'm not a mother-woman. I should love children—to have them, to give them

every free chance to grow. But it would be the same
thing with them: their sewing, their mending, a
good deal of the care of them—I don't know about it,
and I shouldn't like it. I shouldn't be wise about their
feeding, or the care of them if they were sick. And
as for saying that the knowledge comes with the
physical birth of the child, that's sheer nonsense."[59]

Another heroine was a writer. In fact, independent women
were generally featured in all Zona Gale's writing.

At the same time that Zona Gale imbibed the new feminist
views, she still retained enormous respect for her parents
and their wishes. Her mother's disapproval of poet Ridgely
Torrence was probably responsible for her not marrying him.
In 1924, after Torrence married another woman, Zona Gale
wrote him that she still loved him and that she hoped, in the
next life, "we can fall in love all over again—and *that* time,
have enough more star-dust in me, to bring it off."[60] The
First World War disturbed her, as it did so many others. A
devout pacifist, she found it difficult to write or to reason
with people once war and patriotism overtook everyone. She
participated in the activities of the Woman's Peace Party
in New York and contributed articles to its magazine, *Four
Lights*.

In the twenties, she returned to Portage, Wisconsin, to
live. She became a regent of the University of Wisconsin in
1923 and campaigned actively for Robert LaFollette in 1924.
Although she continued to write, her stories dealt with popular themes of love and the problems of romance. Her heroines
were no longer feminists but either strong-willed girls who
learned how to lead their men around or selfish divorcees who
ignored their parents' wishes; they displayed no doubts about
the role women were to play in the modern world. In 1927,
Zona Gale adopted a child and, in the following year, married
an old friend, widower Will Breese. She was fifty-four and
Breese ten years older. Although she traveled to New York
frequently, her life now centered around her beloved home,

family, and town. She died in December 1938, at the age of sixty-four.

"Fannie Hurst is a blend of woman and author," wrote Zora Neale Hurston, a novelist in her own right and one-time secretary to Miss Hurst.

> You cannot separate the two things in her case. Nature must have meant it to be that way. Most career women are different. Their profession is like oil and water. You can see where one stops and the other begins. And then again some women writers are writers and some of them are women. Any time, day or night, you run across Fannie Hurst, you can see and feel her womanhood. And if you read her, you are going to find out that she is an author.[61]

Fannie Hurst has always been known as a woman's writer; her major characters are always women, and the major dilemmas described are always women's dilemmas. But unbeknownst to most, Fannie Hurst was also a feminist writer. Both in her own life and in her writing, she displayed serious and enduring concerns for the full human development of women.

She was born into a comfortable Ohio family of German-Jews in 1889. The Hursts moved to St. Louis, Missouri, when Fannie was a baby; her only sister died when she was five. Fannie Hurst started writing at the age of eight and continued this preoccupation until it became a fruitful occupation. Like Zona Gale, and most writers perhaps, Fannie Hurst's self-definition included a vision of herself as a successful writer. She had a profession she adored, and when the fact that she was a woman interfered with the pursuit of her career, she had to face up to the meaning of womanhood in our culture. The advice she received from her relatives was: "Get married young. Don't educate yourself into a bluestocking. The more you know, the less desirable you be-

come to men. They want a homemaker, not a superior mind."[62]
The power and weight of tradition, of course, was great. The
only meaningful occupation for a woman was marriage and
children. Any woman who deviated from this accepted path
was queer and unstable. This was the basic message drummed
into Fannie Hurst's ears as she grew up. While her father always encouraged her writing and education, as he believed
that knowledge was power, her mother did not agree. Even
after success began to touch Fannie Hurst, her mother was
saying:

> "All right, *The Saturday Evening Post* is a big
> thing. But do you mean to say you hesitate between
> such a life and a home of your own, with say a little
> writing on the side? That is," concluded Mama
> witheringly, "unless *The Saturday Evening Post*
> doesn't believe in marriage."[63]

Persistence is a known trait of writers, and Fannie Hurst
possessed a large dose of it. She left home against her parent's wishes, moved to New York in the early years of this
century, and grubbed for a living until her stories began to
sell. Although she had a pretty face, she was unusually over-
weight and did not date young men. When she did fall in
love with musician Jacques Danielson and he wanted to
marry her, she hesitated. "How could I be certain marriage
would not clip my wings? Besides, I had realistic reasons for
shrinking from it. Mama's and Papa's, the marriage with
which I was most familiar, was good enough as things go,
but certainly unwanted by me."[64] Her indecision almost
caused her to lose Jacques. But finally she agreed to marry
him, in 1915, although their marital arrangement was un-
conventional: they lived separate lives and for the first five
years of their marriage maintained their own apartments
while keeping their marriage a secret.

> Our marital arrangement was certainly not one
> from which to deduce a formula. It happened to fit

> our particular needs. We defied so many of the basic
> laws for the successful marriage. What a list of
> "don'ts" we must have supplied for the marriage
> counselors. Our home life was negligible. We dined
> out, met when we so willed, or went our separate
> ways. We talked wishfully of having children, but
> when it did not happen lived happily and without
> sense of frustration.[65]

Fannie Hurst lived the life many feminists talked about;
she had an independent reason for being—her writing—and
at the same time had a rich and respectful relationship with
the man she loved. She commented in her autobiography that
"every career woman with a private-life mate is faced with
this problem in one form or another: the dignity of her
male."[66] Fannie Hurst and Jacques Danielson seemed to
avoid the problem; he respected her writing although he
knew little about literature and she respected his music
although her musical knowledge was sparse. They had a
profound love-attachment which held them together at the
same time that they had separate interests and concerns
which kept them happy and alive.

In her fiction, Fannie Hurst showed sympathy and concern
for the problems women faced. As her success increased (in
the twenties she was considered the highest paid woman
writer), her novels and short stories became more melo-
dramatic than dramatic, but in her early work she exhibited
feminist themes, themes which would lose their public appeal
by the mid-twenties. Editors wanted stories about gay, irre-
sponsible girls and not about women agonizing over their
life's purpose. In *Star Dust,* however, subtitled "The Story
of an American Girl" (1921), Fannie Hurst created Lilly
Becker, a searching, unsatisfied young woman, a typical
feminist and unflapper-like heroine. In what sounds very
much like autobiography, Lilly grew up in St. Louis and
found herself unsatisfied with the future society had carved
out for her. Her father objected to her going to college:

"Don't spoil a good thing by trying to overdo it,
Lilly. It is as bad for a young girl to permit herself
to be educated into one of those bold, unwomanly
woman's-rights girls as it is for her to be frivolous
and empty-headed. When women get too smart they
get unattractive."[67]

The possible options are clearly drawn in this statement.
A young woman has essentially three choices: to be overeducated and become by implication manly; to be gay and
empty-headed; or to be mediocre, somewhere in the middle,
neither too bright nor too stupid, neither too ambitious nor
too lazy. Hardly desirable choices for a sensitive woman.
"I always wanted to be something,"[68] Lilly exclaimed. But
Lilly did not have a well-defined talent or career choice; she
had casual hopes of being a singer or writer but no clearly
discernible talent or drive in either area. Thus she married
reluctantly but found domestic married life unbearable. "I
just can't rake up enthusiasm over French knots. Something
in me begins to suffocate and I can't get out from under. I
hate it."[69] These are very strong words for the opening of
the jazz age. Lilly Becker did not love her husband and could
not be flip or cool about it. Neither could she adjust to a
future she dreaded.

Against her husband's wishes, she left him (he would not
give her a divorce because of the scandal it would create),
went to New York, and got a job singing. Her boss, noticing
her unhappiness, suggested that a love affair would solve her
problems. Her answer would create pride in the hearts of all
feminists in all periods:

"Oh, there you go again! Is there no limit to sex
self-consciousness? I want to be a person in my
work. An individual. Not first and foremost a woman! . . . I give nothing to you men and I ask nothing
except a fighting chance. I don't believe in all this
pay-the-price business. I don't recognize you as the

arbiters of my destiny. I'll pay my price with my ability, and if I can't pay up that way then I deserve to fail. Women can fight back at the world with something besides their sex. I intend to prove it."[70]

Lilly Becker was trapped, as all women were, in the culture's definition of them. Being a woman meant, first and foremost, being a tempting sex object. In order to get away from this definition, Lilly grasped for another word to describe her desired state—an "individual"—because womanhood was so inextricably tied to sexuality.

It was, in fact, woman's sexuality that brought the next crisis in Lilly's life; she discovered shortly after her arrival in New York that she was pregnant, the very state that defines womanhood. Because she had posed as a single girl, she was evicted from her apartment and went through many trials and tribulations before securing adequate lodging and another job. Lilly questioned the morality of a society that sanctioned marriage under any conditions as being the most desirable state:

> "Married for every reason in the world except love. No marriage ceremony in the world can condone the immorality of that! Society may, but God doesn't. From your point of view, then, I'm a respectable woman. From mine, I'm rotten."[71]

The birth of her daughter, whom she named Zoe, inspired her and gave meaning to her struggles.

> "I don't know which way the vision is pointing. Funny. Oh, but I'm going to clear the way for you, Zoe. No Chinese shoes for your little feet or your little brain. Free—to choose—to be! That's the way I'll rear my daughter! Queer I never think of him, her father."[72]

Lilly subsequently became a responsible secretary and settled down to a quiet life, enjoying her daughter and watching her grow. "I'm the grist being ground between yesterday and to-day,"Lilly mused. "Sometimes I think I must be some sort of an unfinished symphony which it will take another generation to complete. I am a river and I long to be a sea."[73] Later in the novel, after she arranged a meeting between her parents, her husband, herself, and Zoe, she described herself as the grape, with Zoe the wine. "Her arm is long enough to touch what she wants. Mine wasn't. I saw it, but I couldn't reach. I was one generation too underdone."[74] Zoe is the free spirit Lilly had longed to be. Zoe's rebelliousness, in fact, often turned against Lilly; Zoe did not want to see her father or go back to St. Louis. "Do you want to throw me back into that bowl with the greased sides that you managed to climb out of?" she asked her mother. "This from Zoe," mused Lilly, "mixed metaphor and all, who at seventeen kept *Doll's House,* Freud, *Anna Karenina,* and Ellen Key on the table beside her bed."[75]

In the end, because of a complicated set of circumstances, Zoe unknowingly fell in love with the man whom Lilly had long loved (and who had loved her) but whom she could not marry. This climax fitted in with the general theme of Lilly's being the preparation for free-spirited Zoe. While Lilly's struggle for freedom remained incomplete, Zoe fulfilled her life's destiny by marrying a man she loved. This conclusion fails as a feminist statement. Zoe does not become (or at least the reader does not know what she will become) a famous dancer or singer, but rather a woman in love. Lilly found motherhood her main reason for being, and Zoe found love. *Star Dust* begins as an effective exploration of the new woman's search for a self-definition, but it gets lost along the way. Lilly Becker proved to be a successful business woman but she had no faith in herself or respect for her own work. Fannie Hurst recognized that her heroine was an unfinished feminist, but her climax lapsed into the typical romantic ending of a popular melodrama. Whether Zoe, in fact, would become the new woman or not was not clear; the odds are she would not have.

Fannie Hurst frequently lectured on the need for business and professional women to assert themselves, to organize politically, and to propagandize for issues that concerned them. In a 1931 interview for *Independent Woman,* the magazine of the National Federation of Business and Professional Women's Clubs, she stated her long-held belief in the importance of economic independence for women as a crucial part of their freedom. A woman of affairs, she said, was "a salvager of self-respect," and Fannie Hurst became "her ardent champion."[76] Fannie Hurst understood the relationship between economic and psychic freedom in our culture. Women who are economically dependent upon their husbands and/or fathers are also psychologically dependent upon them. Thus career women, with lives of their own, symbolized emancipation.

In the same interview, Fannie Hurst discussed the marriage of the future, which she believed would be based upon surer ground precisely because business women would be self-assured and self-supporting. Future marriages would be a selective process as more and more women came into their own.

> Women will mate with men who are eugenically suited to them. . . . For the mother of that day will be a business woman, and will be able to bring to her children the broader contacts of the outside world, and to stimulate their imaginations as the old fashioned mother, obsessed by small domestic problems, never could do.[77]

Fannie Hurst's views of 1931 were very reminiscent of Henrietta Rodman's 1914 statements. In a sense, of course, the need to justify women's leaving the home by claiming that one of the results would be better motherhood demonstrated the strong hold of traditional views, and the fact that feminists

often thought within the frame of reference of their opponents. Most feminists believed in the inherent natural right of
women to be free, but they never rejected the basic worth
of motherhood. Further, for tactical purposes, they often
adopted the rhetoric and framework of traditionalists.

Fannie Hurst, like most feminists described in this study,
believed that marriage, a home, and a family were positive
goods; but she did not think that they summed up the life
purpose of every woman. They were important needs for
men, as they were for women; but no one considered them
men's main or sole reason for living. Feminists, then, wanted
to apply the same standard to women; they too desired a
family, but many also wanted a career. While Lilly Becker
could not articulate or discover her particular wants, Miss
Hurst suggested that many young women, especially those
of the younger generation, wanted to enlarge their definition
of life. They wanted to live purposefully and fully, according
to standards they helped to carve and not according to the
age-old ones that restricted them.

Fannie Hurst continued writing short stories and novels
into the 1960's. Simultaneously, she found time to chair a
committee in New York on workmen's compensation, to be
a member of the Mayor's Advisory Committee on Unity from
1945 to 1947, a board member of the New York Urban League,
and a United States delegate in 1952 to the World Health
Organization. She died at the age of seventy-eight in 1968,
leaving the bulk of her substantial estate to Brandeis and
Washington Universities. In her life, then, as well as in her
writing, she exhibited the true feminist's concern for the
fate of humanity.

". . . For more than three decades, the *Nation* was Freda
Kirchwey and she was the *Nation*."[78] The *New Republic*
editors, long-time rivals of the *Nation*, wrote these words
upon Freda Kirchwey's retirement in 1955. Freda Kirchwey,
the editor and publisher of the *Nation* for more than thirty
years, typified the upper-middle-class emancipated woman
of this century. She was born and raised in New York City;

her father, George W. Kirchwey, was dean of the Columbia University Law School. She attended Horace Mann School, considered one of the most progressive schools in the city, and went on to Barnard College, the woman's college of Columbia. Freda Kirchwey was always known as a spunky fighter, a person who held strong convictions and was determined to share them with others. In high school, in 1911, she began a suffrage club, and in college she conducted a suffrage campaign in Connecticut. She joined the Socialist Club when she was a freshman, picketed in strikes, and began the movement to abolish sororities at Barnard.

In the Barnard yearbook for 1915, Freda Kirchwey was described as the "best looking, the one who has done most for Barnard, most popular, most militant, and the one most likely to be famous in the future."[79] The prediction came true. A natural flair for writing led her, after college, to become a reporter on the *Morning Telegraph* and then the *New York Tribune*. In 1918, three years after graduating from Barnard, she joined the staff of the *Nation*, one of the nation's oldest intellectual magazines, edited and owned by Oswald Garrison Villard. Within a year, she was foreign editor; in 1922, she became managing editor; ten years later, she was editor and, in 1937, editor and publisher.

Although her career at the *Nation* was a full and time-consuming one, she successfully integrated her career with her private life. A year after college, she married Evans Clark, an economist and later director of the Twentieth Century Fund. Always devoted to the *Nation,* she worked until the day before her son was born, and returned to work shortly thereafter. In recalling those early years, she said:

It really hasn't been any problem. I've always been able to find good competent maids and good schools. I know how difficult it must be for women who live in smaller communities, where expert help is hard to get and where there aren't such good schools. In New York, everything can be made so simple.[80]

Clearly, this reveals the comfortable economic status she enjoyed. In her writing, Freda Kirchwey often showed a deep understanding of the problems of working women, but when she made this statement in 1937, she seemed to have forgotten that she was part of a privileged minority. Most working women in New York City could not afford competent maids at any time, but in the 1910's and 1920's, most middle- and upper-middle-class professional working women could. In this sense, then, Freda Kirchwey's statement accurately reflects the conditions that enabled rich women to work while utilizing the time and talent of working-class girls.

In terms of her career, Freda Kirchwey supported the feministic-pacifists during the First World War; she wrote for *Four Lights,* the New York Woman's Peace Party magazine, supported Crystal Eastman and Henrietta Rodman in their feminist work, and after joining the *Nation* continued her interest in women's rights by writing articles on the subject, conducting a symposium on the changing morality of the 1920's, and in 1927 sponsoring various series of articles on women and their problems.[81]

After 1920, she chose to support editorially the trade union women over Alice Paul's National Women's Party in their fight for the equal rights amendment. She agreed with the Women's Trade Union League that the hard-won protective legislation would be wiped off the books if the amendment passed. In 1928, she criticized the position of the National Women's Party for its support of Mr. Hoover. The NWP had always said that it would never back any candidate who did not come out publicly for the equal rights amendment; Hoover had not done this, although, unlike the Democratic Party candidate, Al Smith, he had not rejected it. Further, Hoover had discussed women and children together as a "natural group," a phrase the woman's movement in general had been fighting for a long time. Thus Editor Kirchwey wondered what the rationale was for the NWP's action.[82]

Her analysis of the NWP convention in 1921 agreed with Crystal Eastman's; Freda Kirchwey disapproved of the high-handed way Alice Paul had controlled the proceedings and prevented any serious dicussion of birth control, disarmament, and better marriage and divorce laws. The reasons for Alice Paul's actions, according to her, were that Miss Paul had lost touch with the mainstream of women and their needs, and that the desire to consolidate her power dominated her thinking.[83] Freda Kirchwey defined herself elsewhere as a "left-wing feminist and internationalist."[84] From her point of view, feminism, in order to be truly effective, had to incorporate itself into a larger world-view. For feminists to discuss disarmament seemed entirely appropriate. A peaceful world, she reasoned, was as crucial to women's freedom as were the vote, equitable laws in every area, and equal opportunity. Alice Paul and the National Women's Party disagreed with this analysis, arguing that the focus of a woman's organization had to be narrow and specific. (This was before Miss Paul changed her own focus.) Further, the NWP believed that an equal rights amendment would eliminate all other laws discriminating against women.

Freda Kirchwey consistently advocated admitting women into the professions. On one occasion, she made a commencement speech at Barnard College in which she criticized Columbia Law School, and her father, for not admitting women. In the thirties, her attention centered upon foreign affairs, and her clear, effective prose became her trademark. She advocated collective security as the world drew closer and closer to another war. While her old-time colleague Oswald Villard staunchly advocated isolationism for America, Freda Kirchwey argued that this country could not ignore world affairs and must materially aid the European nations that shared our tradition of representative democracy. She criticized the lack of U.S. support for the Spanish Republican forces and warned the English and French that they would have to act forcefully and decisively against Hitler's regime.

Early in 1939, she told her readers:

> We are not—most of us—fanatics who fear a fleet of
> Nazi planes over New York or the Panama Canal.

> Rather we fear the gradual crumbling of the eco-
> nomic and political and cultural relationships of
> men and nations in which we all shall be forced, in
> order to survive, to fit into the framework of a Nazi
> world.[85]

She advocated changing the Neutrality Laws so that the
United States could sell supplies to the non-Fascist powers
in case of war. When war descended upon Europe, she advocated military and economic aid to the Allies but believed
that the United States should not intervene directly.

> The consequences of war are so devastating that no
> nation has a right to plunge in unless all other
> means of resistance have failed. It is the tragedy
> of Europe that peaceful means of resistance were
> never applied; instead, surrender was tried as a
> weapon. That is why Europe is at war.[86]

As a young girl at the beginning of the First World War,
Freda Kirchwey had opposed American involvement; twenty
years later she believed that the nature of the threat was
significantly different. The United States could not remain
isolationist in the face of the Nazis, but this country should
try every constructive means to avoid participation in the
war.

In a 1934 editorial, where the appointment of the first
woman, Florence Allen, to the Federal Circuit Court of
Appeals was reported, she commented that F.D.R. ". . . has
recognized her merit and at the same time continued his own
unique record of choosing women for important public offices." But Freda Kirchwey did not stop there; she reminded
her readers:

> . . . Miss Perkins as a Cabinet member and Judge
> Allen as federal judge are only exceptions to the
> general rule that women are still discriminated
> against in the professions and in public life. It is

still fair to say that the woman doctor has to wait
longer, the woman lawyer to work harder, the
woman politician to be more outstanding than the
man who would achieve a correspondingly high
place. The fight for women's rights was not won
when women got the vote; we still need good heads
and stout spirits of both sexes to make equality in
the professions an accomplished fact.[87]

The editor of the *Nation* had not given up her concern for
women's rights; she took a long view of the situation and saw
that professional women still did not receive their due share
of jobs and opportunities. While international affairs consumed most of her time and energy from 1935 on, she always
retained her interest in woman's rights.

Her fresh and cool viewpoint was demonstrated in 1939 in
her attitude toward the formation of the Committee for Cultural Freedom in America, an anti-Communist group led by
such notable Americans as John Dewey and Sidney Hook.
Freda Kirchwey lamented the creation of this group because
the Committee did not openly acknowledge its true purpose
and split the leftist movement unnecessarily. Fully cognizant
of the weakness of the Communists, she still believed that:

With all their faults the Communists perform necessary functions in the confused struggle of our time.
They have helped to build up and to run a string of
organizations—known as "friends" by their opponents—which clearly serve the cause not of "totali-
tarian doctrine" but of a more workable democracy.

The Communist Party, she continued, had postponed its more
"serious revolutionary objectives to some post-next-war millennium . . . to leave them free meanwhile for democratic endeavor in this world."[88] The most radical thing the Communists had proposed recently, she concluded, was a third
term for F.D.R.

Freda Kirchwey had been a Socialist since the 1910's;

when the American Communist Party was formed in 1919, she disapproved of it because of its ties with Moscow. She observed the languid growth of the party during the twenties, its factionalism, and its doctrinal disputes. She did not consider it either as a viable radical force in this country or as a serious threat to the safety of America. One sign of Freda Kirchwey's lack of regard for the activities of the party appeared in her 1933 obituary of Rose Pastor Stokes. Only one sentence was given to Mrs. Stokes's life after the First World War: "The later years of Mrs. Stoke's life were identical with the American Communist Party."[89] This curt dismissal suggested a low opinion of the party and its work during this period. Freda Kirchwey counseled tolerance, however, and advised her colleagues on the non-Communist left to spend their energies in better ways than in attacking the Communists—advice she was to give again in the cold war days of the late forties and early fifties.

Freda Kirchwey remained an active commentator on world affairs throughout the forties and fifties. Her basic commitment to freedom from all tyranny, whether it be the tyranny of a sorority or that of an authoritarian government, remained with her all her long and productive career. As editor of the *Nation,* she continued to be a living example of a whole woman, of a woman who had integrated the wife, mother, and professional roles successfully. Her expertise in foreign affairs grew, and her judgments drew deserved respect from many quarters.

Mary Heaton Vorse continued her labor reporting and fictional writing throughout the twenties and thirties. A woman of forty-six in 1920, she approached the future with maturity and vitality. The two themes that interested her enormously before the war continued to preoccupy her: union efforts and the role of women. Because she was a working mother, she often thought and wrote about the best way to achieve a harmonious synthesis between career and home. Her answers often varied. In some undated manuscripts, thought to be written prior to 1920, she argued that the home was the most important responsibility of a woman and that educated women should relinquish their careers for their husbands.[90] In the duel between the head and the heart, she felt, the heart should always win out. However, as she grew older, and her love of writing and reporting grew rather than diminished, she changed her answer.

In a thinly disguised piece called "Failure," published in 1924 in *Cosmopolitan* magazine, Mary Heaton Vorse declared that she had failed in both enterprises. She had rationalized her reasons for working for many years by saying that, first, it had freed her husband from working so much and then, after she had been widowed, that she simply had to work. But now, years later, she realized that she preferred working because she loved the travel and adventure attached to it. Her failure to do both homemaking and her work well seemed inherent in the nature of things. "No one would come to me and tell me that things had got lost in the laundry," she noted, and "there was nothing between me and my work."[91] The total, all-absorbing quality of her work thrilled her, and she neither could nor would give it up. But guilt feelings were the price she had to pay for the pleasure of working.

More and more women were beginning to experience a joy in satisfying work, she noted in her writings, and they were not going to return to the home. After gaining higher education, most women still married, she wrote in 1924, "and 'settle down.' They find they hate 'settling down.' They don't like housework, they hate the endless ordering of things and seeing that things are kept clean, they hate all the details of running a house." The cruel dilemma women experience has no easy or ready solution. Women

> . . . hate it as much as their husbands would resent giving up their professions when they married, and settling down to grow vegetables, raise hens, and do odd jobs of plumbing and carpentry while their wives made money. And so these women go back to work.[92]

Their return to work created a new set of tensions in the marriage.

This essay, written out of deep personal experience and sensitive thought on the subject, showed Mary Heaton Vorse's awareness of the career woman's problems. She captured the paradox effectively when she continued:

> When she sets up an independent existence of her own, she takes something from him, she ceases to be dependent. This is the most unforgivable crime a woman can commit. Such a woman is competing with her husband. What if she were more successful than he? It would diminish him in his own eyes. It would rob him of his sense of power. If that woman loves her husband, her failure would be measured by her success. One thing all women unite in wanting: love, and the approval of them they love. This does not seem to be obtained through a woman's making a success of her own life, if that success is found outside that woman's home.[93]

She concluded that the younger generation of men and women seemed more equal in their relationships and the men seemed more willing to grant their wives the right of independence. That was the only hope, she grimly ended; women were sure to continue working, especially professional women who loved their work, and the only hope for happy marriages and harmonious human relationships was a radical change in men's attitudes toward women. In a later unpublished study of men, Mary Heaton Vorse discussed the fact that men do not place any value on the role of husband. This view accented a different angle of the same dilemma. Women are defined only as wives; that is the only role for which they receive respect, while men are defined chiefly in terms of their occupation and never praised for their performance of the husband's role. She quoted her black cook, Aunt Sarah, who summarized husbands in our culture in this way: "Dey's only two kin's of husbands, honey, de bad kin' and de worse kin'."[94]

Mary Heaton Vorse recognized, in a period when the subject of women did not receive much serious airing, that conflicting trends were making it increasingly difficult for women to live in modern American society. On the one hand, more women were being educated to recognize life possibilities beyond the home; on the other hand, the cultural definitions remained static and inflexible. The superiority-inferiority interplay in the traditional wife-husband roles accentuated the problem. Mrs. Vorse understood the dominant position held by men in our culture and our families, and how this inhibited the freedom and independence of women. Men had only one center to their lives, their work—as she wrote elsewhere—so they could devote themselves fully to it. Career women had two centers and they were not always sure they could operate in both spheres effectively. "You cannot keep your mind on two things at once."[95] But many women did want to operate in both centers; how to achieve this satisfactorily continues to be the tortuous problem women face in our society.

Men, of course, have not solved, nor have they addressed themselves to, the problem of being good fathers and professionals at the same time. But, typical of our culture's values, women have had to wrestle with this problem while men do not even consider it a problem. The frequent agonizing of sensitive and talented women on the career-family dilemma points up the immense difficulty of the problem, and explains why able women have not contributed their share to society. A good deal of energy is taken up pondering the question—should I pursue my career? If the answer is yes, a good deal of guilt and anxiety prevents the dedication to work that most serious professions demand.

If the answer is no, the unused talent of the woman is channeled into household activities and/or community organizational work. In either case, the married woman with career aspirations consciously faces a problem that men are not required to face. Few demands are made on fathers in our culture; being the family's breadwinner enables them to spend most of their time away from the home. It is expected that fathers will want to relax when they come home and not be faced with petty domestic chores. The old sex roles, first defined in early cultures, still prevail: woman as mother and man as hunter. When women try to break out of their limited role, their actions arouse not only criticism from society's guardians, but gnawing doubts within themselves. The writings of Mary Heaton Vorse on this subject are representative of the thoughts and fears of all working mothers. "I hate having things done for me and I always have," she wrote to a correspondent in the middle twenties. "What I need to have done," she assured this woman, "I like to hire done. The very idea of anyone wanting to take care of me or smooth my way is probably the most offensive idea in the world." For twenty years, she had supported her children and proudly said that she had never had to ask for financial aid from her family.[96] Through her numerous magazine articles for the *New Republic,* women's magazines, and fifty other journals, she earned enough money to send her children to college and help them afterward.

There was no major labor strike in the first fifty years of this century that Mary Heaton Vorse did not cover. In the twenties, she was at the textile strikes in Passaic, New Jersey, and Gastonia, North Carolina; in the thirties, she observed all the auto workers' strikes. Her deep interest in labor was shared by her son, Heaton Vorse, who was wounded in Anderson, Indiana, while he was covering the 1937 General Motors strike for the Federated Press.

She avidly reported the work of the Congress of Industrial Organizations and applauded its success in the late thirties. In 1935 and 1936, Mrs. Vorse worked for the Office of Indian Affairs in Washington and edited *Indians at Work.* She supported the New Deal and Franklin Roosevelt's sympathetic attitude toward labor unions. She considered General Motors' recognition of the United Auto Workers in 1937, as well as the Supreme Court's upholding of the Wagner Act in the same year, to be great victories for the labor unions. Mary Heaton Vorse continued to travel abroad; she had seen the devastation of war in France in 1917, and in 1933 she visited Germany. In two articles for the *New Republic,* she described the oppressiveness of life in Nazi Germany, especially for the Jews.[97]

In fact, until her death in 1966, at the age of ninety-two, Mary Heaton Vorse wrote sketches and essays continually. In one undated manuscript, she answered the question "What Age Would You Like to Be?"[98] by saying that she enjoyed old age: "I have not more leisure, but I live more leisurely and I have time now to imbibe life at all pores. . . . In my former years, the press of events, being both mother and father, breadwinner and housekeeper, I had to rush from one thing to another." In old age, she could contemplate life more fully. Still vital and exceedingly interested in life around her, Mary Heaton Vorse appreciated the difficulty of achieving selfhood as a woman writer and mother in America, but she spent her life working at it.

INTERLUDE

An occasional article would appear in the magazines of the twenties discussing the young women of the period. Infrequently (which in itself is a gauge of the relative unimportance of the issue as a social problem), writers questioned the role of women in American society and wondered what the effects of industrialization and urbanization would be upon the home and family. Elizabeth Porter Wyckoff, for example, asked, "What Is a College Education for?"[99] She argued that women were not receiving vocational guidance and the result was that after college girls ". . . either drudge for years in uncongenial occupations, drift unintelligently from one occupation to another, or fall into makeshift marriages."[100] Unbeknownst to herself, Miss Wyckoff touched a delicate spot: readers of the *Woman Citizen* wrote letters to the editor criticizing her views. Her remedial suggestions were pragmatic and modest, and her tone was cautiously optimistic; but the whole subject of women's education opened up a discussion of the fundamental question: why educate women at all?

Miss Wyckoff *assumed* the value of education for all, an assumption unshared by the majority. Middle-class girls went to college, the traditional argument ran, to cultivate their minds, read the classics, and prepare themselves to be the culture-bearers of the society. Their learning would help them to be better citizens, better wives, and better mothers. How or why this would come about was never fully discussed. The advocates of vocational training for girls, including Miss Wyckoff, argued that a practical knowledge of stenography, typing, and bookkeeping would enable a college graduate to get a job. Neither view considered a college education as a means of preparing a woman for a professional career; rather, her education was to be a temporary, time-filling job; only if misfortune struck would it be preparation for earning a living. The fear of overeducating women was unspoken but real. The dichotomy between the head and the heart, that Mary Heaton Vorse described, applied to women's education. Too much emphasis upon the head robbed women of their natural emotions, warmth, and loving qualities.

A more frequently discussed subject in the contemporary magazines was the role of women in politics. Each year after 1920, journalists interviewed suffragists, surveyed the number of women in politics, and described the gains and losses. Because the fight for suffrage had been such a long and hard one, it was generally assumed that the result would be worthy of the effort. Unfortunately, that did not seem to be the case. However, most women leaders, such as Maud Wood Park of the League of Women Voters and Carrie Chapman Catt, veteran suffragist leader, pointed to the modest gains and cautiously predicted better days ahead. Emily Newell Blair, a vice-chairman of the Democratic National Committee throughout the twenties, defended the women's political record although she recognized that

There is no woman bloc. Those who thought that suffrage would mean that women would organize along sex lines, nominate women, urge special legislation, vote en masse have the right to be disappointed. Woman suffrage has not yielded them their heart's desire. . . . The women who are open to the same prejudices, prey to the same emotions, worshippers of the same ideals as men will not be mobilized by any appeal to which men will prove invulnerable.[101]

The suffragists wanted equal opportunity in politics, Mrs. Blair went on to argue, and that had been achieved. Most woman's organizations were cultural and social in purpose, and could not be expected to become political groups. Women needed training in political action, and the educative role of the League of Women Voters, for example, was important in this respect. Emily Newell Blair's analysis never dealt with the crucial fact that cultural attitudes toward women, held by both sexes, had not changed. Therefore, the passing of a new law and constitutional amendment did not miraculously change women's behavior.

A few perceptive commentators in the twenties did recognize the importance of cultural values regarding women. Leta S. Hollingworth, for example, a professor of educational psychology at Columbia University, had written extensively on women's roles; participating in a symposium on the New Woman in 1927, she summarized human history briskly and pointed to industrialization and birth control as the two key factors that created the new woman of this century. A cultural lag, she argued, prevented harmonious reconciliation between the natural role of motherhood and activities outside the home. "The woman question is and always has been simply this: how to reproduce the species and at the same time to win satisfaction of the human appetites for food, security, self-assertion, mastery, adventure, play and so forth."[102] Professor Hollingworth's succinct statement is surely admirable for its clear and brief expression of the dilemma, but her solution seems pale in comparison. She advocated, as most social critics did, women's increased education and awareness as the resolution of the problem. How to achieve both awareness and behavioral changes she never effectively explained.

Mary Austin, a well-known writer of the period, explained in one article on women, that human cultures had always emphasized the woman's reproductive period as the only meaningful one of her life; similarly, men too had always focused on their sexuality, with the result that the male never grew up and the female felt unhappy once she reached middle age. A "mental unsettling" overcame women when they passed their childbearing period. She advocated that both sexes grow up, undergo maturation, and learn how to adjust to different stages of life. Professional women, Mary Austin suggested, already know this: "There can be no question that for women active in the arts and professions, the best twenty years are those in which the fact that they are females is most completely lost to sight."[103] This particular statement may have thrilled antifeminists who charged feminists with being masculinized women, but the essence of Mary Austin's point was of a different nature entirely: she wanted to lift women above the biological role nature ordained for them and to confer upon them additional reasons for being.

Most writers, however, shared the popular view that women were freer, more open, and more liberated in the twenties than their mothers had been. The writers who held this opinion did not share the concerns of the other commentators described here. Miriam Allen deFord, for instance, called 1928 the beginning of a transitional period, moving from the previous era of male dominance to one of a closer equality between the sexes. Miss deFord pointed to the "approximation of the sexes in dress and appearance," the fact that boys and girls were studying the same subjects (with boys learning to sew and girls participating in sports), and the fact that more women were not accepting alimony unless they had children.[104] The age was egalitarian, she claimed, and the future generation's challenge was: "Will they have the foresight to keep it there, or will the twentieth century see the beginning of a new period of feminine ascendancy?"[105]

Her fears, of course, were unfounded. The examples she presented to support her case, many of which sound like a description of the 1960's and 1970's, were more impressionistic than statistical. If Miss deFord had investigated, she would have learned that fewer women were obtaining advanced degrees in the twenties (there had been a dramatic decrease since 1920, in fact), and the percentage of women in professions such as medicine and law did not increase at all in that decade. Girls may have been playing baseball in school or jumping hurdles, but they still could not participate in male-dominated intramural sports, and they were not trained to compete in athletics. Her prediction of equality, however, seemed to be believed by the flappers. As Mary Heaton Vorse observed the gay young women on board ship in 1928, she was stunned by their lack of interest in anything but themselves. "If they fought for no causes, marched to no slogans, it was because they did not need to. They did not need to with the old idols smacked in the face, not with ferocity or hate, but as a child flicks at something with a whip—absently."[106]

Because the flapper wore lipstick, dated many men before marriage, worked, and traveled freely, she considered herself emancipated; thus, she did not need any crusade or movement. Observers either complimented her frivolity or condemned her for her shallowness; but in either case, the flapper seemed unconcerned. American culture-makers as well as advertisers catered to the young, and the young relished their new freedom. The fact that the overwhelming majority of flappers ultimately accepted the same life roles as their mothers had did not seem relevant while they enjoyed their premarital flings. The flappers had a distinctive style as well as a different attitude toward life; they were less somber than their parents, possessed a healthy amount of generational distrust, and could not conceive that their parents had ever been young. Careful diet, youthful clothes, planned parenthood, and a magazine subscription would assure their perpetual difference from their mothers.

Understandably, flappers with the mentality just described could not understand the lamenters of woman's fate; there was an enormous chasm between them. Mary Austin's discussion of women as reproducers would seem irrelevant to the flapper, with her belief (it is not sure how much *knowledge* she really had) in birth control. Leta Hollingworth's interest in seeing women achieve identities outside the home would also seem inappropriate to the flapper, since the home, after marriage, with its new appliances and dainty furniture, was her ideal. And what was the fuss about politics anyway? Mr. Harding was handsome, that was for sure; but Mr. Coolidge and Mr. Hoover did not inspire an interest in politics, and the tariff was too boring to comprehend. It was still considered "cute" for women not to know about economic matters and to stare wide-eyed when men explained international relations.

For those interested in the Soviet experiment regarding women, Anne O'Hare McCormick, a distinguished journalist for the *New York Times,* reported that the majority of women in the Soviet Union did not approve of the liberal marriage and divorce laws instituted under the Communists. "Women are instinctive philistines," she argued.

> To say that the Revolution affects their lives more than the lives of men is only to say that women are more tangled in the ties that must be broken if the consistent Communist society is to be established. With the most revolutionary will in the world, only in exceptional cases do women reject the idea of romance in love, permanence in the family, stability in the home.[107]

Thus, according to at least one reporter in 1928, Soviet women did not desire radical changes in their life styles.

Perhaps there was an interesting similarity here between the Soviet women and the American flapper; on the surface, they both appeared radically different from the previous generation, but below the surface they shared quite traditional views about womanhood.

ELEANOR ROOSEVELT: A LIVING SYMBOL OF FEMINISM

The only woman in this whole century who emerged as a popular example of a fully realized human being was Eleanor Roosevelt. Not only the nation but the world came to know her toothy smile, high-pitched voice, and, most important, her deep commitment to mankind. Although she always had her critics, Eleanor Roosevelt became the first First Lady in our history who achieved a completely separate identity while being the wife of the President. She was not only Mrs. Franklin Delano Roosevelt but Eleanor Roosevelt; she was not only a mother of five, and a grandmother, but a teacher, a radio broadcaster, a syndicated columnist, and part owner of a furniture manufacturing company. But more than these separate activities, she was a woman whose independent judgment and opinion were respected, who, indeed, had opinions all her own. Given the fact that F.D.R. was such a dominating personality, her feat is even more extraordinary. The wife of a meek man can often overshadow him, but the wife of a charismatic President rarely can share equally in the limelight.

When her husband was governor of New York in the late twenties, Eleanor Roosevelt was already known as an active and energetic worker in humanitarian causes.[108] In fact, many astute political observers later said that had not Eleanor Roosevelt participated actively in Democratic Party affairs after 1921 (when Franklin contracted polio), F.D.R. would not have had a political future. Working with Molly Dewson, a dynamic and knowledgeable political organizer, Eleanor Roosevelt has been credited with gaining women

equal representation on the New York State Democratic
Party committee in 1926. In the 1932 presidential campaign,
Molly Dewson and Eleanor Roosevelt worked out an organizational scheme in which a vice-chairwoman in every state
headed up the women's division and a committeewoman was
chosen in every county.[109] Eleanor Roosevelt had assidu-
ously cultivated the traditionally Republican counties of
upper New York State, knowing how important it was to
meet and talk with people in their own communities. She
also knew that women, with their newly obtained political
power, could become impressive forces for a candidate's election once they became committed to him.

Eleanor Roosevelt wrote many of the pamphlets distrib-
uted by the Democratic women and, with her invaluable
co-worker Molly Dewson, oversaw the entire women's divi-
sional work during the campaign. Joseph P. Lash, Eleanor's
most recent and thorough biographer, noted that no wife of
a presidential candidate had ever played such an active part
in her husband's campaign, "but in Eleanor's case it seemed
the natural thing to do."[110] As First Lady, Eleanor Roosevelt
continued her multiple activities and bewildered all who
watched her. Throughout the twenties, she had taught at the
Todhunter School, lectured extensively, written articles for
popular magazines, and entertained graciously at the State
House in Albany as the governor's wife from 1928 to 1932;
New Yorkers had got used to the most energetic and sweetly
disposed first lady they had ever known. After 1933, the
whole nation became shocked, amused, and very much impressed with the intense activity of their First Lady. Her
grace and charm, her refusal to get angry with either her
critics or F.D.R.'s made her a legend in her own time. Reporters continually asked her how she could maintain such a
hectic schedule and yet never lose her good humor, how she
could smile when asked a hostile question, and how she could
invite critics of the New Deal to the White House for dinner.
To all of them she replied that hating was a waste of good
energy and that people who faced each problem honestly and

with faith could become useful people—and that was all of our purpose on earth, to be useful.

While First Lady, Eleanor Roosevelt established many firsts on her own. In her first fifteen months in the White House, she traveled more than fifty thousand miles.[111] She would board an airplane as casually as another person walked; she drove her own car and refused Secret Service protection unless she was with the President. Jokes about her seemingly infinite energy erupted everywhere. A *New Yorker* cartoon of June 1933 showed two coal miners working deep in the earth; one looked up and said, "For gosh sakes, here comes Mrs. Roosevelt!" Eleanor Roosevelt visited coal mines, homes for delinquent children, and slum sections of the big cities. Admiral Byrd was reported to have set two places for supper in his South Pole shack, "just in case Mrs. Roosevelt should drop in."[112] Her reputation as a speaker and a traveler increased, and requests were often received at the White House which read: "If we cannot have the President, may we have Mrs. Roosevelt?"[113]

Impeccably honest, Eleanor Roosevelt always faced her critics squarely. Her behavior, argued many traditionalists, was unbecoming to a lady and especially the First Lady. She answered these comments by saying, "I am sorry if I hurt anyone's feelings, but one must do in this life the thing that seems right to oneself."[114] And in a letter to a friend in 1941, she wrote: "Somewhere along the line of development we discover what we really are and then we make our real decision for which we are responsible. Make that decision primarily for yourself because you can never really live anyone's life, not even your child's. The influence you exert is through your own life and what you become yourself."[115] In addition to being her own person, and living according to her own lights, which is the essence of feminism, Eleanor Roosevelt played a key role in educating American women to the fuller possibilities of their own lives. She wrote a syndicated column called "My Day" as well as frequent articles in the popular magazines. In one article, she reminded her readers that the home is not an isolated unit; it ". . . is so closely tied, by a million strings, to the rest of the world."[116] The activities of the community, of the nation, and of the world should be of concern to women in the home. Their lives as well as their children's were inextricably a part of the larger world around them.

In her writings, Eleanor Roosevelt stressed the importance of women's education and preparation for multiple roles in our society. She characterized her philosophy in this way:

> I am old-fashioned enough to believe that every girl ought to marry and have a family. I am also modern enough and progressive enough to believe that it is as much the function of the school to prepare her for that job as it is to prepare her for the expression of other phases of her life.[117]

During the depression, when women were being discouraged from working because it was said that they took jobs away from men, the First Lady recognized the importance of financial remuneration for the self-image of the woman. "It would be well if men realized the need that some women have for a little financial independence."[118] Women performing domestic chores in the home every day are doing important work, she hastened to add, but they are not paid for it. From her experience with young girls at the Todhunter School, Eleanor Roosevelt came to realize that the young women growing up during the thirties expected to work, hoped to find it rewarding, and planned to work during the early years of their marriages.

A constant theme in Mrs. Roosevelt's writing was her urging of women to become knowledgeable about politics and government and to vote intelligently. She said at one point that it was more important to have one million women vote wisely than to elect one woman to office.[119] In 1940, in a three-part series on women in politics, Eleanor Roosevelt surveyed the political achievements of women and found them wanting. In the decade 1929-1939, the number of women in elected positions had declined, although the number of women appointed to government posts had increased. "Women have used this suffrage, as far as I can tell, approximately as much as men have."[120] The one area where women had made a positive contribution, she noted, was social welfare. Since 1920, the government has become aware of the importance of labor legislation, educational provisions for all people, and health care for the citizenry. This awareness, and the concrete accomplishments made on the basis of it, can be credited largely to women's efforts. Ever the realist, however, Mrs. Roosevelt acknowledged that ". . . there has been no really great change in government and . . . there is no sign that when moral questions come up, women rise in a body to bring about certain reforms."[121]

The achievements of women might not have justified suffrage, she confessed, but some would say that neither have men's accomplishments justified their voting rights. In proposing a new direction for the future, Eleanor Roosevelt suggested a woman's crusade—that is, women uniting *consciously* (as they do not unite *naturally*) for causes that deeply affect them; a war against war would be one appropriate example of a cause that touched women intimately. "I believe women can be educated to think about all humans and not so much about their own individual humans."[122] This is not a new idea, of course, but it demonstrated Eleanor Roosevelt's devotion to reform and her belief that women could be educated to work for social change.

"I have heard people say that the United States is a matriarchy—that the women rule. That is true only in nonessentials." In her own sweet, nonhostile way, Eleanor Roosevelt frequently reminded her magazine readers that the status of women in America needed improving. "Considering women as persons must begin with women themselves," she reminded her readers.[123] Always encouraging women to fulfill their human potential, she answered those who asked her whether wives should work by saying that they were asking the wrong question. The question should be: "Are you able to carry on two full-time jobs?"[124] If you are healthy, well organized, and have a supportive husband, you will probably succeed. If any of these factors are missing, Mrs. Roosevelt counseled, you will have problems. Women with professional careers should never abandon them, she said, because they may need to work sometime in the future, because their knowledge and ability will rust without use, and because they will miss the joy of professional activity.

Eleanor Roosevelt always distinguished carefully between the various categories of women. She never forgot that the majority of women who worked did so out of economic necessity and only a minority out of desire. Improved labor laws, social security benefits, and better public education could help the majority of working women. Through the Civil Works Administration's Women's Division, 100,000 women received employment. Mrs. Ellen S. Woodward, director of that division, frequently consulted with Eleanor and worked to increase the number of women employed by government agencies.[125] Eleanor Roosevelt believed that rich women with household help should always do something constructive outside the home; otherwise they were idlers—and that would never do. Because she practiced what she preached, and continually used examples in her writing from her own life, Eleanor's words were respected and her advice frequently sought. One cartoon in the *Ladies' Home Journal* showed a column of soldiers standing at attention as the commanding officer said: "And hereafter if there is anything you don't like, come to me—don't write to Mrs. Roosevelt."[126]

"But how do you do it, Mrs. Roosevelt?" people continued to ask. "How do you maintain your incredibly busy and hectic schedule and remain calm and sweetly disposed?" The answer, she wrote her avid readers, was self-control. "This control is not a gift from the gods, but must be acquired patiently. A placid disposition can achieve calm more easily than a highly strung one. Self-control can be acquired under any circumstances, I think."[127] Whether every woman could successfully emulate Mrs. Roosevelt's style is questionable, but because of her down-to-earth manner of writing, her interest in the specific details of life, and her descriptions of the concrete problems women faced, her numerous columns were well read and well loved. Further, Eleanor Roosevelt's constant concern for the welfare of women and for their difficulties showed an inimitable sensitivity of spirit.

The First Lady's humanitarian nature took many forms and directions. She was a most enthusiastic advocate of the National Youth Administration, one of the many agencies developed under the New Deal. She vigorously supported the Social Security Act, old age compensation, and improved health and education measures. She also encouraged women to participate in politics and took a keen interest in the careers of her women friends. In 1934, she campaigned for her good friend Mrs. Caroline O'Day, who ran for representative at large from New York. Eleanor Roosevelt's numerous speeches in her behalf surely helped Mrs. O'Day win. She encouraged the President to appoint qualified women to public office; the presence of Secretary of Labor Frances Perkins, the first woman to hold a Cabinet position, owed something to the urging of Eleanor Roosevelt.

She believed that women could make a unique contribution to public office. In one discussion on the subject, she said, "I think emotion is *the* contribution which women have to make. They can at times be objective and analytical, but they can also feel things and in a way that is rarely given to men to feel."[128] She went on to note that women, by the nature of their work in the home, are familiar with a great number and variety of things. "In the political field, she can be of very great value by interpreting the human element in a machine age."[129] Eleanor Roosevelt believed that everyone who entered public life did so in response to a creative instinct, "that fundamental instinct to leave something behind us which we ourselves have made."[130] Creativity was not solely a womanly characteristic, but women surely knew what creation was all about and they wanted to express themselves creatively in many ways—not only as mothers.

Eleanor Roosevelt became a familiar sight, "boarding an air-plane with her bulging brief-case and her knitting bag."[131] She was the first First Lady to hold weekly press conferences; in fact, her list of firsts grew and grew the longer she occupied the White House. By carving out her own definition of the role of First Lady, she continued to be a living example of what a woman could be in our society. She refused to be influenced by the fashion-makers of the day and wore one of the two evening gowns she bought each year to numerous functions. Conscious of her plain appearance, she chose to ignore it rather than accentuate it. Her earnings from her writing were regularly given to her favorite charities, most notably the American Friends Service Committee, which received the receipts of a sixteen-week radio broadcast series. Her autobiography, *This Is My Story*—another first, incidentally, because no First Lady had ever written her memoirs while still in the White House—also provided funds for her numerous philanthropies.

Rose Schneiderman and the Women's Trade Union League had been old friends of Mrs. Roosevelt's. One story has it that after F.D.R.'s election in 1933, Eleanor Roosevelt visited Rose Schneiderman and asked her about the WTUL's budget. Upon hearing that money was short, the First Lady pledged to give three hundred dollars a week for twelve weeks to the organization.[132] Eleanor Roosevelt had a long-standing commitment to working women and their need for protective legislation; thus she did not support the equal rights amendment.

By the end of the thirties, columnists talked about Eleanor Roosevelt as a force unto herself; *Look* magazine called her one of the ten most powerful people in Washington, "a cabinet minister without portfolio."[133] In an interview in 1940, Eleanor Roosevelt said that she believed the American people were not ready for a woman President.[134] A *Fortune* poll in 1940 asked: "What Do You Think Eleanor Roosevelt Should Do If She Does Not Return to the White House Next

Year?" The results showed that nearly 50 percent of the women surveyed and 39.1 percent of the men thought she should continue writing and lecturing; only 7.3 percent of the women and 5.8 percent of the men believed she should be elected or appointed to some high government office; while 17.7 percent of the women and 30.3 per cent of the men thought she should retire.[135] As powerful and influential as she was, the First Lady did not change the dominant view of Americans that women were not equipped for responsible and important positions in our society. The slight difference between men's and women's views regarding Eleanor Roosevelt as an elected official effectively confirmed the fact that both sexes still shared the traditional image of women—although more women than men believed that Mrs. Roosevelt should remain active.

Eleanor Roosevelt never acted like a politician. She always took a clear-cut and committed stand on all issues. Perhaps because she was the wife of the President, she could get away with this type of behavior; conversely, however, if her position was an unpopular one, it could hurt the President's popularity. She did become the target of much criticism for her dignified announcement of her son Elliott's divorce and her subsequent statement that divorce may, at times, be necessary; her well-publicized resignation from the D.A.R. when it refused to let black singer Marian Anderson use Constitution Hall in 1939; and her growing advocacy of international responsibility after 1939. However, she never wavered in her beliefs. Her honesty made her acknowledge at the end of the decade that the New Deal had not solved all the social problems of the era—a truly unpolitical statement—but that it had tried, and moved in the right direction.

When Europe plunged into a second world war in 1939, Eleanor Roosevelt expressed a growing concern over America's isolationism. In her column, "My Day," she wrote on September 13, "All we can do is to judge things we wish to preserve in the world and to throw our weight into the development and accomplishment of these things, first at home and then abroad." And on September 19, "Hundreds of thousands of men, women and children are dying. Are we going to think only of our skins and our own pockets?"[136]

Critics became alarmed; was Mrs. Roosevelt testing out new ideas for the President? Was she seeing what the reaction would be to shifts in American foreign policy? Isolationists fervently hoped not, and refuted Mrs. Roosevelt's views. The war in Europe was not of our making or of our concern, they argued, and the First Lady should not interfere in such matters. Her critics found many other views worth attacking in the following years.

In May 1941, for example, Eleanor Roosevelt proposed a year of national service for young girls, as was required for young men.[137] Girls should devote a year of service to their communities (she did not recommend sending them off to camps like the boys), such as work in hospitals. She anticipated her critics by saying that this idea was not dictatorial or fascistic; people could vote on whether young boys and girls should give a year of service to their country for the benefit of both the country and themselves. Girls could obtain training during the year of service that would be useful to them later on. "I believe that girls, if it is decided to require of them a year of service, should be placed on exactly the same footing as men, and they should be given the same subsistence and the same wage."[138]

Bold and forthright, her suggestions sound today like an early version of the Job Corps of the sixties. Or, closer to her own time, it was a version of the Civilian Conservation Corps applied to girls. Mrs. Roosevelt was aware of the criticism leveled by some feminists and women's organizations that young girls were not obtaining a fair share of the government assistance programs. A year of national service for them would help to redress that particular grievance. It would also recognize, by its very existence, that young girls have a human potential as well as young men and that the government owed the female portion of the population the same consideration and aid that it owed to the male portion.

This scheme, then, was another example of Eleanor Roosevelt's concern for women and her recognition that they were a seriously neglected part of the nation.

Eleanor Roosevelt's credo always remained disarmingly simple: ". . . to care unselfishly not only for personal good but for the good of those who toil with them upon the earth."[139] "She believes," wrote one of the many admiring women reporters who covered her activities throughout the thirties, "in the new education and the old religion."

> She is only a Right-Wing feminist. She utters New Deal preachments in pure Brahmin accents. She hasn't entirely escaped Old New York, tho she looks forward to a kindlier social order. And she has no intention of relaxing her efforts to bring it about.[140]

Her efforts continued into the forties and fifties. Never faltering or tiring, she devoted herself to the United Nations with the same zeal she gave to the United States. Her magnetic smile, shy but firm manner, and engaging friendliness, coupled with her fundamental humanism, made her a much-loved person to millions. Eleanor Roosevelt had a deep love for all human life and the right of each person to live fully; her life epitomized this belief.

The Great Depression of 1929 affected women as well as men. While the National Women's Party continued to agitate for the equal rights amendment and the League of Women Voters educated women to understand political issues, the working women of America still suffered to a greater extent than their husbands and brothers. The built-in discrimination policy of unequal pay for equal work, the long hours, and the sweatshop conditions of the early 1900's became even more intense during the depression. The Women's Trade Union League, though its leader Rose Schneiderman served on the Labor Advisory Board of the NRA, did not seem to make a positive impression on administrative actions. The

National Consumers League, another key woman's group, advocated wage boards in every state to set a minimum wage for women workers. One source claimed that seventy-one codes devised by the NRA had lower wages for women doing the same work as men; the differences ran from five cents to twenty-five cents an hour.[141] In Fall River, Massachusetts, in the garment factories that had traditionally employed women, women were working a forty-eight-hour week earning a maximum of 15 cents an hour for a total weekly wage of $7.20. A study of Baltimore male garment workers showed that their wages ranged from $8.25 for a forty-hour week to $10.19 for a fifty-four-hour week.[142] In the textile mills of the South, women worked nights and suffered under terrible conditions.

New Deal agencies such as the Civilian Conservation Corps did not employ women, although over 4,000,000 of the unemployed were women. In 1935, out of 1,600,000 workers engaged in government projects, only 142,000 were women.[143] The Economy Act of 1932, especially Article 213, discriminated against women when both husband and wife worked for the government; the article stated that if layoffs were necessary, the wife should be dismissed first as an economy measure. According to the federal Office of Education, married women were barred from teaching in more than 50 percent of the representative American cities. Various states passed laws barring jobs to married women whose husbands had incomes above $100 a month.[144] The situation, indeed, looked dire for the working women of America.

At the same time, however, Franklin Roosevelt appointed Florence Allen to the federal judiciary and Frances Perkins to the Cabinet. Compared with the total absence of women in prominent positions prior to his administration, his accomplishments seemed noteworthy and progressive. Emily Newell Blair wrote of numerous women in Washington who occupied significant appointed posts.[145] Nellie Tayloe Ross, ex-governor of Wyoming, became the first woman director of the U.S. Mint. Other prominent women included Marion

Banister, as Assistant Treasurer of the United States, Rose Schneiderman, as member of the NRA Labor Advisory Board, Josephine Roche, millionaire heiress to Colorado coal mines, as Assistant Secretary of the Treasury, and Stella Akin, as Special Assistant to the Attorney General. These were only a few of the many professional, talented women occupying positions in Washington.

The contrast was great, of course, between women working for five cents an hour in an unventilated textile mill and Frances Perkins as Secretary of Labor. It is truly tragic that at the moment in our history when a President and his wife were committed to women's rights and when there existed a significant number of women's organizations and leaders who could provide the talent for responsible government positions, a serious economic depression prevented the realization of women's equality in every sphere. The dilemma of working women, however, was also tied to the whole labor union movement; as labor won its right to organize and to bargain collectively under the New Deal, union women, especially in the International Ladies Garment Workers Union, benefitted too. But even union women did not receive identical pay and benefits with union men. Unorganized working women, however (as well as unorganized workingmen, for that matter) were the greatest sufferers during the depression. And one critic of women's organizations argued that the majority of women's groups did not pay heed to working women.[146]

The charge against women's groups could be leveled fairly against the General Federation of Women's Clubs, the League of Women Voters, and the National Federation of Business and Professional Women's Clubs; all of them dealt with their own middle-class issues, primarily of a cultural, educational, and social nature, and ignored the industrial women. The National Consumers League and the Women's Trade Union League, the only two woman's groups committed to working women, were too weak and underfinanced to be effective propagandists during the thirties. The National Woman's Party blithely pursued its own goal. Thus there was no significant leadership (except for that of Eleanor Roosevelt, who was a symbol rather than a leader—she espoused no single cause exclusively) for working-class women or, for that matter, for the numerous feminist concerns of a decade before. Generally, men and women thought about how they were going to earn a living in the dark days of the thirties; the young girls abandoned the flapper image of the twenties for somber dress and sober action.

In an extensive survey of women's views on marriage and divorce as well as other issues, the *Ladies' Home Journal* discovered in 1938 that American women believed in divorce (69 percent), in birth control (79 percent), and in motherhood (98 percent of the mothers were glad they had children).[147] Only 20 percent of the women interviewed believed that a woman should be elected President, and those who believed in birth control also believed that four children was the ideal number for an American family. Middle America had not substantially changed its views on the role of women; women still accepted their place in the home as the only meaningful one and did not think highly enough of themselves to favor a woman President. Further, they did not think about the working woman in the textile factory.

Margaret Mead, the famous anthropologist, in one analysis of the American woman during the 1930's, cogently explained why this traditional way of thinking persisted. Each culture, she wrote, determined identity and roles according to sex; girls are taught to be nonachievers in male areas in order to retain their femininity, while boys' achievement is a fulfillment of their human potential. If women try to achieve in a male-designated area, they deny their womanliness and their opportunity to love and marry. "Until this dilemma," she concluded, "this identification of achievement and masculinity, is resolved, the world will be able to use only half of its gifted, and always the best chefs will be men."[148] Eleanor Roosevelt understood the problem well; women had to be educated to view themselves as people before they could expect men to see them as people. Apparently, American women of the thirties, whether they understood the situation in anthropological terms or not, accepted their sex-determined roles and did not want to risk, as Sara Teasdale's old maid had, the loss of love.

Notes

1. Eleanor Wembridge, "The Girl Tribe—An Anthropological Study," *Survey*, 60 (May 1, 1928), 157.

2. Mary Heaton Vorse, "Tourist Third," *Harper's Magazine*, 158 (March 1929), 514.

3. Charlotte Perkins Gilman, "The New Generation of Women," *Current History*, 18 (August 1923), 735.

4. *Ibid.*, p. 737.

5. Frederick Lewis Allen, *Only Yesterday* (New York, Harper, 1931), pp. 94, 107.

6. *Ibid.*, p. 101.

7. The United States Department of Commerce's annual *Statistical Abstract of the United States* provides information on a wide variety of social concerns.

8. Henry Ruggles, "Fashions and the Female," *Independent*, 116 (February 20, 1926), 219-220.

9. See the table on p. 88.

10. For a detailed discussion of Margaret Sanger's thoughts and actions, see David Kennedy's *Birth Control in America: The Career of Margaret Sanger* (New Haven, Yale University Press, 1970).

11. Margaret Sanger, *Woman and the New Race* (New York, Blue Ribbon Books, 1920).

12. *Ibid.*, p. 94.

13. Margaret Sanger, *The Pivot of Civilization* (New York, Brentano's, 1922), p. 11.

14. Richard Drinnon's *Rebel in Paradise* (Chicago, University of Chicago Press, 1961) is a good summary of Emma Goldman's life as well as the particular tribulations she suffered after 1920.

15. Elizabeth Gurley Flynn to Mary Heaton Vorse, May 16, 1930, MHV Collection.

16. *Ibid.*

17. Elizabeth Gurley Flynn to Mary Heaton Vorse, March 22, 1937, MHV Collection. Joe Ettor and Carlo Tresca were fellow Wobblies with whom she had worked in the 1910's.

18. "Red Leader Testifies," *New York Times,* October 4, 1952, p. 24.

19. Elizabeth Gurley Flynn to Mary Heaton Vorse, September 28, 1939, MHV Collection.

20. *Ibid.,* January 7, 1940.

21. Corliss Lamont, ed., *The Trial of Elizabeth Gurley Flynn by the American Civil Liberties Union* (New York, Horizon Press, 1968), p. 14.

22. Reported in the *New York Times,* October 19, 1925, p. 1.

23. Rose Pastor Stokes, "There Are Few Bad Divorces," *Collier's,* 77 (February 13, 1926), 49.

24. Richard Drinnon, *Rebel in Paradise,* p. 204.

25. *Ibid.*

26. *New York Times,* May 6, 1922, p. 11.

27. Reports in the *Times* from May 1922 to March 1923.

28. See James Weinstein's *The Decline of Socialism in America, 1912-1925* (New York, Monthly Review Press, 1967) for a more complete discussion of this subject.

29. Obituary notice, *New York Times,* January 12, 1948, p. 19.

30. Maud Wood Park, "What the American Woman Thinks," *The Woman Citizen,* n.s. 8 (April 19, 1923), 20.

31. "What Women Voters Want—Report of the League of Women Voters Convention," *The Woman Citizen,* 8 (May 3, 1924), 10-11.

32. James S. Lemons, "The New Woman in the New Era: The Woman Movement from the Great War to the Great Depression," Ph.D. thesis, University of Missouri, 1967, deals with this subject. Note especially pp. 182-184, 261.

33. *Bulletin of the Illinois League of Women Voters,* 7 (January 1927), 1-3.

34. *Congressional Digest,* 3 (February 1924), 153-158.

35. *Ibid.,* p. 155.

36. Mary Anderson, *Women at Work,* p. 163.

37. Carol A. Rehfisch, "The Woman's Party Is Right," *New Republic,* 36 (September 26, 1923), 124.

38. "Miss Alice Paul Retires," *New York Times,* February 20, 1921, p. 3.

39. Ernestine Tittle, "Women in the Washington Scene," *Century Magazine,* 106 (August 1923), 514-515.

40. Frances Kellor, "Women in British and American Politics," *Current History,* 17 (February 1923), 823.

41. *Ibid.*

42. Edna Kenton, "The Ladies' Next Step—The Case for the Equal Rights Amendment," *Harper's Magazine,* 152 (February 1926), 366-374.

43. Quoted in John B. Dawson, "The Program of the National Woman's Party from the Point of View of Connecticut Social Workers," *Family,* 3 (January 1923), 226.

44. Ernestine Tittle, p. 515.

45. John Dawson, p. 227.

46. Genevieve Parkhurst, "Is Feminism Dead?" *Harper's Magazine,* 170 (May 1935), 736.

47. Cornelia S. Parker, "feminists and Feminists," *Survey,* 56 (August 1926), 204.

48. Alice Paul, "Women Demand Equality in World Code of Law," *Congressional Digest,* 9 (November 1930), 279.

49. Quoted in "Pan-American Delegates for Rights of Women," *Christian Century,* 51 (January 3, 1934), 7.

50. Mary Hornaday, "Promoting a World Crusade," *Christian Science Monitor Magazine,* December 28, 1938, p. 4.

51. *Current Biography* (New York, H. W. Wilson, 1947), p. 500.

52. *Ibid.*

53. "What Women Think About the Vote," *Woman Citizen,* n.s. 8 (March 22, 1924), 29-30.

54. Rose Schneiderman had met, and worked with, Eleanor Roosevelt during the twenties when Rose was head of the New York WTUL. They became good friends in the course of the decade.

55. Miss Schneiderman sued Dr. Wirt for libel; the incident is reported in *School and Society,* 40 (October 27, 1934), 549.

56. Zona Gale, *Miss Lulu Bett* (New York, D. Appleton, 1921), p. 4.

57. *Ibid.* p. 46.

58. August Derleth, *Still Small Voice: The Biography of Zona Gale* (New York, D. Appleton, 1940), p. 100.

59. *Ibid.,* p. 116.

60. *Ibid.,* p. 84.

61. Zora Neale Hurston, "Fannie Hurst," *Saturday Review,* 16 (October 9, 1937), 15-16.

62. Fannie Hurst, *Anatomy of Me* (New York, Doubleday, 1958), p. 105.

63. *Ibid.,* p. 188.

64. *Ibid.,* p. 221.

65. *Ibid.,* p. 272.

66. *Ibid.,* p. 308.

67. Fannie Hurst, *Star Dust: The Story of an American Girl* (New York, Harper, 1921), p. 54.

68. *Ibid.*

69. *Ibid.,* p. 58.

70. *Ibid.,* p. 144.

71. *Ibid.*, p. 199.

72. *Ibid.*, p. 227.

73. *Ibid.*, p. 266.

74. *Ibid.*, p. 420.

75. *Ibid.*, p. 402.

76. Mary Carroll, "This Freedom," *Independent Woman*, 10 (April 1931), 149.

77. *Ibid.*

78. *New Republic,* September 26, 1955, p. 7.

79. Evelyn Seeley, "Editing for Tomorrow," *Independent Woman,* 16 (November 1937), 340.

80. *Ibid.*, p. 357.

81. *Our Changing Morality*, edited by Freda Kirchwey, was published in 1924; it was a collection of articles first written for the *Nation*. Also, see the Spring-Summer 1927 issues of the *Nation* for another series on women.

82. Unsigned editorial, "The Woman's Party and Mr. Hoover," *Nation,* 127 (October 3, 1928), 312.

83. Freda Kirchwey, "Alice Paul Pulls the Strings," *Nation,* 112, (March 2, 1921), 332-333.

84. Freda Kirchwey, "The Pan-American Conference of Women," *Nation,* 114 (May 10, 1922), 565.

85. Freda Kirchwey, "Loving Hitler Less," *Nation,* 148 (March 25, 1939), 338.

86. Freda Kirchwey, "America Is Not Neutral," *Nation,* 150 (May 18, 1940), 614.

87. Editorial, *Nation,* 138 (March 21, 1934), 317.

88. Freda Kirchwey, "Red Totalitarianism," *Nation,* 148 (May 27, 1939), 605-606.

89. *Nation,* 137 (July 5, 1933), 3.

90. Mary Heaton Vorse, "The Confessions of a College Woman," November 1909, unpublished manuscript, MHV Collection.

91. Mary Heaton Vorse, "Failure," manuscript draft, MHV Collection, pp. 3-4.

92. *Ibid.*, p. 6.

93. *Ibid.*

94. Mary Heaton Vorse, "Men, Some Reflections On," undated manuscript, the chapter on "The Husband" contains this quote at its beginning.

95. Mary Heaton Vorse, "Working Mother," undated manuscript, MHV Collection.

96. MHV to Winnifred (no last name), October 3, 1926, MHV Collection, pp. 1-2.

97. See *New Republic,* June 14, 1933, issue, "Germany: The

Twilight of Reason," and July 19, 1933, issue: "Getting the Jews Out of Germany."

98. From an undated manuscript, MHV Collection, p. 2.

99. Elizabeth Porter Wyckoff, "What Is a College Education for?" *Woman Citizen*, 6 (July 2, 1921), 13.

100. *Ibid.*

101. Emily Newell Blair, "Are Women a Failure in Politics?" *Harper's Magazine*, 151 (October 1925), 514.

102. Leta S. Hollingworth, "The New Woman in the Making," *Current History*, 27 (October 1927), 15.

103. Mary Austin, "The Best Twenty Years," *Survey*, 60 (April 1, 1928), 9.

104. Miriam Allen deFord, "The Feminist Future," *New Republic*, 56 (September 19, 1928), 121-123.

105. *Ibid.*, p. 123.

106. Vorse, "Tourist Third," p. 515.

107. Anne O'Hare McCormick, "Marriage in Soviet Russia," *Women's Journal*, n.s. 13 (September 1928), 38.

108. Joseph P. Lash's marvelous study, *Eleanor and Franklin* (New York, W. W. Norton, 1971), contributes mightily to our knowledge of Eleanor's development prior to 1933.

109. Lash, *Eleanor and Franklin*, Part Three, "The Emergence of Eleanor Roosevelt," deals extensively with her political activities in the twenties.

110. *Ibid.*, p. 351.

111. Stories and articles by and about Eleanor Roosevelt were numerous; she wrote frequently for women's magazines, most notably the *Woman's Home Companion* in the early thirties and then the *Ladies' Home Journal*. One of the best articles about her was "Tireless Lady," *Literary Digest*, 123 (January 23, 1937), 4-5.

112. *Ibid.*, p. 5.

113. Dorothy Dunbar Bromley, "The Future of Eleanor Roosevelt," *Harper's Magazine*, 180 (January 1940), 135.

114. Emma Bugbee, "A New Interpretation of the 'First Lady's' Role," *Literary Digest*, 116 (September 16, 1933), 22.

115. Lash, *Eleanor and Franklin*, p. 238.

116. Mrs. Franklin D. Roosevelt, "In Defense of Curiosity," *Saturday Evening Post*, 208 (August 24, 1935), 8.

117. Anna [Eleanor] Roosevelt, "Today's Girl and Tomorrow's Job," *Woman's Home Companion*, 59 (June 1932), 12.

118. Eleanor Roosevelt, "Should Wives Work?" *Good Housekeeping*, 105 (December 1937), 212.

119. Roosevelt, "Today's Girl and Tomorrow's Job," p. 12.

120. Eleanor Roosevelt, "Women in Politics," *Good Housekeeping*, 110 (March 1940), 45.

121. *Ibid.*, p. 68.

122. Eleanor Roosevelt, "Women in Politics," *Good Housekeeping,* April 1940, p. 201.

123. *Ibid.*, p. 202.

124. Eleanor Roosevelt, "Should Wives Work?" p. 28.

125. Lash, *Eleanor and Franklin,* pp. 388-389.

126. *Ladies' Home Journal,* 58 (June 1941), 23.

127. Eleanor Roosevelt, "Twenty-Four Hours," *Ladies' Home Journal,* 57 (October 1940), 20.

128. "Trialog on Office Holders," *Independent Woman,* 17 (January 1938), 18.

129. *Ibid.*

130. *Ibid.*, p. 31.

131. Bugbee, "A New Interpretation of the "First Lady's' Role," p. 22.

132. **Bromley,** "The Future of Eleanor Roosevelt," p. 132.

133. Raymond Clapper, "The Ten Most Powerful People in Washington" (condensation of article), *Reader's Digest,* 38 (May 1941), 48.

134. Bromley, pp. 129-139.

135. *Fortune,* 21 (May 1940), 77.

136. Reported in *Time,* 34 (October 9, 1939), 12-13.

137. Eleanor Roosevelt, "Defense and Girls," *Ladies' Home Journal,* 58 (May 1941), 25, 54.

138. *Ibid.*, p. 25.

139. Eleanor Roosevelt, "What Religion Means to Me," *Forum,* 88 (December 1932), 323.

140. Emma Bugbee, "America's Most Travelled Lady," *Literary Digest,* 117 (April 28, 1934), 39.

141. Parkhurst, p. 743.

142. Josephine Goldmark, "The New Menace in Industry," *Scribner's Magazine,* 93 (March 1933), 141.

143. Parkhurst, p. 744.

144. Alma Lutz, "Why Discharge Women First?" *Independent Woman,* 10 (December 1931), 569.

145. Emily Newell Blair, "A Who's Who of Women in Washington," *Good Housekeeping,* 102 (January 1936), 38-39, 166-168.

146. Parkhurst, pp. 739-740.

147. Henry F. Pringle, "What Do the Women of America Think About Marriage and Divorce?" *Ladies' Home Journal,* 55 (February 1938), 14-15, 82-85; (March 1938), 14; (November 1938), 22-23, 48.

148. Margaret Mead, "Sex and Achievement," *Forum,* 94 (November 1937), 303.

4

The Bleak and Lonely Years, 1940-1960

I DON'T WANT TO SMOKE CIGARS OR GO TO STAG PARTIES, WEAR JOCKEY SHORTS OR PICK UP THE CHECK.

—Shelley Winters, 1950

MOST LEGISLATIVE BODIES ARE COMPOSED OF MEN. CONSEQUENTLY IT IS NECESSARY TO PERSUADE LARGE NUMBERS OF MEN TO CHANGE THEIR POINTS OF VIEW BEFORE THE DESIRED LEGISLATIVE END IS ACCOMPLISHED. OFTEN, AFTER BEING WOOED AND WON, THE MEN BELIEVE THAT THE LEGISLATION WAS THEIR OWN IDEA. WHEN THE DUST OF BATTLE HAS CLEARED AND REPORTERS AND PHOTOGRAPHERS ARE CALLED IN, THE WOMEN ARE LEFT OUT OF THE PICTURE. BUT THAT IS ALL RIGHT WITH US AS LONG AS OUR OBJECTIVE IS GAINED.

—Mrs. John G. Lee, President,
League of Women Voters, 1957

The most depressing fact about the 1940's and 1950's regarding feminism was its lack of appeal to educated, middle-class women as well as to the average woman. Not only did the Shelley Winterses of America reject the feminist image, but those traditionally pragmatic feminists, the organization women, did too. The above quotation from the president of the League of Women Voters typified the American middle-class woman's attitude toward activism, toward making a militant fuss over rights; it was bad form. As long as women did good work, they did not have to receive recognition for it. Standing in the background, unobserved, was entirely appropriate. In other words, the traditional role of women remaining *behind* men prevailed. The fire and spirit of the 1910's had disappeared; the cautious but serious work of the League women and the trade union women of the twenties and thirties had also gone; and the middle- and lower-class women who had formerly been active slipped quietly into oblivion.

The 1940's should be distinguished from, and separated from, the 1950's by the extent of civic involvement. The Second World War brought women into the factories of America in great numbers; it saw the creation of Rosie the Riveter and the donning of military uniforms by thousands of women. Women left the home in wartime to pitch in and work for the national good. In contrast, women returned to the home in the 1950's and lauded domesticity rather than civic participation. But in terms of attitudes, the two decades were of one piece. Those women—and their numbers were steadily increasing—who remained in the work force after the war held lower paid jobs in the factory and semiskilled positions in the office. Women did not advance in the medical and legal professions; they did not become bank executives; they did not become decision-makers in the corporations of America. The quality of employed women's work did not rise in proportion to their numbers.

The women of the middle class, the major recruiting ground for feminists, went to college in the forties and fifties, but they were fewer than in the past. In 1930, for example, 43.7 percent of all college students were women; in 1940, 40.2 percent and in 1950, 30.2 percent. While 15 percent of all Ph.D. degrees went to women in 1920, in the early 1950's women earned only 10 percent.[1] These statistics are crucial in explaining the lack of leadership for feminist organizations in these same years. The middle-class woman, who in the past had the time, education, and inclination to work for women's causes had lost all of these qualities. She no longer went to college in the same numbers; she married earlier, had children, and became absorbed in suburban living, that new phenomenon that removed women from city life and gave them a self-contained, totally time-consuming set of activities, such as car pooling, volunteering to address envelopes for the school board, and attending girl scout meetings. Women continued to be joiners, but the nature of the organizations they joined changed materially. Neither the National Women's Party nor the Women's Trade Union League interested or attracted the suburban woman; the local PTA became her major organizational effort.

What about the women who did go to college? In one study of more than a thousand 1934 women graduates of the leading women's colleges,[2] the results were not hopeful for believers in feminism. The woman college graduate of 1934, who was in her middle thirties in 1949, when the survey was taken, had married (82 percent), had a husband who was a professional or business man, and had an average of 2.16 children. For the most part, the women had enjoyed their college years but as one woman said, "I have discovered in most of my friends and, I must admit, in myself, a feeling of frustration and of having been prepared for something better than the monotonies of dusting, sweeping, cooking and mending."[3] But these discontented, overeducated women did not become feminists. Rather, 88 percent of the married group still believed that marriage was more important than a career, although 87 percent did believe that the two could be combined provided six conditions existed: (1) The children were old enough. (2) The woman had energy and talent. (3) The husband was cooperative. (4) Her career was a part-time one. (5) There was enough money for household help. (6) Her career was kept subordinate to her marriage.

Truly, a demanding set of criteria to be met before a woman could venture forth, away from her dusting and chauffeuring. Further, imposing the explicit condition that the career be subordinate to the home severely restricted the case for a career. How could a wife pursue a serious career under the conditions set forth? Why weren't similar demands imposed upon a husband's career? The 1949 interviewer did not even consider these questions. Instead, he concluded his survey with a quotation from the retiring president of Wellesley College, Mildred McAfee Horton, who said, "College failed to teach these women that most people accomplish most in the world by working through established social institutions, and that the family is entirely respectable as a sphere of activity."[4] Dr. Horton was in good company when she said that the family was *the* social institution for women's work. The question that must surely be raised, however, was, Why bother with a college education, then? Indeed, many traditionalists have always said precisely that. A liberal arts education does not prepare women for the domestic chores of the house; it only raises expectations that are later dashed. Home economics or nothing is suitable fare for women's education. Colleges were not the breeding ground for rebels in the forties and fifties. Marriage still constituted the sum total of a woman's dream. Indeed, the irony was that a liberal arts education failed to produce independent women thinkers, and so the critics' fears were unfounded.

Thus women who went to college in the thirties, forties, and fifties shared the same value system with those women who did not attend college. They agreed that marriage was the prime occupation of all women, and that professional careers were secondary in their field of vision. If and when college women worked, they did so in a part-time, temporary manner. The majority of college-trained women did not pursue a career seriously. They shared, knowingly or unknowingly, the perspective of working-class women who worked out of economic necessity without love for, or commitment to, their work. Work outside the home, then, was not an all-consuming or truly meaningful experience for American women. The home remained, as always, the main center of their lives. Advanced education did not change this basic pattern. Volunteer organizations, usually child and community centered, replaced both remunerative work and social-welfare-type work for most middle-class women.

Most social commentators on American women in the forties and fifties misread the evidence they looked at. Because Americans are generally beguiled by statistics, they immediately equated growth with progress. When the numbers of working women increased during the Second World War and continued to increase after it, observers interpreted this as progress, when it was nothing of the kind. Quantity and quality are not synonymous terms; more women working as office clerks (the occupation with the largest increase in women workers from 1940 to 1960) does not signify progress. Women continued, and continue, to be paid less for the same work as men do; they continued to be discriminated against in terms of promotions and raises; and they did not increase their share of responsible and higher skilled jobs. Cultural attitudes did not change during this period. Indeed, they have not changed substantially during this whole century. Roles for women remained the traditional ones of wife, mother, and, very incidentally, temporary worker.

There were a few popular writers who suggested that institutions in our society would have to change in order to accommodate working women. Mary Heaton Vorse, still actively interested in the world, wrote in 1944 that if the government wanted women to work, it had to provide child-care centers and flexible working arrangements for them.[5] And Gertrude Samuels agreed, in an article for the *New York Times Magazine,* that nursery facilities should be established in factories.[6] Neither of these women saw their suggestions implemented. Factory owners had no difficulty finding cheap female labor without providing child-care centers; neither was there an organized, articulate protest from working women on this issue. Similarly, there were no Feminist Alliances during the forties and fifties; nor were there effective lobby organizations for quality education for all, the elimination of infant mortality, or the right to abortion. Middle-class women's organizations focused upon civic matters rather than women's matters and no lower-class women's groups arose to deal with the difficulties they faced.

Life magazine, hardly a radical journal, recognized in 1946 that women had not truly achieved equal opportunity in America. It editorialized that the American woman ". . . is still not a full partner in the national scheme of things. The immense and positive power that women should exert is still not effectively applied over the full social and political arc."[7] Although there were one million more women voters than men in 1946, women did not use their political power to achieve their rights. The *Life* editor continued,

> Our urban industrial society, which rests on a division of labor, even tends to freeze women in their subservient social role. This very danger makes political equality the essential means to their final emancipation. For politics, in a democracy with weak social traditions, shapes our customs and manners, as well as our laws. So if ours is to be a whole and healthy civilization, our politics needs the feminine touch. It needs our woman power.[8]

But women did not realize their power during this period, and they found precious few articulators or supporters of their cause. Indeed, most men and women did not even see the problem.

FEMINIST WRITERS AS CRITICS AND VISIONARIES

As in every period throughout this century, there were a few women who perceived the problem of their sex and wrote about it. The feminist writers of the forties and fifties were intellectual shakers rather than activistic movers. They expressed their concerns in writing and hoped to arouse their readers to action. They did not organize any women's groups; they were professional writers and attacked the problem in the only way they knew how: they wrote about it. Their presence in the inactive environment of the forties and fifties, however, made them stand out even more than in earlier decades. The current generation of feminist activists have not paid their respects to the particular feminist writers I am going to discuss in the following pages. All these women were famous and well known as writers, but their fame does not rest on the feminist books they wrote. In fact, these works are virtually unknown to modern readers, a comment in itself on the value of feminist writing during an uncongenial time.

Pearl Buck, for example, is popularly known for her many novels on China; she was a noted prizewinner and household name whose readers could identify many of her most famous books. But one title they surely never read was *Of Men and Women*. Published in 1941 for the American Association of University Women, this book cogently and at times eloquently presented a strong feminist case. Reminiscent of the writings of Crystal Eastman and Henrietta Rodman, it took a comparative approach to the problem of women. Having lived in China for many years, Miss Buck knew both Chinese and American culture and, in her comparison, often found American cultural attitudes wanting. "In China," she wrote, "the home was not what it is in our country, a thing apart from men's lives except when they return to it for food and sleep. The real life of the nation went on in the home."[9] After the revolution in China in the 1920's, women were given equal opportunity, and observers found women in many professions as one result of their newfound freedom.

In the United States, in contrast, there is only a myth of freedom and opportunity for women. Child-raising practices in America discourage the development of independent, fully human women. Mothers, in fact, degrade their own sex. "Don't be a sissy girl," boys are told in our culture. "If a certain kind of male is desired, I can understand this education, but what is one to think of women who deliberately teach their sons to despise women?"[10] Equal child-raising methods for both sexes, she argued, was necessary. American women held a low opinion of themselves. With the degrading position women held in Nazi Germany and Japan as a reminder of how women are treated in fascist countries, Pearl Buck feared that the natural subservience of American women made them vulnerable to similar treatment.

"If all women could be born with inferior minds and men with superior ones, the scheme of women for the home would doubtless be perfectly satisfactory. But unless that can be done, it is not satisfactory."[11] Systematically, the novelist scrutinized all aspects of the American culture—the home, child-raising techniques, educational practices, and general values—and found all of them wanting in their attitudes toward women. Women, in Miss Buck's view, were as guilty as men in preserving the outmoded view of themselves. Both sexes had to be educated to the life possibilities of women in the mid-twentieth century.

> American children are reared almost entirely by women. Men excuse themselves from it as once they excused themselves from responsibility for conception. Actually they are as inexcusable in the one matter as in the other. They have an equal responsibility with women for the development of the children they begat. It sounds naive and ignorant to say that they have not. So they say instead that they are too busy making a living for the family.[12]

Of Men and Women continually points out the cultural inconsistencies that were endemic in the culture. If woman persists in being interested in things outside the home, Pearl Buck noted, we insist that she must be neglecting her home. If she still persists and makes a success through incredible dogged persistence, we laugh at her. We even sneer at her, and sometimes we treat her with unbelievable rudeness.[13]

American women could be categorized, she continued, into three major groupings: (1) those women who were born talented and surmounted all the obstacles to success in their respective professions (a minority, after all, as the number of naturally talented people in any population is small) ; (2) the women who were born domestic and loved their home and caring for it; and (3) the "gunpowder" women, the largest single group, who were unhappy but were not sure why, or how to alleviate their anguish. The "gunpowder" women were not committed to any particular cause or profession. The middle-class status which most of them enjoyed gave them economic security but no emotional security. Their motivation was deadened and their energy channeled into nonproductive and nonsatisfying activities.[14]

"A man is educated and turned out to work. But a woman is educated—and turned out to grass."[15] For work, Pearl Buck felt, was crucial to personal happiness and fulfillment—meaningful work, that is, not time-filling work. A human being with ability in a variety of areas needs the opportunities to express it. The wife and mother roles, which are not discussed extensively in the book, but rather are assumed, do not appear to Miss Buck to be satisfying professions for all women. Monogamy, she argued, had never truly been practiced. Because girl babies always outnumber boy babies, there is a natural surplus of women over men in every population. The Chinese killed their girl babies to keep the population in balance; in other cultures polygamy solved the problem. In Western society, however, the solution has been a very unsatisfactory one: prostitution and the double standard, as well as scores of unhappy women who never marry but who hope to, since the culture does not provide any other respectable life choice for them.

It is simply not decent, Pearl Buck claimed, for society to promise marriage to all women when it is not feasible.

> The only sensible course, therefore, is to educate women into independent human beings, ready to take their place in the work of nation and world, and to educate men in allowing them to do that work. For the only other alternative is polygamy, the recognized and legal polygamy of the East or the furtive American polygamy of illegal relationship. . . .[16]

In the best American tradition, then, in the interests of pragmatic harmony, Pearl Buck asked for a new orientation toward women. In addition to the practical considerations of the matter, however, she offered a number of other reasons for allowing women to become human. Real monogamy, for example, would be possible "if economic pressure and [avoiding] social stigma" were removed as the reasons for marriage. On the moral level, women should be freed simply because they are human beings like men. In the ideal environment, women and men would marry only if they truly cared for each other, and those women who never married could live individually and socially useful lives, free of the stigma traditionally attached to an unmarried woman.

Miss Buck also attacked the two myths that have prevented the emancipation of women: the home myth and the angel myth. The promise of economic security made women agree to remain dependent homebodies. By attributing heavenly, angel-like qualities to them, men further confirmed their dependency role. Women were supposed to be soft, ethereal, and better than men. Translated in real terms, this meant that women were either superior or inferior to men, these myths and by getting the women to accept them, men but under no circumstances equal to them. By perpetuating completed their dominance over women. Pearl Buck believed that they did this out of resentment: women as mothers had chastised them, and as teachers had reprimanded them, and so with women as wives, they sought and achieved revenge. Wives as surrogate mothers and teachers received the punishment that men had received as children and young adults. Whether this analysis was based upon good psychology or not, the willingness of women to succumb to the punishment suggested that the victims accepted their oppressors' views.

In a later reference to the angel myth, Pearl Buck dispelled its power by saying that women have not kept the world purer and have not materially affected the well-being of mankind. The only way to bring peace to the world, she wrote in the very unpeaceful year of 1941, was for women to go out into the world and work with humane men to bring about peace.

> Yet to continue to bear children only to have them slaughtered is folly. But to take as a solemn task the prevention of war would be an achievement unmatched. In the process women would become inevitably concerned in human welfare, to the betterment of all society as well as of themselves. It is the only hope I see of the end of war.[17]

"Where is this moral superiority that will do nothing but knit while heads roll off in revolutions and war crashes upon our great cities so that ruins are all that we shall have left if the world goes on as it now is?"[18] Miss Buck did not assign to either sex absolute virtues or vices. Rather, she believed that the mothers of the race had a stake in peace, a stake that they could be educated to understand. Both sexes, of course, would benefit from a peaceful world.

Historically, women had fulfilled themselves by having babies and men by destroying them. "There ought to be some other more profitable form of pleasurable sacrifice for the human race than this sacrifice of the innocents."[19] The only hope for mankind, concluded Miss Buck, is true equality between the sexes, a condition never tried anywhere to her knowledge. In a period when the popular view held that women had unlimited opportunity and had made significant progress, Pearl Buck declared:

Profound as race prejudice is against the Negro American, it is not practically as far-reaching as the prejudice against women. For stripping away the sentimentality which makes Mother's Day and Best American Mother Contests, the truth is that women suffer all the effects of a minority.[20]

At a time when the rights of black Americans were also being ignored, Miss Buck had the perception to draw the comparison and to judge women as the greater sufferers at the hands of American democracy. Although the next generation would produce both black and feminist militants, Pearl Buck's 1941 *Of Men and Women* stands as a forceful and still relevant feminist statement.

Finally, the novelist proposed a radical change in our educational system to meet the needs of sexual equality. Both sexes, she said, should be educated together according to ability; homemaking courses, child-care subjects, and vocational subjects should be coeducational. History courses should present women leaders as well as men, in order to elevate the image of women. Foreshadowing some of the suggestions made twenty-five years later, Pearl Buck asked her readers how many of them knew who Elizabeth Cady Stanton was; if they didn't, that proved her point.[21] "Men and women should own the world as a mutual possession."[22] Psychology courses should recognize the mental differences of the sexes but should be taught in such a way as to distinguish between the inherited and environmental factors that made up the human personality.

"Let woman out of the home, let man into it, should be the aim of education. The home needs man, and the world outside needs women."[23] This succinct view summarizes the essence of *Of Men and Women*. Perhaps because 1941, the publication year, was a war year, the book did not receive widespread attention. Given the climate of opinion of the era, however, it is dubious whether women readers would have recognized themselves in Pearl Buck's descriptions of

American women. It took a bolder time for this message to catch on. But a later age produced its own spokeswomen, and Pearl Buck's contribution to feminism has gone unrecognized and unregarded. Pity, because it still expresses the problem eloquently.

Dorothy Sayers, a well-known mystery-story writer, wrote one essay for *Vogue* magazine in 1947 called "The Woman Question,"[24] which also captured the essence of the woman problem. Beginning with the basic premise that women and men are more alike than different (a crucial foundation to the whole argument), Dorothy Sayers continued by reminding her readers that the term *homo* described both male and female; however, culturally, the terms man (*vir*) and woman (*femina*) have been used in such a way that men have been considered both *vir* and *homo* and women as only *femina*. In this brief scheme, she showed how women have always been judged solely by their feminineness and never their humanness, the result being that women have always been dependent, passive, and indecisive.

> If, after a few centuries of this kind of treatment, the male was a little self-conscious, a little on the defensive, and a little bewildered about what was required of him, I should not blame him. If he traded a little upon his sex, I could forgive him. If he presented the world with a major social problem, I should scarcely be surprised. It would be more surprising if he retained any rag of sanity and self-respect.[25]

The Russians, she said, seemed to realize the human potential of women in a way that other societies did not. "But are revolution and blood the sole educational means of getting this plain fact into our heads?" Concluding in much the same way as Pearl Buck, Dorothy Sayers expressed the woman's paradoxical position well:

> They are far above man, to inspire him, far beneath
> him, to corrupt him; they have feminine minds and
> feminine natures, but their mind is not one with
> their nature like the minds of men; they have no
> human mind, no human nature.[26]

Dorothy Sayers's essay was pointed as well as poignant. It captured the essential feminist arguments. It based its appeal on the hope-assumption that if (and when) readers accepted the cultural nature of the feminist argument, they would respond by changing the unfeminist features of the culture. In logic, the argument was faultless; but in practice, it failed. *Vogue* readers in 1947 were hardly the discontented women that the writer hoped to reach; the advertisements in the same issue of the magazine occupied far more space than the serious copy. Readers of *Vogue,* the pages seemed to say, were faultlessly dressed and carefully poised ladies. The models, surely, had no cares in the world. The faces peering forth from *Vogue* were not discontented faces. It is surely a marvel that the editors of this fashion magazine consented to publish a feminist article. Perhaps their purpose was two-fold: they assuaged their consciences with the inclusion of a socially significant piece while knowing that the message would go unheeded and therefore not endanger the sale of their magazine.

Audience awareness, of course, is the major goal of the polemical writer. It is the necessary precondition to any kind of action. If the feminist writer can hit a responsive chord in her reader's mind, she has achieved, she hopes, the first step toward change. But it is a long first step when you are dealing with something as large and significant as attitudes toward women. The sophisticated manner in which Dorothy Sayers presented the problem made it even more difficult to communicate the message. Finally, of course, the positive advantages of women as *femina* cannot be airily dismissed. To many women, feminine wiles are legitimate and desirable tools in the battle of the sexes. Rather than abandon them, many women work at strengthening them. Thus the problems faced by a feminist writer are numerous: an unsympathetic and puzzled audience, a hostile and threatened audience, and/or an amused audience. In any and all cases, the beauty and power of Dorothy Sayers's "The Woman Question" pleased the few who shared her feelings but missed the many who did not.

Dorothy Thompson, one of the best known women journalists of the century, wrote frequently on the woman question during this period. At times, it is true, her message must have infuriated feminists. For example, in her monthly column in the *Ladies' Home Journal* for September 1939, she told her women readers that

> Society, at this moment, has a greater need of good mothers than it has of more private secretaries, laboratory assistants, short-story writers, lawyers, social workers and motion-picture stars. It is a better thing to produce a fine man than it is to produce a second-rate novel, and fine men begin by being fine children.[27]

But she changed her tune considerably during the war and thereafter. In an important article in 1943,[28] she looked ahead to the postwar period and envisioned a number of notable changes in the structure of society, changes that would be essential to the changed role of women.

The home, the factory, and the school, she prophesied, would alter their traditional patterns to accommodate the working woman. The large numbers of women working during the war would continue after the war, she predicted, and our society would adapt to the new conditions. Factories, for example, would be decentralized and move to small communities (and to the new suburbs) so that women workers could be closer to home. Schools would serve hot lunches to children and provide after-school programs until their parents returned from work. The home would be fully mechanized to simplify domestic chores, and both parents would participate equally in child raising. Dorothy Thompson's scenario would create a peaceful revolution in all major social institutions. So she hoped.

But the dream did not come true after the war. The women who remained in the factories remained under the same conditions that already existed. The government and the factory ignored the children; and the parents, in our individualistic culture, continued to be responsible for the welfare of their own children. Baby-sitting costs remained high, and working women found themselves discriminated against in other ways as well: income tax laws prevented their deducting baby-sitting expenses if the joint income of the couple exceeded $4,500 a year. In 1948, the government instituted the $600-a-year exemption for each child, thereby encouraging parents to produce more children; the federal government, however, did not inform parents how they were going to afford more children unless both parents worked; and if both did, how they were going to provide adequate care for their children, especially preschoolers. In typical American fashion, only a fragment of the social problem was faced while the larger, more comprehensive problem was ignored.

"Are Women Different?" asked Dorothy Thompson in 1951. A truly fundamental question and one upon which most feminist and antifeminist arguments have been based. In women's search for equality, she wondered why they had assumed the rightness of male standards of excellence. "They do not assert their *own* experience, affirm their *own* instincts, believe in their *own* wisdom, or struggle for their *own* values. And therefore, they do not release for society the unique power which is in them."[29] The basis for the differentness of women, according to Dorothy Thompson, was largely in their reproductive capacity.

Women will, I think, have fulfilled the woman's

revolution when they are not only equal in external status, but when they dare to be equal in real power —in the power generated in their wombs, their nerves, their maternal experiences, and not only in their heads. Then they will contribute to bring humanity into equilibrium, which is harmony, and peace.[30]

Many feminists, especially among the current generation, would reject the womb definition of women because this has always been the culture's view of them—as mothers. If, however, the basis for the woman's differentness is not biological, what is it? The romantic traditionalists laud the woman's power to be a mother as her sole claim to uniqueness—and as the major reason for her spending her life in the home; the feminists claim women are more like men than different from them but can't explain why they don't organize to gain their equal share of society's opportunities. Those feminists who claim that women are indeed different from men, in other than maternal ways, can never define the nature of the differences. And so the problem of clear-cut premises leading to clear-cut solutions never emerges.

Dorothy Thompson's belief in women as mothers did not further the analysis. Mothers, as Pearl Buck suggested, have not contributed to humanity's health except by being in the home—which is what they have always done with little measurable improvement in society, or in the home for that matter. Dorothy Thompson grappled with the problem; after more thought and reading on the subject, most notably the works of Ashley Montagu and Simone de Beauvoir, she changed her mind.

One cannot get around the fact that a child is begotten by its father in a few seconds, but must be carried by its mother for nine months. That its mother is thereafter its natural source of nourishment for some months more, and its intimate guard-

ian and protector for at least several years. The
woman with children is "tied down."[31]

Motherhood now appeared to be an unjust burden placed
solely upon women. Some women, of course, choose not to
have children, thereby avoiding this whole syndrome of in-
volvements; but, she commented, that is a high price to pay.
"No man has to give up being a complete male in order to
be a full-time concentrated artist, engineer, executive or
worker." With a new perspective in the apathetic year of
1953, Miss Thompson succinctly captured one significant
aspect of the woman's dilemma:

> But the woman who is talented and intellectually
> equipped for a demanding art or profession is, if
> she be fully feminine, torn between two functions.
> The feminist movement never really faced up to this
> fact.[32]

The final statement, I believe, is very important. Dorothy
Thompson noted a major flaw in feminist organizations.
With the exception of Henrietta Rodman's 1914 collective
apartment house scheme, most feminist activity concentrated
upon specific laws rather than a whole program that would
enable women to be both mothers and professionals. Certainly, feminist writers had always been plagued with the
impossible task of succeeding in all areas of human life. Mary
Heaton Vorse finally concluded that you could not have two
centers to your life, while Freda Kirchwey had good domestic help that freed her to continue her career. While individual feminists had to come to terms with the career/family
dichotomy, no feminist organization provided a comprehensive answer.

Elizabeth Gurley Flynn believed, along with most feminist
activists, that her work for the Wobblies superseded her
work at home. Her resolution was a personal one. Feminists
never publicly discussed how a conscientious mother could

also be a conscientious, practicing doctor; or how a feminist mother could run a successful business enterprise simultaneously. The collectivizing of the home, in a socialist setting, was viewed as the answer by most socialist feminists, but the discussion of this subject, couched in socialist terms, was often vague and abstract. Crystal Eastman's vision of a centralized government that would care for its children and would recognize each human being sounded utopian at best and subversive at worst. Thus the feminists who did consider the problem of motherhood and careerhood usually skipped a number of steps; they leaped over the present, where the dilemma seemed insoluble to thousands of women, into a future society where all would be well. Indeed, Dorothy Thompson's criticism of the feminist movement on this ground seems apt.

Harking back to an earlier theme, Dorothy Thompson argued in 1953 that factories and offices should provide nurseries and flexible working schedules. She saw no reason, for example, why secretaries could not take their work home. "Neither businesses nor schools are run to suit the hours of the working mother." She wondered ". . . why women with all their political and economic power cannot force from society more consideration of their own special problems."[33] The only group in our society that benefited from the present arrangement, she wryly concluded, were the psychiatrists. "Whether or not there's anything wrong with American women, their environment is not yet adjusted to their needs."[34] Dorothy Thompson persistently asked why women did not organize and utilize their power for their own good. In 1960, she noted that "Women have had the vote for over forty years and their organizations lobby in Washington for all sorts of causes; why, why, why don't they take up their *own* causes and obvious needs?"[35]

Contrary to Betty Friedan's later charge that the women's magazines contained only articles lauding domesticity, Dorothy Thompson's monthly column in the *Ladies' Home Journal* throughout the forties and fifties continually reminded women of their unfulfilled possibilities. The message was clearly, and often dramatically, stated. But her call to action went unheeded, not because, as Betty Friedan argued, men controlled the women's media, but because women in the post-World War Two period gladly cherished their wifely and motherly roles and enjoyed the new prosperity that gave them a home in the suburbs with an aqua-colored kitchen. Women believed, as they had in the 1910's, that only crazy spinsters praised a life outside the home. Normal women enjoyed the comfort and security of their newfound middle-class status and would be damned before they gave it up. The cultural attitudes, the core of the issue, had not changed substantially at all. In fact, things had gone downhill for women in the forties and fifties. The college-educated women of the 1910's became the backbone of many critical reform movements, including feminist ones, while the college-educated women of the 1950's returned to the home. Those who pursued a particular profession showed little or no concern for the woman's rights issue. The middle-class woman who had been a feminist in the 1910's became a personally ambitious career woman in the 1950's or a busy suburban mother involved in a whole range of volunteer community projects. Rather than looking outward, the educated women of the fifties looked inward, back to their families and small communities and not out toward the larger society.

Margaret Mead continued writing about women, too. Indeed, she is still, in the early 1970's, actively contributing ideas to this and other topics of interest. As a cultural anthropologist, of course, she had studied many different cultures, most notably the exotic tribal cultures of Samoa and New Guinea; she had been impressed with the contentment preliterate women seemed to have as mothers of their people. However, when she studied the American situation, she did not arrive at the same conclusion. American women were not blissfully content with their roles. The signs of dissatisfaction were apparent in the continually rising divorce rate, the mounting alcoholism among women, and the increase in juvenile delinquency. Unhappy American women, further, did not do a good job in their assigned roles as wives and mothers.

Margaret Mead's articles during the post-World War Two years showed her concern with giving women a larger self-definition. The gap between educational expectations and life opportunities for women was growing, not narrowing. Girls were taught in school, she noted in one essay, that they had freedom of choice, but it was denied them afterward. "If a man's choice of a girl doesn't carry with it a compulsory sort of job, why should a girl's choice of a man prescribe a compulsory job for the next thirty years?"[36] Women became confused in our culture because of this apparent problem. "Should she (a woman) see herself as a person or primarily as a woman?" Sounding much like Pearl Buck, Margaret Mead said that there were two possible solutions: either return women to their narrow biological role as producers of life—a solution she immediately rejected—or change social institutions to accommodate them. She then made three specific suggestions to accomplish the latter goal: men should participate more in the raising of children; technology should help to ease the drudgery of household chores; and neighborhood, collective units should aid in raising children. Margaret Mead did not favor large child-raising institutions but believed that small community units, where everyone knew each other, might be a feasible idea.

> When men take a greater part in these activities
> that we call living, as opposed to making a living,
> we shall approach again the sort of balance between
> the sexes that we had in early America, on our
> American farms, when both worked together at the
> same tasks, often within earshot of each other.[37]

Margaret Mead's hope for feminist success sometimes led her to claim victory when it did not exist. For example, she argued in one article that men were, in fact, turning away from their careers in greater numbers so that they could spend more time at home with their families. In convincing his wife that the home was important, she stated, the husband had also convinced himself. This idea seemed more in the vein of wishful thinking than of describing reality.[38] Elsewhere, in discussing modern marriage, she argued that women in middle age should "individualize their marriage, to think more about each other's rhythms, each other's capacities for change and fulfillment."[39] The vagueness of the suggestion made it less than helpful, and the readers had to draw their own conclusions as to its meaning.

But the dominant message of Margaret Mead's advice to American women was in the best feminist tradition. "The only way to break the deadlock is to reinstitute the range of ideals without which any civilization perishes. . . . People, not just men. By hamstringing women at the point where some of them can make the contributions we need, we have hamstrung men also."[40] As late as 1960, she was reiterating the same theme:

> This future must include a new image for and of women beyond her primary role of home making. The present image is built on loss—loss of children, loss of one's figure, loss of zest, loss of one's husband. Built out of the negations of the present, it means no banging doors as children come from school, no occasional nights out with one's husband, nothing to look forward to.[41]

She recommended careers in nursing, teaching, and other womanly professions as women's life's work. At the same time that Margaret Mead could say, "So, we had the paradox of having women educated like men and of according them all the rights of men, except one—the right to dedicate themselves to any task other than homemaking,"[42] she also could resort to the typical view that woman's work was inextricably tied to her maternal capacity. Human work, which has always meant man's work, still seems to be man's work in Margaret Mead's analysis; woman's work still carries with it the traditional biological restrictions that society has always imposed.

However, Margaret Mead's frequent discussions of the role of American women in our culture and the need to allow them free expression of their talents fall within the feminist frame of reference. Her belief that men are, in fact, participating in greater numbers in the home and in child raising has proven false. Her suggestions that woman's work should be related to her motherly capacity would not be received favorably by feminists who want to break out of the biological-social role definition. In earlier treatments of the subject, Margaret Mead showed an awareness of the connection between sex and achievement in all cultures; she recognized that it was the culture that assigned certain traits to each sex and expected all members to conform to the established pattern. Frequently, as she noted, the differentiations were not legitimate but rather perpetuated discrimination against the female sex. But in her own mind, apparently, she still believed that there was a legitimate reason for assigning all the nurturing roles to women and all the non-nurturing roles to men. She could not make the break entirely. She could write eloquently about how unfair it was to educate women and then bury them in the home, but her vision of their usefulness outside the home still retained the traditional view of women as nurses and teachers.

The nature and purpose of college education for women became the subject of sociologist Mirra Komarovsky's book *Women in the Modern World* (1953). Professor Komarovsky taught sociology courses on the family and marriage at Barnard College for over twenty-five years. Her book dealt with the problems faced by college-educated American women and proposed ways of harmonizing an authentic, intellectually stimulating college education with homemaking. Using case studies from many of her students as the basis for her study, as well as statistical and psychological data, she illustrated the now familiar dilemma faced by college-educated women: a sense of loss after marriage, of frustration at the dull drudgery of household chores, and of inadequacy.

Mirra Komarovsky presented statistics on the marriage rate of college women that effectively demonstrated how she, too, was the captive of the culture. While the college women of the 1910's generation did not marry in the same proportion as the female population as a whole, the college women of the 1940's were marrying in greater numbers.[43] As a sociologist, she wanted to show her readers that graduating from college would not lessen a woman's chances for marriage— still the major profession of all women. But women college graduates who married, her evidence also showed, felt unhappy and unsure of the role of wife and mother. Frequent examples illustrated the restrictiveness of the domestic roles for the sensitive, educated young woman. Her self-image declined; no one asked her opinion about any subject of import any longer. As a college student, she had held her own in conversations. As a housewife, she felt isolated, removed from the world, and uninformed. Many of these women relied upon their husbands to provide them with information about the outside world. They accepted the dependency role, either gladly or guiltily, but in either case they accepted it.

Mirra Komarovsky surveyed numerous studies to prove that there was no substantial intellectual difference between the sexes, thereby giving support to her view that men and women should be given the same educational opportunities. She reviewed the child-raising techniques in our culture as evidence of the sex stereotyping that fostered woman's dependency as an adult. In short, she covered the now familiar ground on how the American culture restricts women. Perhaps because the book was a sociological effort, an attempt at scholarly objectivity, it did not contain the passion or the verve of Pearl Buck's treatment of the same subject, and surely none of the polemics of the next generation's feminist writers.

It is frequently asserted that today's co-eds have rebelled against the feminism of earlier college generations and have returned to the traditional feminine role. Though no comparable attitude studies
exist to test this assertion, it does appear that
feminine militancy is absent from the campus and
that, moreover, the traditional role is defended with
new weapons drawn from the arsenal of psychoanalysis, and with what appears sometimes a defen-
sive emotion. Like the girl who feared that she
would make a successful career woman and would
thereby jeopardize her future marriage, some girls
appear to espouse the traditional role all the more
passionately because they feel tempted by other
goals.[44]

Young college women may, indeed, have experienced guilt in
rejecting a career, fear of the uncertainty of a future without
a husband, and defensiveness in discussing their conventional
choice of wifehood. But Mirra Komarovsky offered little
solace for the career-oriented woman. She agreed with traditionalists that "the deepest satisfactions in the life of a
woman are bound up with child raising" and that this
"hardly requires the support of statistics."[45] In her recommendations for college-educated women, she proposed part-
time jobs and understanding husbands as essential parts of
the solution.

Like the other feminist writers described in this section,
she believed that husbands who participated in child raising
would materially alter the family structure and contribute
to the happiness of women. Although she correctly identified
the problem as being one of cultural attitudes, she wanted to
change the wrong attitudes. Surely, she concluded, homemaking "is one of the several equally reputable careers for
college women."[46]

It is quite true that building bridges, writing books,
and splitting the atom are no more essential to so-

ciety or more difficult than child raising. But, in our
opinion, women cannot be made to believe it unless
men believe it too; unless, that is, the whole of our
society becomes oriented towards values quite different from those which dominate it today.[47]

Mirra Komarovsky wanted homemaking and child raising
to be given a dignified place in human endeavors. Rather than
changing cultural values to allow women an equal place in
the larger world, she suggested uplifting the image of the
home. Women do not have to leave their homes to receive
high status recognition; the culture merely has to truly re-
vere, not just pay lip service to, the importance of the home.
Women who did not share her commitment to child raising
found no solace or advice in *Women in the Modern World*.

In practice, achieving any value change is a mighty task.
However, while the majority of feminists wanted the value
change to be toward freeing women to work and live equita-
bly in the larger society, Mirra Komarovsky proposed keeping women, including college women, in the homes but giving
the homemaking profession a higher status. In all fairness
to her, she also recommended collective nurseries to aid
working mothers and more part-time jobs for women; but
she disapproved of women's complaining and expressing discontent with their lot.

And if life later frustrates the love of ideas acquired
in college, and if women find themselves so preoccupied with the "raw materials of daily living" that
they lose sight of the wider intellectual and civic
horizons, it may be healthier that they should remain dissatisfied and apologetic until some sounder
solution than the philosophy of "sour grapes" is
found.[48]

This statement could not have been written after 1965, but it
clearly reflects the climate of opinion of the 1950's. While

Mirra Komarovsky must be credited with discussing the role of college women in America as a problem, she still accepted the traditional values of the society and did not consider novel or heretical ways to upset the status quo.

In the bleak 1950's, Mirra Komarovsky and Margaret Mead, however moderate their feminist expressions were, presented conscious and sensitive statements about women when the public and the intellectuals generally ignored the subject. True, Pearl Buck's contribution, Dorothy Thompson's hard-hitting plea for women to organize on their own behalf, and Dorothy Sayers's brief but powerful feminist essay would rate above the Komarovsky and Mead contributions to feminist writing and thought during the period. But at a time when the subject was largely neglected, their efforts cannot be dismissed. The deeply ambivalent quality in their writing effectively portrays the conflict that even sensitive women possessed. Reconciling motherhood and a professional career, as Dorothy Thompson had suggested, was the crux of the matter. The fact that both Mirra Komarovsky and Margaret Mead tried to reconcile the two by suggesting that the woman's career was homemaking, motherhood, and/or the nurturing professions was understandable, if somewhat annoying and unsatisfying to women who may have desired a career in physics. Further, as long as women continued to adjust their lives to existing patterns, they would be faced with the low image and status society accorded them. Only when societal institutions changed, as Dorothy Thompson suggested—thereby recognizing and acknowledging working women as heavily burdened human beings—could there be any hope of meaningful change.

THREE KEY REPORTS ON WOMEN

Despite the sterility of the forties and fifties for feminist thought and action, three very different but interesting studies of the modern woman emerged in that period: Ferdinand Lundberg and Marynia Farnham's *Modern Woman: The Lost Sex* (1947), Simone de Beauvoir's *The Second Sex* (translated into English in 1953), and Alfred Kinsey's *Sexual Behavior in the Human Female* (1953). Lundberg and Farnham, using a Freudian perspective, attacked feminism; de Beauvoir presented the most comprehensive defense of the feminist position in modern history; and Kinsey provided scientific data that described woman's sexuality in new ways. Indeed woman's sexuality had been successfully ignored for a very long time by most of the medical profession.

Lundberg and Farnham lamented the material forces of the nineteenth and twentieth century that took women out of the home and deprived them of their traditional biological-cultural roles. The industrial revolution drove women into the factories, and the French Revolution gave them false ideas about themselves and the sources of their happiness. "It is our contention," the authors gravely stated, "that with the principal machine man built, the steam engine, the proper use of which he has not yet been able to figure out, he destroyed his material earthly home."[49] Women became emulators of men as a result of the industrial revolution, and unsatisfied with their domestic roles. Those who actively espoused feminism became the villains in this study. The feminist neuroticism, as the authors called it, was most effectively expressed in their ideology:

1. that women are identical with men (equal)
2. they should receive the same education as men
3. should be governed by the same moral standards
4. should have the same work opportunities and
5. should have the same political rights[50]

The mere statement of feminist beliefs, in the authors' views, damned it to eternity. Women who wanted to be like men, who wanted to compete equally with men, were denying their basic psychosexual natures. The culture of the West, Lundberg and Farnham reminded their readers, is phallic and is man determined, and women entering this man's world are therefore phallic imitators. Since women can never have a penis, they can never achieve equality with men.

Why don't women recognize this fact? Why don't they acknowledge their basic physiological difference from men and live within the sexual and cultural confines of the home, a place suited to their natures? Lundberg and Farnham's answer to these questions, of course, was that the feminists' sickness, their neuroticism, was precisely due to their inability to own up to their true natures and live contentedly in domestic bliss. Feminists who try to make men acknowledge their equality are displaying their basic hostility toward men. "Whatever *was,* to the feminists, was wrong, and had to be changed."[51] This statement, taken out of context, could be interpreted as a positive sign of the healthy reformer wanting to right society; but to the Freudian authors of this book, that statement of purpose was a pejorative one. The dissatisfaction and the restlessness of women were signs of their maladjustment. Society, of course, contributed to the feminists' sickness. By removing the functions of the home, by reducing the responsibilities of the mother in regard to her children and the care of her home, the woman had been robbed of her traditional functions. Thus she left the home in search of a new identity. "The 'successful woman,' as success is measured on the contemporary phallic standard, is successful as a man."[52]

Lundberg and Farnham pointed to the irony (and the tragedy) of feminists' trying to succeed according to a male standard of success. Recognizing the reduced work load of the modern home, they recommended part-time jobs for women outside the home—but only jobs that were closely linked with the nurturing (that is, the natural) functions of women. Nursing, teaching, counseling, and doctoring were acceptable, but engineering, truck driving, the law, and professional athletics were not. Ironically, the Freudians' suggestions for positive improvement came close to Margaret

Mead's and Mirra Komarovsy's. Although Mead and Komarovsky would not describe woman's discontent as penis envy,
they would share the view of specific womanly occupations.
Using the sexual act as the analogy for all women's roles,
Lundberg and Farnham developed a highly rigid and deter-
ministic analysis. Woman's biology determined her cultural
roles, and the inextricable tie could be broken only at the risk
of extreme neuroticism.

Modern Woman pleased the conservatives, who had always
shaken their heads disapprovingly at the career women, and
buoyed the spirits of Freudian psychiatrists, whose couches
were occupied by similarly diagnosed women. To the majority of women—that is to say, the apathetic women of
America who did not study the question—penis envy was an
undesirable characteristic and one to be consciously avoided.
Channeling your surplus energy, therefore, into the next
PTA luncheon was a safer and healthier way to express
yourself than to take additional courses to complete your
college education. No upstanding American woman wanted
to be called mannish or masculine, an epithet to be avoided
at all costs. The vicious circle that feminists had always
complained about was effectively closed in the Lundberg and
Farnham study: women who sought careers in man's world
were mannish and denied their true natures; their only
solace was in nurturing tasks. The life options for women
were decidedly different from those available to men. That
was that, and any woman who thought otherwise was mentally ill.

Simone de Beauvoir, a famous French woman novelist
and existentialist philosopher, contributed the most exhaustive study of women published to that date.[53] *The Second
Sex* explored mythology, psychology, literature, and history
to demonstrate the second-sex status of women in Western
culture. From the Old Testament's view of woman as primarily the creator of life to descriptions of child-raising practices, de Beauvoir proved that women have been raised to be,

in existentialist terminology, immanent creatures, while men have been raised to be transcendent beings. Men are taught to reach beyond themselves, to strive for greater and greater development as well as power, while women are trained to be inward, passive, and simply present. Women are the in-gatherers of the culture, and men are the discoverers and strugglers. Excitement, discovery, fulfillment are manly possibilities; woman's satisfactions derive from her absorption of the immediate environment. The mothers of the race receive pleasure from their sons' accomplishments. They bask in the glory of others. ". . . It is civilization as a whole that produces this creature, intermediate between male and eunuch, which is described as feminine."[54]

In the most complete and serious analysis yet of the woman's role in Western society, de Beauvoir explained how love was woman's total *raison d'être,* while for men it was only a part of their life's purpose. Love, then, perpetuates the dependency role of women, a role that prevents all women from attaining authentic separateness as human beings. "On the day when it will be possible for woman to love not in her weakness but in her strength," concluded de Beauvoir, "not to escape herself but to find herself, not to abase herself but to assert herself—on that day love will become for her, as for man, a source of life and not of mortal danger."[55] True love for women, argued the French writer, can only come when they have had a meaningful existence outside of the home. Work was a crucial means of self-identification in de Beauvoir's frame of reference; satisfying work had always been the means by which men achieved personal happiness and recognition in our society. Women needed the same experience in order to achieve selfhood.

Further, in a most trenchant and penetrating discussion of motherhood, de Beauvoir argued that only working women —that is, women who had had rewarding work experiences— could be good mothers. Women had to be engaged in life in order to bear children in a meaningful way; women had to love life to want children, and the only way this could happen was by doing professionally exciting work. Working and raising children, she acknowledged, was a difficult task, but society could and should create the necessary institutions to make the double chore feasible. There was no God or man-made law that required women and children to belong exclusively to each other.[56] Simone de Beauvoir questioned the mother role of women in a way never before attempted by feminists. She relentlessly attacked all the time-worn views and myths on the subject and concluded that all mothers, if they faced themselves honestly, would recognize an ambivalence in their attitude toward motherhood. De Beauvoir, contrary to her critics, did not renounce motherhood but claimed that only whole women could accept motherhood enthusiastically. Existentially, women had to become human beings before they could become mothers.

Predictably, the reception that *The Second Sex* got in this country demonstrated the very traditional commitments of most Americans. Two major critics called the work paranoic,[57] while Margaret Mead, who acknowledged its basic soundness, expressed annoyance with de Beauvoir's denigration of the mother role.[58] She believed that the French writer envied men their transcendent place in the universe and wished she had been born a man. Given de Beauvoir's discussion of the life possibilities for men in Western culture, in contrast to the limited life styles open to women, Margaret Mead's criticism was probably accurate. But to the Frenchwoman, it would not have been the damning statement that it was to Mead and to American readers. To say that a woman wants to be like a man, with Lundberg and Farnham as respectable evidence, proved to most people that she was sick and sad. But to de Beauvoir, it was a simple case of justice for women to have equal opportunity with men; she envied the power and opportunity men had, not their penises. Further, for the deprived to envy the powerful may not be an attractive trait, but it is surely a normal, not an abnormal, one.

Margaret Mead believed that the novelist's strong antipathy toward male domination was largely a result of the French culture, which still accepted marriages of convenience and discouraged birth control. Thus she believed that de Beauvoir's book only described the feelings of a brilliant woman bound to a traditional culture. Paradoxically, at the same time that Margaret Mead wrote articles describing the maddening gap in America between the promises made to women and their life expectations, her review of *The Second Sex* showed no awareness of the fact that there was more similarity than difference between woman's status in America and in France.

Typical of the times, *The Second Sex* did not create the public interest that *Sexual Politics,* a book modeled upon it, did in 1970. In 1953, a select number of intellectuals read the book and that was that. The press did not feature articles on the subject, nor did television produce talk shows to discuss women's rights. Brendan Gill in *The New Yorker* called it a work of art, ". . . with the salt of recklessness that makes art sting."[59] However, *The Second Sex* did not sting enough readers to have a significant effect upon the American consciousness.

Kinsey's *Sexual Behavior in the Human Female* (1953) did not receive the attention it deserved either, while his earlier report on male sexuality had received much popular notice. The reason for this lack of interest is tied to the traditional cultural attitudes toward women and sex. The old belief, and it has not materially changed in the twentieth century, was that men are sexual creatures—aggressive, outward, and domineering. Woman, as expressed sublimely in the Victorian era, endured the male's advances if he were her husband and repudiated them if he were not. Sexual activity was sanctioned only for its resulting maternity; concomitantly, to many women, it was dreaded for this reason as well. But in any case, women were not supposed to possess sexual desires or feelings. If a woman secretly experienced sexual longings, she kept it a secret. She felt shame, guilt, and remorse for her perverse body that made her shudder in unexplainable ways.

Dr. Kinsey's study revealed, unknowingly perhaps, much about cultural attitudes toward women's sexual nature and behavior. In studying the marital histories of a sampling of women, he discovered, among other things, that "those females who had not responded to the point of orgasm prior to marriage, failed to respond after marriage three times as often as the females who had had a fair amount of orgasmic experience before marriage."[60] The significance of this statement, culturally, is that the 36 percent of the women in the sample who had not experienced any kind of orgasm prior to marriage demonstrated the inhibited, nonexploratory nature of American women regarding their own sexuality. While masturbation leading to orgasm, a meaningful prelude to adult sexual activity, was a common practice among adolescent boys (93 percent in early adolescence and 99 percent in the teens), 62 percent of the adolescent girls masturbated and only 20 percent experienced orgasm.[61] The fact that fewer women had orgasmic experiences prior to marriage resulted in unfulfilled married women, incapable of full sexual satisfaction. The technical literature, as Kinsey pointed out, referred to these women as frigid.

> We dislike the term, for it has come to connote either an unwillingness or an incapacity to function sexually. In most circumstances neither of these implications is correct. It is doubtful whether there is ever a complete lack of capacity, although individuals appear to differ in their levels of response. In general, females and males appear to be equally responsive to the whole range of physical stimuli which may initiate erotic reactions and the specific data show that the average female is no slower in response than the average male when she is sufficiently stimulated and when she is not inhibited in her activity. Females may not be so often aroused

by psychologic stimuli but if there is any sufficient physical stimulation, it is probable that all females are physiologically capable of responding and of responding to the point of orgasm.[62]

Throughout the study, Kinsey repeatedly said that women had the same capacity for sexual expression and fulfillment as did men. In discussing the anatomical differences between the sexes, he parted company with the Freudians. "The genitalia of the female and the male," he told his readers,

> originate embroylogically from essentially identical structures. . . . The penis, in spite of its greater size, is not known to be better equipped with sensory nerves than the much smaller clitoris. Both structures are of considerable significance in sexual arousal.[63]

The larger size of the penis, Kinsey claimed, had a psychological effect on the male and caused him to focus on it. Anticipating much of the women's liberation literature of the 1960's Kinsey dispelled the view, for those who read and accepted his findings at least, that the existence of the phallus determined everything, from coitus to culture.

> The female may find psychological satisfaction in her function in receiving, while the male may find satisfaction in his capacity to penetrate during coitus, but it is not clear that this could account for the more aggressive part which the average male plays, and the less aggressive part which the average female plays in sexual activity. The differences in aggressiveness of the average female and male appear to depend upon something more than the differences in their genital anatomy.[64]

Men feel *psychologically* dominant, enjoy that feeling, and, by extension, consider the sex act as a metaphor for all of their life's roles. Kinsey's report disputed the determinism of the Freudians. Sexual anatomy and physiology did not decide cultural roles. Rather, psychological attitudes played a large part in determining human roles; if both sexes feel, think, and view themselves in terms of the sex roles they play in coitus, if they project the qualities they display in bed to all their nonsexual activities, then the power of sex to determine all human roles is indeed strong. But psychological attitudes can be changed; biological ones cannot. Herein lies the difference.

Kinsey's report should have made people reconsider the airtight equation of sex anatomy and human role behavior. Women did not have to remain entirely passive during sexual intercourse. Both men and women could enjoy sexual fulfillment; it did not have to remain primarily a male experience. Kinsey and his staff were concerned with describing what was, although they also established a normative goal: sexually fulfilled females. The evidence suggested that premarital sexual experience, either in the form of masturbation or of coitus, led to more sexually fulfilled married women, and consequently happier women. Fewer divorces, fewer screaming wives, happier children, and pleased men might result. Both sexes stood to benefit, as did society as a whole, from the realization of this goal.

An interesting example of the cultural values implicit in Kinsey's report was his observation that men divorce adulterous partners far more frequently than do women. True to the double standard in our culture, women accept their husbands' sexual infidelity, while men divorce their wives for committing the same sin.[65] The wife in our culture, the mother, is the keeper of the family and the preserver of its sanctity. She sees herself in this role and is willing to forgive her erring husband rather than break up the family. Men, on the other hand, uncommitted to the role of family preserver (even though they are the breadwinners), are willing to sacrifice their homes if their wives commit adultery. The difference in each sex's response to the other's impropriety aptly reflects the culture's different attitudes on the subject. Adulterous women wear the scarlet letter, while adulterous men become playboys.

Kinsey's study, then, offers much of interest to the feminist, indeed much of interest to all men and women. He rejected the Freudian theory of vaginal orgasm, provided evidence to suggest that women are fully as capable of enjoying sexual relations as men are, and that female sexuality is a human subject worthy of study. Sexual fulfillment, according to this scientist's view, is healthy and essential; women should not be afraid or ashamed of their own sexuality. Perhaps his charts and statistical summaries scared away many readers. That was unfortunate because his study, although not answering all significant questions regarding woman's sexuality, contributed mightily to a subject deserving more attention than it had previously received.

The authors of *Modern Woman: The Lost Sex* criticized the feminist trend in modern society, de Beauvoir criticized the Freudians and many others, and Kinsey offered a dispassionate survey of women's sexual behavior. Kinsey and de Beauvoir were compatible and both rejected the Lundberg-Farnham view of women. Although the Kinsey report and the de Beauvoir translation appeared in the same year, 1953, no serious and constructive interchange of ideas was presented for public consumption. Scholars tucked away the insights they may have gained from these volumes, and potential women activists buried the books in their bottom drawers. It remained for their children, born in the late forties, to mine the jewels of de Beauvoir and arm themselves with the discoveries of Kinsey.

ELIZABETH GURLEY FLYNN:
THE DEMISE OF A RADICAL FEMINIST

Elizabeth Gurley Flynn, a Wobblies organizer at the age of fifteen, was still going strong after 1940. Illness had kept her relatively quiet in the middle and late 1920's as well as the early 1930's, but by the middle of the 1930's, she was feeling better and eager to get back into the fray. In 1937, she joined the Communist Party because, she later said, she "wanted to advance a political party of the working class."[66] Her devotion to the class of her origins, as well as to women, never left her. She began writing political pamphlets for the Communist Party and became one of its chief spokeswomen. One magazine sketch about her, written in 1946, called her "a public speaker in a class with Billy Sunday, William Jennings Bryan, and other brass-lunged giants of Chautauqua days." She had delivered nearly ten thousand speeches in her life and considered herself a "professional revolutionist and agitator."[67]

In 1940, her name received much attention in the press when she was expelled from the board of directors of the American Civil Liberties Union. Elizabeth Gurley Flynn had been a charter member of the ACLU, committed to the cause of civil liberties for all. Her work in establishing a Workers Defense Union during the early 1920's was done in conjunction with the ACLU. But the climate of opinion had changed significantly since then. Many liberals, although traditional defenders of individual rights, had been appalled by the Nazi-Soviet Pact of August 1939, and lost sympathy with American Communists. The ACLU's behavior toward Mrs. Flynn was heavy-handed and unwarranted. She had announced her decision to become a member of the Communist Party at an ACLU board meeting in 1937; two years later, she had been unanimously reelected to the board for a three-year term. A pamphlet entitled *Why We Defend Free Speech for Nazis, Fascists and Communists* was put out by the ACLU a month before Elizabeth Gurley Flynn was asked to resign from the board. Thus, the irony of the ACLU's action was unbelievable. The *Nation,* in an editorial, wondered why the board had reelected her in 1939 if they did not want Communists in their midst. Surely the editors suggested, it did not serve the cause of civil liberties to start a hullabaloo over the presence of one Communist.[68]

Corliss Lamont, a pro-Flynn member of the ACLU board, charged that she was being used as a sacrificial lamb so that the organization could receive a clean bill of health from the House Committee on Un-American Activities. In her defense before the board (for she refused to resign and demanded a hearing in which they would have to expel her if they wanted to be rid of her), Mrs. Flynn said:

> If this trial occurred elsewhere it would be a case for the ACLU to defend! I am fighting for civil liberties in the ACLU! This charge violates every principle we fought for in the past. Unless the ACLU returns to its original position, its future record is likely to disgrace its past. I have a moral duty, as a charter member of the ACLU, to fight against this danger and to maintain my status.[69]

Despite the death of her only child just two months before, Elizabeth Gurley Flynn appeared undaunted in the face of the board. Lamont described her at the time as

> . . . a warm, vital person, all Irish, with crystal blue eyes, a clear white skin and shining black hair which she parted in the middle and rolled back softly in a knot at the back. Her spirit and enthusiasm were contagious. . . . Elizabeth was now in her fifties, still beautiful; her blue eyes were calm, her manner self-possessed. . . . There was no question that Elizabeth was respected by everyone around the table, even by those who had instituted these proceedings, for her life-long concern for the oppressed and her passionate sense of justice.[70]

After six hours of deliberation, the board voted to expel her, a member with twenty-three years of service.

Elizabeth Gurley Flynn continued her propaganda work for the Communist Party and produced three pamphlets in the next few years that tried to convince American women of their potential role in bringing peace to the world. Her doctrinaire devotion to the Communists, however, made it difficult for her to maintain her long-held pacifistic philosophy. In 1940, she wrote *I Didn't Raise My Boy to Be a Soldier for Wall Street,* a pamphlet that accurately reflected her long-standing commitment to pacifism and the still-acceptable party line that the war was started by imperialistic bankers to further their own selfish capitalistic aims. But when the Soviet Union was attacked by the Nazis and entered the war on the Allied side, she abandoned pacifism for active involvement in the war and encouraged Americans to buy savings stamps. She chastised John L. Lewis, head of the United Mine Workers, for hedging on his war stand. She appealed to the mine workers to go over their leader's head and pressure for a second front to relieve the Soviet Union.[71]

In a pamphlet describing the lives of Ella Reeve Bloor and Anita Whitney, two old-time Communist leaders, Elizabeth Flynn harked back to a favorite theme: "Once women understand and accept their important co-equal role in society they will give to it the deep emotional as well as intellectual absorption which these two great American women have displayed throughout their life time."[72] And in *Women Have a Date with Destiny,* the revolutionary writer told her readers that voting women could decide the 1944 election. Supporting Franklin D. Roosevelt's bid for reelection, she reminded American women that they outnumbered men voters and should use their political power accordingly.[73] After the war, in still another pamphlet, *Woman's Place—In the Fight for a Better World,* she told American women to organize politically so that disarmament, lasting peace, and justice for all could be achieved. Capitalism kept women in an inferior position as it did the working class. The Communist Party, Elizabeth Flynn argued, had as the first plank in its platform, "Equality of women in the political, economic, legal, professional, cultural, and social life of our country."[74]

Along with this pledge, maternity benefits, child-care centers, and job equality were all Communist proposals.

Elizabeth Gurley Flynn was able, in her role as propagandist for the Communist Party, to integrate her long-held commitment to women with her devotion to the working class. The injustices suffered by both groups, as she saw it, were the result of the capitalistic system; both women and workers would benefit from Communism. But Mrs. Flynn's writings, rather than recommending the overthrow of the American government, urged the election of F.D.R. and the buying of savings stamps. However, during the Communist witchhunting days after World War Two, the United States government prosecuted Elizabeth Flynn for her known affiliation with the Communist Party. At sixty-two years of age, she was tried with twelve other Communist leaders in 1952 under the Smith Act for conspiring to teach and advocate the violent overthrow of the United States government. After a long trial, with repeated delays and postponements, she was sentenced to the women's federal reformatory at Alderson, West Virginia, in January 1955.

Asked by the judge whether she would be willing to go to the Soviet Union, if it could be arranged, rather than serve a prison term, she answered no:

> I said we would all be happy to visit the Soviet Union. But we would not accept exile from our own country. We did not feel we had any right to go there to enjoy socialism which somebody else had worked to build. This is our country and our duty is to stay right here and help to build socialism here.[75]

During her twenty-eight-month prison term, Mrs. Flynn wrote poetry, took notes on the prison environment which would later become part of a book on the prison, and participated in the desegregation of a cottage made up predominantly of black women. She also wrote an article for the

July 4 issue of the prison quarterly, which received public attention. Columnist Murray Kempton wrote in the *New York Post:*

> Miss Elizabeth Gurley Flynn, who was convicted under the Smith Act during the campaign year of 1952, has been in a West Virginia Federal Prison for women. Last July 4th the prison authorities asked her to write a patriotic editorial. Neither she nor they seemed to think it odd for a July 4th piece to come from a woman convicted of conspiracy to advocate the overthrow of the government of the United States; she wrote it and they printed it. She is regarded by all parole boards as unrepentant and therefore unfit for mercy; she is only fit to tell Federal prisoners why they should love America. I would like to say that Thomas Jefferson would have been proud of this story; but I am more sure that he would have wondered what she was doing in jail in the first place. Jefferson, bless him, was better than most of us because he had no need for the sense of irony.[76]

An unrepentant Elizabeth Gurley Flynn was released from prison in May 1957. She remained unflappable. At the age of sixty-seven, an ex-convict, she returned to her work for the Communist Party, as determined as ever to spread the party's philosophy to all Americans and to see the repressive restraints upon its activities removed. But first, according to one story, she went to her local Social Security office to collect her ninety dollars a month. She explained to a bewildered woman clerk that the reason she had not come to register two years before was that she had been in prison; she further startled her by saying that her employer for the past twenty years had been the Communist Party. "It doesn't matter," retorted the clerk, "just fill out the forms." She did and subsequently received her monthly payments. In 1961, at the age of seventy-one, Mrs. Flynn was given the highest position in the United States Communist Party—chairman of the national committee. She continued to work for the repeal of the Smith Act and to ease the restrictions imposed upon the Communist Party. Her only success was the Supreme Court decision to grant passports to Communists. As a result, she was able to pay a visit to the Soviet Union. While there in 1964, she died, at age seventy-four. She was given a full-scale state funeral in Red Square, with Premier Khrushchev standing in the honor guard.

Thus ended the long and active career of Elizabeth Gurley Flynn. In her later years, she had tried to recapture, through her work for the Communist Party, the drama, excitement, and joy in struggle that she had known as a young participant in the coal miners' and textile workers' strikes of the 1910's. No one could ever say that Elizabeth Gurley Flynn had not spent her earthly years working for the causes she believed in. And that was more than can be said for most of us.

FREDA KIRCHWEY:
COLD WAR ANALYST, 1945-1955

Feminist editor Freda Kirchwey spent her last decade as publisher and editor of the *Nation* commenting upon American foreign policy in her magazine's pages. Historians of the post-World War Two period point to Walter Lippmann and George Kennan as major critics of American foreign policy, and ignore the perceptive writings of Freda Kirchwey. While George Kennan was first a supporter of cold war policy and later a recanter of it, Miss Kirchwey saw the folly of the cold war strategy from the beginning. She questioned the future use of the atom bomb shortly after Nagasaki, and wondered how the oil and coal industries would react to the peacetime utilization of atomic energy.[77]

Miss Kirchwey recommended sharing the secret of the

bomb with the Russians for numerous reasons: because they would discover it sooner or later anyway (as their scientists were already at work on it), and because it would prevent the creation of needless tensions and lessen the risk of future trouble in the world. "The differences between Russia and the West," she wrote in November 1945 (and repeated frequently during the next decade), "are real differences; they existed long before the first bomb was dropped and they would still exist if Russia had the secret. But the bomb has intensified them and stalled efforts to solve them."[78] Reconciling, or at least conciliating, the differences between the two superpowers became Freda Kirchwey's major theme.

As she looked at the world after the devastating war, she remembered the problem-filled aftermath of the First World War. Long a critic of colonialism, she spoke out against the British presence in Palestine in 1945 as well as the French return to Indochina. She interpreted the Truman Doctrine, with its aid to Greece and Turkey, as a colonial action. How could the United States, she asked, very self-righteously of course, criticize the Soviet intervention in Rumania and Bulgaria when it supported reactionary governments in China, Greece, Spain and Latin America? How could America decry Soviet interference when it was guilty of precisely the same thing?[79] "Put baldly, Mr. Truman's message was a plain declaration of political war against Russia. Nothing more, but also nothing less."[80]

Freda Kirchwey viewed Henry Wallace (the former Secretary of Commerce whom Truman had fired for his criticism of the Truman foreign policy) as a well-meaning but unrealistic progressive. She shared Wallace's criticism of the bellicose foreign policy of the administration but eschewed third-party hopefuls, having seen the demise of the Bull Moose Party and LaFollette's Progressive Party. Rather, Miss Kirchwey suggested that all progressives should rally around like-minded candidates in the Democratic Party. Another enduring theme of the *Nation* editor was the call to the left, to all liberals, progressives, and radicals, to agree to disagree with one another but to unite against the growing conservatism in the country. Senator Joe McCarthy's rise drew critical notice in the pages of the *Nation*. Freda Kirchwey's memories of firsthand experiences with Attorney General A. Mitchell Palmer in 1919 made her aware of the power of anti-Communist-radical hysteria in the country and the danger it would hold for all progressives.

> McCarthy's open and calculating use of false denunciation to spread fright and reinforce with public suspicion his own political forays against the party in power has so much in common with totalitarian tactics everywhere that decent democrats have to fight it as they would fight an invading army.[81]

Elsewhere she noted that "the threat of communism in this country is insignificant; while the threat of reaction is explicit in the Washington red-hunt and implicit in Mr. Truman's new foreign policy."[82] President Truman's approval of the Internal Security Act of 1950 almost put her in despair; she feared that the administration was trying to outdo the McCarthy wing of the Republican Party in its routing of mythical Communists. The fear in the left wing, the willingness, in fact the eagerness, with which liberals denounced any radical sympathies they may have had in the thirties, put terror in her heart. Whereas in the twenties, the members of the left stayed together and weathered the storm of administration prosecution and persecution, they seemed to fall apart in the late forties and early fifties. It seemed to be very difficult to be against American foreign policy and not be labeled a Communist sympathizer. Freda Kirchwey tried to preserve the delicate balance, and she commended Henry Wallace for his attempts to put an end to the cold war mentality.

> It's only to say that Henry Wallace would end, promptly and forever, the school-yard-bully tech-

nique in dealing with Russia. "We'll sail our ships
wherever we blank blank please" is not a useful
slogan for the times we are living through. In other
words, Wallace would avoid provocations; he would
make every legitimate effort to draw Russia back
into the Big Three fraternity with all the rights and
privileges of membership.[83]

Freda Kirchwey recognized the tyrannical and authoritarian ways of the Soviet Union, but told Americans that
they should clean their own house and conduct their own
affairs properly before they hurled abuse at others. The cold
war strategists surely found this advice naive, stupid, and
possibly downright subversive. But Freda Kirchwey kept
giving it. She worried about the growth of the military—an
understandable phenomenon during wartime but a trouble-
some and disturbing one in peacetime.[84] During this same
period, she traveled widely throughout Europe, the Middle
East, and Latin America. Her firsthand reports confirmed
her basic philosophy. The British presence in Palestine
fomented rebellion among the Arabs and mistreated the Jews.
Long an advocate of Jewish rights, Freda Kirchwey wrote
sympathetic reports in 1947-48 about the partition and the
Jewish effort to create a peaceful state.[85]

"But one thing seems certain: we shall not successfully
defend American capitalism by costly attempts to patch up
the capitalism of Germany or Greece or by trying to perpetuate feudalism in the Balkans or the Middle East or
China."[86] The 1948 election gave liberal-progressives little
choice or hope for comfort. Truman was unacceptable, so
was Dewey; Wallace was unrealistic, and Norman Thomas
was a visionary. The best the liberals could hope for, Miss
Kirchwey counseled, was the election of liberals to Congress
to effect a positive legislative program.[87] A new deal in
foreign policy was what the country needed; whether it
would get it seemed unlikely. Freda Kirchwey's analysis of
American policy in Asia sounds prophetic today; the genera-

tion of the 1960's has seen all the dire consequences that she predicted in 1950 come true. Immediately after the success of Mao's revolution in China, Editor Kirchwey advocated recognition of Red China so as to create workable relations with the new China and prevent further alienation.[88] A long-time critic of Chiang Kai-shek's regime, she believed that the United States had to reckon with the Communists in China, just as they had to reckon with the Communists in Russia. The continued support of the French in Indochina and the Rhee government in Korea were all part of a plan ". . . to keep the troublemakers out and the willing stooges in." Further, everything the United States did, she accurately predicted, would be "tagged 'defense of national independence' instead of being plainly marked 'military prescription for licking the Communists.' "[89]

The Truman administration in 1950 did not communicate its goals to the American people except in anti-Communist slogans. They did not offer a constructive debate on the North Atlantic Treaty Organization, or on American involvement in Korea.

> Still less do we know how far the Administration plans to carry its aid to France in Indo-China. The mounting successes of Ho Chi Minh's army offer grim evidence of the struggle that lies ahead. . . . Will our government continue to throw arms and money into this most ugly of all colonial wars, or will it use its influence to bring about a settlement through the good offices of the U.S., as was done in Indonesia?[90]

The credibility gap, much heralded as a new phenomenon in the sixties, harked back at least to the early fifties. The pursuance of foreign policy goals that were clearly in the European colonial tradition and not the American tradition did not receive public discussion or analysis. The national interest and patriotism, as phrases rather than serious concepts to be studied, substituted for clear thinking. "The Russians may be bad boys to the last commissar," she wearily reiterated to her readers in 1951, "insincere and aggressive, and ready to take advantage of an immediate weakness on the part of the West. What should be considered in Washington, however, is whether by saying this and only this, over and over, we have discharged our duty toward peace and Western security."[91] Unfortunately, the readers of the *Nation* (and the circulation decreased during this period) probably agreed with her already; the unbelieving either did not read the *Nation* or, if they read it, repudiated its views as being weak-minded.

After 1952, Freda Kirchwey wrote less and less. One of her few contributions in 1953 was a theatrical review on an old and favorite subject: the role of women in American society. The play under scrutiny was *The Ladies of the Corridor*, written by Dorothy Parker and Arnaud D'Usseau. Its theme was the loneliness of women in a New York residential hotel. To Miss Kirchwey, the play's critics had missed its camouflaged moral; rather than seeing it as it really was, "a comment on a society that enjoins upon intelligent, energetic women a quarter-century or so of idle uselessness," critics avoided the bitter statement about woman's role entirely. "What kind of a system is this," asked Feminist Kirchwey as well as the women in the play, ". . . that makes it the normal, expected thing for men to spend their days piling up funds to enable the wives who outlive or divorce them to survive without any effort except that involved in 'filling' empty lives?"[92]

Indeed, some very strong questioning statements are made by the women in *The Ladies in the Corridor*. Mrs. Ames, for example, a recent widow who has left Akron for the excitement of New York (as well as to be close to her only child), says to her son Robert when he asks her about her future plans: "Bob, there really isn't a thing I can do. And because I know I can't I've come to believe I don't want to. And by now my son, I believe that very firmly."[93] Surely a perceptive comment about the power of psychological conditioning in our society. At a later point in the play, the same woman expands the point to include the effects of cultural upbringing upon personal psychology:

> I don't know how to get myself fixed up. There's something lacking. I guess there's something lacking in a lot of women; nobody's ever one of a kind. We were told you grew up, you got married, and there you were. And so we did, and so there we were. But our husbands, they were busy. We weren't part of their lives; and as we got older we weren't part of anybody's lives, and yet we never learned how to be alone. It's different with girls now. But that's the way it was with me.[94]

Surely a succinct summary of the mammoth wrong American society does to the female sex. Mrs. Ames's assumption that the young girls growing up were free of her dilemma was wrong. The young women of the forties and fifties shared the same narrow upbringing with her.

Another woman in the play, an alcoholic who eventually commits suicide, calls the trio who sit in the lobby and observe other people's lives: "vegetables . . ., sitting there in their bins, waiting for the garbage collector to come and get them. So I get drunk and fall on my ear. Well, at least I'm not sitting down waiting."[95] *The Ladies of the Corridor* effectively portrayed how American society treated a significant, and growing, segment of womanhood, the widows and divorcees; it rejected them. Most of the drama critics believed that the play consisted of unrelated episodes, and despite some good lines from Dorothy Parker, their judgment was negative; the play closed after forty-five performances.

Freda Kirchwey retired as editor and publisher of the *Nation* in 1955. Her vitality never flagged, and her belief in vigorous reporting and advocate journalism never stopped. Upon her retirement, her friendly rivals, the *New Republic* editors, complimented her on her superb job of managing and writing, and also noted: "Through it all, her private life has been proof that it is possible to combine a career in journalism with successful activity as wife and mother."[96] Of course, no tribute to a male reporter or editor ever includes a statement praising his devotion to fatherhood; but given the cultural setting of this country, any woman who does venture forth into a career is a brave woman indeed, and any woman who succeeds at both her career and her marriage is a rarity and deserving of praise. In the hierarchy of values, then, an accomplished woman like Freda Kirchwey deserves double praise.

The war years of 1940-1945 demanded discipline and commitment for all Americans. Women joined the Wacs, worked in factories in previously male-defined jobs, and folded bandages for the Red Cross. They behaved as women had always behaved during wartime, with patriotism and courage. But the display of energy and self-discipline ceased with the war's end. Many women continued to work but, as already indicated, not in decision-making positions. The Eisenhower years of the fifties resembled the twenties more closely than the forties. Consumerism replaced war work as the primary activity of middle-class American women. They left the home only to purchase new goods for it; they debated only the advantages of a blender over a Mix-master. Electric toothbrushes, finned Cadillac cars, and automated kitchens occupied their minds and imaginations. Women became consumers with a vengeance. Madison Avenue depended upon this, husbands lamented it, and Bob Hope made jokes about it. But in any case, consumerism became the major way of life for American women, and the way in which they defined themselves and, in turn, were defined by others.

The grandfather-image of President Eisenhower lulled everyone into an even greater apathy than usual in peacetime America. Women's organizations and college women were no exception. Perhaps feminist reform, in fact all reform movements, need a fertile environment in which to operate—one in which many different social reforms are competing for the public's attention. No one reform can survive effectively without the survival of others. The 1910's had seen suffrage, feminism, temperance, progressive politics, Negro equality, and pure food and drug laws all thrive in the same atmosphere. The decade of the 1950's, in contrast, was silent, with its conspicuously quiet college generation, its career-oriented populace, and its devotion to the fulfillment of the material aspects of the mythical American dream.

Slight efforts were made, of course, to rouse women to social involvement. As early as 1943, Anne O'Hare McCormick, a distinguished foreign correspondent and editorial writer for the *New York Times,* chaired a meeting, sponsored by the *Times,* of the leading women's organizations held for the purpose of formulating a postwar program. "Something is wrong either with women," she told the representatives, "or with the processes of political thought when democratic Governments summon only the occasional woman to help solve the greatest human problems that ever overwhelmed mankind."[97] Why were not women's organizations contributing leaders to government service? "While women are mobilized into industry, into the Wacs and Waves and Spars and other auxiliary military services, they hold very few administrative posts."[98] It was the fault of women themselves, argued Mrs. McCormick; women had to assume responsibility for the well-being of the society.

While another meeting was held a year later, it only produced a statement of resolve that sounded like the many similarly worded documents issued by well-intentioned organizations throughout human history. Calling themselves by the impressive title of Women's Action Committee for Victory and Lasting Peace, the delegates recommended that Mrs. McCormick and Dorothy Thompson be chosen to represent the United States at the peace conference.[99] Although this suggestion was not implemented, Mrs. McCormick became part of the five-person delegation to the Paris meeting of the United Nations Educational, Scientific, and Cultural Organization in 1946. Ignoring Mrs. McCormick's criticism of them, women's organizations contented themselves with having one undeniably able woman represent all American women.

Another reason for the unusual lull during the fifties was the mistaken belief, referred to earlier, that women had achieved not only complete equality but in some cases superiority. Philip Wylie established his reputation by attacking Mom as the vile and potent destructive force of modern civilization. Mom was lambasted as the evil force in society, not the traditionally creative one. Historian Arthur Schlesinger, Jr., wrote about the American man's lack of identity and reviewed the typical 1950's array of reasons for it—the major one being the ascendance of women. And even Eleanor Roosevelt, in her honest and gentle way, assumed that the woman's position was better than ever.

> I think it might still be said that if a woman wants really to succeed she must be better than a man, for she is under more careful scrutiny; but this is practically the only handicap under which women now labor in almost any field of endeavor.[100]

Statistics describing the amount of stock American women owned provided irrefutable evidence, in the minds of the statisticians, of the tremendous power women had. Legal and political equality were also pointed to as evidence of women's equal status.

To critics of women's rights, equality is always negatively equated with superiority. Reflective of American values, men's power is never defined as dominant or overbearing, but if women achieve any power, it is always viewed as dangerous. The irony of all this, of course, is that women of the fifties did not realize any meaningful influence. A common joke, turned upside down, effectively captured the point:

A husband comments to a male friend, "My wife is the boss in the family—she decides whether Red China will enter the U.N., while I handle the everyday matters." Women did not vote as a politically conscious unit; they did not act as a viable consumer group using their economic power effectively; and they did not exercise power in the councils of government. The Big Mama myth, as Eve Merriam pointed out,[101] was only a myth, albeit a powerful one.

Historian Mary R. Beard contributed to the confusion by reminding readers, in a 1947 women's issue of the *Annals of the American Academy of Political and Social Science* that you cannot talk about women as a monolithic group. "Every day's events demonstrate that woman's role in society is women's roles in societies. . . ."[102] Arguing this way makes it pointless to try to deal with women's problems as common ones or to organize women politically or economically. The majority of people, apparently, shared this perspective; the individualistic bent of Americans prevented any concerted activity on the part of women *as* women *for* women. "The working wives of 1951," another reporter noted, "are not motivated by feminism, but by common sense applied to economic dilemma."[103] Whatever that means. American women, like American men, were practical people who took each specific and concrete problem as it appeared and tried to deal with it individually.

At the end of the fifties, women's problems were no closer to a solution than at the beginning of the forties. The philosophical approach of the *Christian Century,* written in 1940 in an editorial on disillusioned feminists, still captured the point of view of the majority, a point of view which gave comfort and support to continued inaction:

Her disappointment is natural; but considering the unreasonable hopes she entertained, it was inevitable. The granting of suffrage was a matter of simple justice, but it was no short cut to political perfection. Men had been making something of a

mess of politics for generations, not because of
qualities peculiar to their sex but by reason of
human frailties which (be it said with all defer-
ence) women share with them.[104]

Simple justice apparently did not include allowing the female
part of the population to decide their life roles for themselves. The Christian view of ultimate imperfection could
become a respectable reason for sensitive people to avoid
doing anything about real human problems. The majority,
of course, did not reflect on or rationalize this question; for
them material progress, a goal which women shared with
men, was the only kind of progress worth anything anyway.
Because there were not too many critics who shrilly preached
the feminist message, most people could placidly avoid considering the issue. The 1950's ended on a quiet note. There
was no hint of the roar of the sixties that was to come, except
perhaps in the publication of *The Three Faces of Eve* in 1957.
Was the schizophrenic personality of Eve White symbolic of
the sensitive woman's dilemma in an unfeminist society?
Only the future would tell.

Notes

1. Mabel Newcomer, *A Century of Higher Education for
American Women* (New York, Harper, 1959), p. 46.
2. John Willig, "Class of '34 (Female) Fifteen Years Later,"
New York Times Magazine, June 12, 1949, pp. 10, 51, 53.
3. *Ibid.,* p. 53.
4. *Ibid.*
5. Mary Heaton Vorse, "Women Don't Quit, If—" *Independent
Woman,* 23 (January 1944), 8-9, 24-25.
6. Gertrude Samuels, "Why Twenty Million Women Work,"
New York Times Magazine, September 9, 1951, p. 134.
7. Editorial, "The American Woman," *Life,* 21 (October 21,
1946), 36.
8. *Ibid.*
9. Pearl S. Buck, *Of Men and Women* (New York, John Day,
1941), p. 12.

10. *Ibid.*, p. 16.

11. *Ibid.*, p. 25.

12. *Ibid.*, pp. 53-54.

13. *Ibid.*, p. 59.

14. *Ibid.*, pp. 77-78.

15. *Ibid.*, p. 86.

16. *Ibid.*, p. 107.

17. *Ibid.*, p. 143.

18. *Ibid.*, p. 152.

19. *Ibid.*, p. 155.

20. *Ibid.*, p. 170.

21. *Ibid.*, pp. 179-180.

22. *Ibid.*, p. 183.

23. *Ibid.*, p. 184.

24. Dorothy Sayers, "The Woman Question," *Vogue,* 109 (January 15, 1947), 86, 128, 133.

25. *Ibid.*, p. 128.

26. *Ibid.*, p. 133.

27. Dorothy Thompson, "If I Had a Daughter," *Ladies' Home Journal,* 56 (September 1939), 41.

28. Dorothy Thompson, "Women and the Coming World," *Ladies' Home Journal,* 60 (October 1943), 6, 156.

29. Dorothy Thompson, "Are Women Different?" *Ladies' Home Journal,* 68 (November 1951), 11, 14, 137.

30. *Ibid.*

31. Dorothy Thompson, "What Is Wrong with American Women?" *Ladies' Home Journal,* 70 (August 1953), 75.

32. *Ibid.*

33. *Ibid.*

34. *Ibid.*

35. Dorothy Thompson, "It's All the Fault of the Women!" *Ladies' Home Journal,* 77 (May 1960), 19.

36. Margaret Mead, "What Women Want," *Fortune,* 24 (December 1946), 175.

37. *Ibid.*, p. 223.

38. Margaret Mead, "American Man in a Woman's World," *New York Times Magazine,* February 10, 1957, pp. 11, 20, 22-23.

39. Margaret Mead, "Modern Marriage, the Danger Point," *Nation,* 177 (October 31, 1953), 350.

40. Mead, "American Man in a Woman's World," p. 23.

41. Margaret Mead, "The Secret of Completeness," *Good Housekeeping,* 150 (May 1960), 162.

42. Mead, "American Man in a Woman's World," p. 11.

43. Mirra Komarovsky, *Women in the Modern World: Their Education and Their Dilemmas* (Boston, Little, Brown, 1953). Chapter IV in particular deals with this subject.

44. *Ibid.*, p. 94.

45. *Ibid.*, p. 124.

46. *Ibid.*, p. 287.

47. *Ibid.*, p. 291.

48. *Ibid.*, p. 124.

49. Ferninand Lundberg and Marynia F. Farnham, *Modern Woman: The Lost Sex* (New York, Harper, 1947), p. 91.

50. *Ibid.*, p. 144.

51. *Ibid.*, p. 165.

52. *Ibid.*, p. 202.

53. De Beauvoir is the only non-American woman writer included in this study; her work is so significant to feminist thought that it could not be ignored. Also, it greatly influenced subsequent American feminists.

54. Simone de Beauvoir, *The Second Sex,* trans. and ed. by H. M. Parshely (New York, Bantam Books edition, 1970), p. 249.

55. *Ibid.*, p. 629.

56. *Ibid.* Chapter XVII, "The Mothers," treats this subject fully.

57. C. J. Rolo in the *Atlantic Monthly* and Dr. Karl Menninger in the *Saturday Review* called her paranoic (*Atlantic Monthly,* 191 [April 1953], 86; *Saturday Review,* 26 [February 21, 1953], 26-31).

58. Margaret Mead, "A SR Panel Takes Aim at 'The Second Sex,'" *Saturday Review,* 26 (February 21, 1953), 26-31.

59. Brendan Gill, "Books in Review," *The New Yorker,* 29 (February 28, 1953), 97.

60. Alfred C. Kinsey, *et al., Sexual Behavior in the Human Female,* Institute for Sex Research, Indiana University (Philadelphia, W. B. Saunders, 1953), p. 172.

61. *Ibid.*, p. 173.

62. *Ibid.*, pp. 373-374.

63. *Ibid.*, p. 591.

64. *Ibid.*, p. 592.

65. *Ibid.*, p. 436.

66. "Red Leader Testifies," *New York Times,* October 4, 1952, p. 24.

67. "Hoarse," *The New Yorker,* 22 (October 26, 1946), 25.

68. *Nation,* 150 (May 18, 1940), 610.

69. Corliss Lamont, ed., *The Trial of Elizabeth Gurley Flynn by the American Civil Liberties Union* (New York, Horizon Press, 1968), p. 99.

70. *Ibid.*, p. 14.

71. Elizabeth Gurley Flynn, *I Didn't Raise My Son to Be a Soldier for Wall Street* (1940) and *Coal Miners and the War* (1942) (New York, Workers Library Publishers).

72. *Daughters of America: Ella Reeve Bloor, Anita Whitney* (New York, Workers Library Publishers, 1942), p. 14.

73. *Women Have a Date with Destiny* (New York, Workers Library Publishers, 1944).

74. Elizabeth Gurley Flynn, *Woman's Place—In the Fight for a Better World* (New York, New Century Publishers, 1947), p. 14.

75. Elizabeth Gurley Flynn, *The Alderson Story—My Life as a Political Prisoner* (New York, International Publishers, 1963), p. 185.

76. *Ibid.*, pp. 72-73.

77. All the references in this section are from the *Nation*. Freda Kirchwey, "More About the Atom," 161 (August 25, 1945), 170-171.

78. Freda Kirchwey, "Russia and the Bomb," November 17, 1945, p. 512.

79. Freda Kirchwey, "The Challenge of Henry Wallace," September 28, 1946, pp. 337-339.

80. Freda Kirchwey, "Manifest Destiny, 1947," March 22, 1947, p. 317.

81. Freda Kirchwey, "The Cohorts of Fear," April 14, 1951, p. 339. See also "Notes for a New Year," January 11, 1947, pp. 33-34; and in December 13, 1947 issue, "What Are We Afraid Of?"

82. Freda Kirchwey, "Liberals Beware!" April 5, 1947, p. 384.

83. "The Challenge of Henry Wallace," p. 337.

84. "Toward a New Beginning," November 16, 1946, pp. 544-545.

85. From July to December 1947, she wrote reports on Palestine; see also "America and Israel," May 22, 1948, pp. 565-566.

86. "What America Wants," May 3, 1947, p. 506.

87. "How Are You Going to Vote?" October 23, 1948, p. 452.

88. "China, Blunder upon Blunder?" January 7, 1950, pp. 1-2.

89. "America's Asian Policy," July 22, 1950, p. 73.

90. "Unanswered Questions," October 28, 1950, p. 377.

91. "Proof of the Pudding," August 18, 1951, pp. 122-123.

92. "Theater," November 7, 1953, p. 378.

93. Dorothy Parker and Arnaud D'Usseau, *The Ladies of the Corridor* (New York, Samuel French, 1952), p. 50.

94. *Ibid.*, p. 87.

95. *Ibid.*, p. 100.

96. *New Republic*, September 26, 1955, p. 7.

97. *New York Times*, October 28, 1943, p. 26.

98. *Ibid.*

99. *Ibid.*, May 4, 1944, p. 16.

100. Eleanor Roosevelt, "Women Have Come a Long Way," *Harper's*, 201 (October 1950), 76.

101. Eve Merriam, "The Matriarchal Myth," *Nation,* 177 (November 8, 1958), 332-335.

102. Mary R. Beard, "Woman's Role in Society," in "Women's Opportunities and Responsibilities," *Annals,* 251 (May 1947), 3.

103. Nancy Barr Mavity, "The Two-Income Family," *Harper's,* 203 (December 1951), 63.

104. "Feminist Disillusioned About Women in Politics," *Christian Century,* 57 (May 22, 1940), 661.

5

The Resurgence of Feminism:
Movers and Shakers
in the Sixties

I AM MYN OWENE WOMAN, WEL AT ESE.
   —Chaucer's Criseyde (quoted in Mary McCarthy's
         "The Man in the Brooks Brothers Shirt")

YOU CAN'T EXPECT A MAN TO GIVE YOU YOUR IDENTITY
ON A SILVER PLATTER, WHICH IS WHAT SOCIETY
WOULD HAVE US BELIEVE. THAT'S DISHONEST, AND IT
HAS PRODUCED A LOT OF BITTER WOMEN. BECAUSE I
HAVE WORK TO CARE ABOUT, IT IS POSSIBLE THAT I
MAY BE LESS DIFFICULT TO GET ALONG WITH THAN
OTHER WOMEN WHEN THE DOUBLE CHINS START TO
FORM.

                                        —Gloria Steinem

I STILL THINK EVERY MALE SEES A CUNT AS A VELVET-
LINED SAFE-DEPOSIT BOX. WHAT'S VALUABLE IS WHAT
they PUT IN THERE, AND HOW NICE IT FEELS. SO UN-
FAIR—IT'S ALL SO UNFUCKINGFAIR.
                        —Lois Gould, *Such Good Friends*

Nineteen-sixty was still Eisenhower's year and the liberated
sentiments just expressed were yet to come. The woman
voter of 1960, technically the majority, was conservative and

229

uninterested in politics and government.[1] Anyone who cared to look would have found that the textbooks of America included only sparse mention of women,[2] and a survey of *Who's Who in America* revealed that only 4 percent of the listings in 1958 were women, while 8.5 percent had been women in 1902[3]. The second-class status of American women prevailed. Despite their legal and political equality, women were not, in fact, equal, since neither women nor men perceived them as equal—and this was the crux of the whole matter. Women did not venture forth from the home or assert themselves because they believed their traditional roles were their sole reasons for living. If some women secretly hated the limited nature of their lives, they feared doing anything about it. Self-doubt paralyzed many. The dependent nature of women's roles had succeeded, indeed, in making them dependent. Women favored the Republican Party over the Democratic and shied away from reformist politics.[4] They did not see themselves as a group and so did not behave like one.

To many, the election of John F. Kennedy seemed to suggest a new departure in all areas. In terms of the First Lady image, Jacqueline Kennedy appeared as a vision of youthful chic after the grandmotherliness of Mamie Eisenhower. Not since the days of Eleanor Roosevelt had a First Lady created the excitement and interest that Jackie did. The nature of the interest, however, was different. While Eleanor Roosevelt's prominence rested upon her intense involvement in social matters, Jackie Kennedy's activity centered on fashion and style. Eleanor Roosevelt became a respected leader because of what she said and did, not because of how she looked. In contrast, Jackie Kennedy's bouffant hair style, her pillbox hat, and her simple but elegant suits became the aspect of her that was imitated and admired. "I think the major role of the First Lady," Mrs. Kennedy was quoted as saying, "is to take care of the President."[5] The President might pioneer a new frontier but his wife would follow the old trail. She would continue to be an upper-class clotheshorse, a tradition with a long history in America, albeit a novelty in a First Lady.

Regarding women, John F. Kennedy did not blaze new trails. Ted Sorensen, in his study of Kennedy, said that J.F.K. would not appoint a woman Cabinet member "merely for the sake of show."[6] The President seemed uncomfortable at times in personal encounters with assertive women. At one White House reception for the women representatives from the United Nations, the President was taken aback by the Burmese delegate's remark that a woman President would surely invite the male United Nations representatives to the White House some day. Well, the President replied, he had not expected "the standard of revolt" to be raised in the Rose Garden; he also admitted that he was "always rather nervous about how you talk about women who are active in politics, whether they want to be talked about as women or as politicians."[7] Surrounded by impressive women, especially his mother, the President may have been both respectful of and awed by independent women; because the Kennedy females were very much their own women, perhaps he assumed that all women, if they wished, could achieve the same kind of independence.

THE PRESIDENT'S COMMISSION

Kennedy's establishment of the President's Commission on the Status of Women, in December 1961, became his one major contribution to women's rights. Esther Peterson, director of the Women's Bureau and later Assistant Secretary of Labor, had proposed this Commission to the President so that a full-scale investigation could be made of the laws and practices regarding women in our society. In announcing the creation of the Commission, Kennedy said, "Women should not be a marginal group to be employed periodically, only to be denied opportunity to satisfy their needs and aspirations when unemployment rises or a war ends."[8] He instructed the Commission to report to him by October 1963. The topics to be studied included the federal government's employment and wage policies and practices; the effects of the federal social insurance program and tax laws on women's net earnings; an appraisal of federal and state labor laws; differences in the legal treatment of men and women in regard to political and civil rights, property rights, and family relations; and possible new or expanded services for working wives and mothers.

Eleanor Roosevelt, although old and frail, accepted the chairmanship of the Commission. Of the other twenty-five members, fourteen were women. Senator Maurine Neuberger, Representative Edith Green, Mary I. Bunting, president of Radcliffe College, and Margaret Hickey of the *Ladies' Home Journal* were among the prominent women members. Esther Peterson was executive vice-chairman and Professor Richard A. Lester of Princeton, vice-chairman. President Kennedy expressed his hope that the Commission would take the necessary steps "to demolish prejudices and outmoded customs which act as barriers to the full partnership of women in our democracy."[9] He asked the federal government to become the model for the nation as a whole and to practice equality of opportunity in employment, with efficient public service as a criterion. The Commission held its first meeting in February 1962; the President attended and recommended that the Commission investigate working conditions for women in relation to equal pay for equal work.

The federal government attempted to enact the goals of the Commission. The chairman of the Civil Service Commission asked all government heads to review their hiring policies for women. Deputy Attorney General Nicholas Katzenbach announced in April 1962 that all civil service offices, in requesting candidates for promotion, were to consider women on an equal basis with men. In July 1962, the President sent a memorandum to all executive department heads saying that all promotions should be made on the basis of individual merit. And on June 10, 1963, President

Kennedy signed into law the Equal Pay Act. Representative Edith Green of Oregon had sponsored this bill, which provided for equal pay to women working for any company that was subject to the Fair Labor Standards Act. At the bill-signing ceremony, President Kennedy discussed the need for day-care centers for children of working mothers, another objective of his administration. Congress had appropriated $800,000 to state welfare agencies for expanded day-care centers, but Kennedy commented that more was needed. He recommended grants of $4 million to the states in 1963 and $10 million yearly thereafter to aid in the establishment of local day-care programs.[10]

Eleanor Roosevelt died in November 1962, eleven months before the work of the Commission was completed. In October 1963, when the Commission submitted its final report, President Kennedy paid tribute to her as well as to Esther Peterson, Richard Lester, Maurine Neuberger, and Edith Green for their work on the report. He hoped that the day would soon come when women would be able to realize their potential. He quoted one of his favorite sayings, the Greek belief that true happiness resided in the fullest use of one's powers "along the lines of excellence."[11] The Commission's report, published under the title *American Women*,[12] presented a most comprehensive compendium of information that confirmed women's second-class status. It also provided a list of recommendations on how to improve that status. Among them were continuing education and vigorous counseling services for women; federal and local agencies to provide financial assistance for married women so that they could complete their education after their children were in school; flexible residence requirements to ease the mother's return to college; and child-care facilities for all income levels. Finally, the Commission recommended that the federal government itself review its stricture against employing part-time workers, so that qualified women could be hired.

The Commission did not recommend support for the equal rights amendment; this amendment, first proposed by Alice

Paul's National Women's Party in 1923, was still being presented to Congress forty years later with little hope of success. The Commission's rationale for rejecting it was that the Fifth and Fourteenth Amendments to the Constitution embodied the principle of equality for women. The Commission recommended that test cases be brought under these two amendments so that the Supreme Court could interpret whether they indeed included discrimination on the basis of sex. If the Court rejected this interpretation, then perhaps a new amendment would be necessary. But the Commission recommended acting upon the existing amendments to gain equal rights for women, before proposing a new amendment.

At the conclusion of its report, the Commission also recommended the creation of a committee made up of Cabinet members, as well as a citizens' advisory council, to mobilize the federal government's resources in behalf of women. On November 1, 1963, President Kennedy signed Executive Order 11126 creating the Interdepartmental Committee on the Status of Women. Willard Wirtz, Secretary of Labor, was its chairman, and the six other members included the Attorney General and the chairmen of the Civil Service Commission and the Equal Employment Opportunity Commission. All the states followed the lead of the federal government and created their own interdepartmental committees and citizens' advisory councils to deal with the interests of women in their respective states.

In the best American tradition, the Commission had presented a report that suggested improving educational opportunities for women and allocating more money for child-care facilities. Money and education have traditionally been advocated as the most effective ways to create desired social reform. Surely they are significant and essential ingredients in effecting any change in our society. However, the Commission's recommendations remained just that. Its members were not a lobbying force in Washington for the implementation of its suggestions; the women to whom they appealed did not organize effective support for desired legislation. James Reston, the *New York Times* columnist, asked President Kennedy in January 1962 to mobilize educated American women in behalf of the federal aid to education bill, a bill which would have provided financial support to women returning to school, but women did not respond to the call.[13]

The domestic legislation proposed under President Kennedy, much of which would have benefited women, did not pass through Congress under his administration. John Kennedy, however, must be credited with creating the Commission on the Status of Women and publicizing its results. Further, the passage of the Equal Pay Act of 1963 was a worthy product of the Kennedy years. Although his interest and concern for the young, the blacks, and the space program made his attention to women appear minimal, his accomplishments laid the foundation for much of the action of the late sixties.

Foreign and domestic crises consumed Kennedy's energies. Yet one of the great social issues of the sixties, civil rights for black Americans, did lead inevitably to women's renewed interest in themselves as well as to the interest of other deprived groups in their own welfare. Group assertiveness, militancy on one's own behalf, became the tenor and tone of the late sixties. The mood for women's liberation was conceived, at least, in the early sixties when John F. Kennedy encouraged people to cry out against oppression. More than the Commission and the Equal Pay Act perhaps, the Kennedy mood contributed mightily to the creation of an activist college generation of young people. J.F.K. may not have anticipated the various directions and causes his posture would lead to, but the Peace Corps message and the New Frontier rhetoric paved the way for militant youth. The Commission's findings, on the other hand, provided the necessary data for those middle-class activists who wanted facts along with rhetoric. All in all, the Kennedy years renewed the faith of young America in social and purposeful action; and the deprived, the blacks, the poor, the chicanos, and the women later translated these words into action. John Kennedy's contribution to renewed feminist interest was explicit in his support of the Commission on the Status of Women, and implicit in his general philosophy and style.

WOMEN AND PEACE

Simultaneously, in the Kennedy years, there was the creation of a new woman's movement, Women Strike for Peace, in response to the growing dangers associated with nuclear testing and the mounting arms race. The women of WSP said that they were simply mothers who want their children to grow up and live in peace. Most of the women who marched for peace, one reporter noted, "are wives and mothers, which is why they became involved in the first place."[14] Appealing to the ostensible natural desire of women to work for peace and to reject war (a sentiment shared by women's peace groups during World War I as well), Women Strike for Peace asked President Kennedy in 1962 to remove one missile base on foreign soil as a good-will gesture.[15] "Women, who are daily involved almost by biological definition in what are the true, deep issues of life—food, shelter, care of the young"[16]—should work for peace. This women's movement—and they insisted upon being considered a movement with a loose, unformed organization rather than a structured group—accepted the traditional definition of the womanly role and built upon it their justification for peace work.

Women Strike for Peace did not develop a feminist rationale. Its members did not argue that women could become a powerful ideological force in and of themselves; rather, they believed that "Women have more free time and can be more straightforward—i.e., they don't have to be logical, but can be emotional. This is an accepted image."[17] WSP accepted the society's definition of women. One representative admitted that they had "no special competence in international politics." "But," a reporter commented, "these women care, and when people really care they seem to acquire wisdom and power and an instinct for making the right moves."[18] Women as emotional, irrational, but well-intentioned beings was the projected image. Women were not capable of rational analysis, the WSP leaders suggested, but rather were emotional and maternal peace-niks.

Apparently not everyone considered the WSP harmless. The House Un-American Activities Committee, for one, believed that the women's peace movement was Communist inspired and worthy of investigation. Dagmar Wilson, a famous illustrator of children's books and one of the representatives of WSP, was subpoenaed to testify before the Committee in December 1962. Mrs. Wilson alarmed the Committee, and fortified its suspicions, when she said that she would welcome everyone and anyone into the peace movement: Communists, Nazis, and Fascists. The *New York Times* quoted her as saying that "unless everybody in the whole world joins us in this fight, then God help us."[19] The audience found many of her remarks more amusing than threatening. Two years later, at another HUAC hearing, Mrs. Wilson was cited for contempt of Congress, but the court later reversed the decision.[20] At a peace rally in November 1963, Mrs. Wilson pleaded for disarmament and peace as the essential condition for a free and vital society. She and her supporters carried signs calling for a "Peace Economy with Jobs for All" and vowed to gain wide acceptance of their views.[21] Unfortunately, the enthusiasm and commitment of the few women in Women Strike for Peace did not infect the majority. Later in the same month, President Kennedy was killed, and a new war was already brewing in Southeast Asia.

The standard women's organizations plodded along in their predictable and traditional ways. Women Strike for Peace was a new effort at stirring American women, albeit a modest one. No one, man or woman, could object to women's organizing for peace; at best, they would be praised for their idealism and selflessness, and at worst (with HUAC effectively representing this end of the spectrum), they would be considered dupes of subversive organizations. Indeed, the belief that women (and liberals and blacks) could be easily deceived provides another illustration of society's deprecatory image of woman. The fact that the women were asking for the removal of one missile base was considered naive and indicative of their ignorance of power politics. Women Strike for Peace encouraged this image of themselves; they actually professed it. Ultimately, of course, it was a self-defeating pose; how can anyone take a movement seriously if it does not take itself seriously—or, rather, if it does not claim knowledge as well as truth on its side? Being right has never been sufficient claim for redressing grievances; but knowing the facts and presenting them in a reasonable and impressive way may have an effect upon the powers that be. Just as the League of Women Voters contented itself with doing good work while remaining in the background, so Women Strike for Peace, a brief eruption in the early sixties, accepted the very same set of values. Similarly, and predictably, they suffered the same fate: they were shrugged off or ignored.

THE FEMININE MYSTIQUE

The Feminine Mystique broke the literary calm in 1963 with its message of unhappy women who sought relentlessly and futilely for a meaning to their lives. The women described in Betty Friedan's book were college educated, middle- to upper-middle-class married women, whose responses to Friedan's questions demonstrated that the domestic role did not live up to their expectations. The book appeared when statistics showed that the average age at which women married was 19.8 years. In fact, it was predicted in 1963 that the unmarried woman, the traditional spinster in our society, was a passing phenomenon. Ninety-three per cent of all American women in their thirties had been married.

Thus Betty Friedan's book spoke to the majority of American women—married women—who had become wives at a young age and often found, at the age of thirty, that life was boring and without meaning.

The mystique of woman as biological creature, best suited to wifely and motherly chores, was a snow job, argued the author. While Mirra Komarovsky's study of college-educated married women a decade earlier advised unhappy educated women to cope and to seek part-time jobs, Betty Friedan crisply recommended that women devote themselves to a lifelong career (preferably a career that could be interrupted intermittently for childbearing), but one that would provide them with professional satisfaction. Meaningful work, traditionally the domain of men, was what educated women needed in order to find satisfaction in life. Betty Friedan's message appealed to middle-class women readers. Her book was a popular success; within a year, 65,000 hardcover copies and 700,000 paperback copies had been sold. Although her solution to the woman's dilemma was not materially different from the one advocated by Mirra Komarovsky in 1953 or Pearl Buck, for that matter, in 1941, women seemed to be more receptive to this subject in 1963.

More American women were middle class; more were going to college than ever before; and more were finding that their liberal arts education had become an obstacle to domestic life. College did not prepare them for life in the suburbs; indeed it hindered it. But what were the alternatives? Home economics courses were not intellectually challenging and did not appeal to the majority of liberal arts students. College had become a socially essential prerequisite for the middle-class girl. True, it had become a mating ground and not a scholarly pursuit, but girls wanted to go to college, take interesting courses, and then marry. But if intellectually exciting courses which turned women on to abstract levels of thinking and acquainted them with literary and philosophical ideas would be abandoned upon graduation, what good were they? Could housewives continue their studies in neighborhood book clubs, literary teas, and cultural societies? Could they find adequate satisfaction in a once a month book club? Clearly Betty Friedan said no; women turned to drink, sex, and overpossession of their children as outlets for their excess energy. The home did not consume their attention or interest. Ironically, as the home became more and more automated, the culture told women that their place was in the home. As the community took over more and more of the child-raising tasks, women were told that motherhood was still their major reason for being.

Betty Friedan's belief that the praise of domesticity was a conspiracy on the part of men editors returning to the women's magazines after World War Two, however, was unconvincing. Some of the few feminist writings during this century had appeared in the women's magazines, including Dorothy Sayers's article in *Vogue* in 1946 and Dorothy Thompson's frequent articles in the *Ladies' Home Journal* in the postwar period. Betty Friedan's description of middle-class educated women's unhappiness was accurate enough; but her reason for it was not. Rather than a conspiracy of men editors to make domesticity seem attractive to unsuspecting women readers, the real reason was more fundamental: men and women had not changed their traditional belief in the importance of motherhood for women. After World War Two, women gladly abandoned the war production factories for a kitchen and home of their own. They were glad to be reunited with their husbands and have children.

Women's magazines did not change; they continued to laud domesticity while offering slight pickings to the career woman. Contrary to Betty Friedan's belief, the women's magazines had *always* favored the traditional roles for women while presenting an occasional story about the career girl. That pattern had remained unchanged throughout the century. Recipes and descriptions of a bride's wardrobe always dominated the pages, and the adventuresome single girl who worked appeared infrequently. Career women have rarely been portrayed as married mothers in any of the popular literature of this country. Lucy Freeman suggested, in her review of the book, another culprit:

> It is superficial to blame the "culture" and its hand-maidens, the women's magazines, as she does. What is to stop a woman who is interested in national and international affairs from reading magazines that deal with those subjects? To paraphrase a famous line, "The fault, dear Mrs. Friedan, is not in our culture, but in ourselves."[22]

Betty Friedan's message did not deal with working-class women or black women. Like most feminist writing, it appealed to the class of the writer: the middle class. Just as Henrietta Rodman's collective apartment house appealed to professional middle-class women, so Betty Friedan's words affected the college-educated women of America. Trade union women, such as Elizabeth Gurley Flynn, Mary Anderson, and Kate Richards O'Hare, did not emerge to speak directly to the needs of poor women in the early sixties. Whether she knew it or not, *The Feminine Mystique* fit into the feminist genre: of Crystal Eastman's essays on women, of Pearl Buck's *Of Men and Women*, and of Simone de Beauvoir's *The Second Sex*. The scope of *The Feminine Mystique*, in fact, is slight compared to the mammoth work of de Beauvoir or the comparative analysis of Pearl Buck.

Mrs. Friedan's chapter criticizing Freud and Margaret Mead for their contributions to the woman as mother image anticipated some of the women's liberation writings of the late sixties. Freud especially, with his doctrine of anatomy determining destiny, would be severely attacked by radical feminists later; but the attack upon Margaret Mead does not seem entirely justified. True, as Betty Friedan pointed out, the anthropologist's descriptions of primitive cultures were admiring ones (in which woman as mother was the single and most satisfying role played) ; but Margaret Mead also wrote forthrightly that American culture, with its democratic ethos, did not live up to its promises to women. Although she advocated the nurturing professions for working women, and thus restricted women's opportunities, she did believe in meaningful work for women other than that of wife and mother; she did accept equal educational opportunities for women and equal pay for equal work. Betty Friedan oversimplified Margaret Mead's position. Miss Mead did not recommend that American women bear children every year, although she did admire nursing mothers.

Margaret Mead would more accurately be classified as a moderate feminist, one in the same category with Mirra Komarovsky. Both of these academicians believed in expanding the roles of women, but they did not accept the wide-ranging views of full-fledged feminists who wanted all barriers, all restrictive definitions of women, to be removed. Engineering, soldiering, and street-sweeping were all possible womanly occupations, according to the feminist position, if they were human occupations. In the opinion of total feminists, the words "human" and "woman" could, and should, be interchanged. Margaret Mead did not go the entire route in her thinking about women precisely because she still believed in the vital importance of motherhood for women. Indeed, to the young feminists of 1967, Betty Friedan's 1963 *The Feminine Mystique* appeared moderate and even conservative. She did not advocate the abandonment of the family unit; nor did she speak about woman's sexuality or advocate the end of capitalism.

It is often difficult to label a certain piece of feminist writing in terms of the spectrum of feminist thought: so much depends upon its relationship to what has gone before. Crystal Eastman was a radical feminist in relation to Jane Addams, while Emma Goldman was more radical than both of them. Compared with literary discussions of feminism in the unspectacular fifties and early sixties, Betty Friedan was bold and forthright. She presented the subject of women in a way that aroused interest and attention, and argued that, contrary to the popular view, women had not made it in America. But though *The Feminine Mystique* briefly awakened interest in the subject of women, it was not self-sustaining. Four years after the appearance of this book, a younger generation of women, women who could be the daughters of those described in *The Feminine Mystique,* would mobilize their own interest in the subject and write their own feminist views.

THE GREAT SOCIETY

In 1964, Lyndon Baines Johnson became the first Democrat in twenty years to win the majority of women's votes. Having Barry Goldwater as his opponent, of course, helped a lot. According to Louis Harris' poll, women feared that Goldwater, if elected, would get the country into war (53 percent of the women polled, as opposed to 45 percent of the men). Further, women seemed to be less fearful of civil rights for black Americans than men. While women had previously supported General Eisenhower and had favored Richard Nixon in 1960 over John F. Kennedy (52 percent for Nixon, 48 percent for Kennedy), the posture of L.B.J. as peacemaker in contrast to Goldwater's bellicosity made him more attractive to women voters.[23] Indeed, women's predilection for peace seemed to have some validity in voting behavior.

Although the women's trust in L.B.J.'s peace promises turned out to be misplaced, he contributed mightily, more than any other President, to the cause of women's rights. Modeling the Great Society after F.D.R.'s New Deal, he hired more women and worked for the rights of more minority groups than had any previous President. Lady Bird Johnson, as First Lady, more nearly resembled Eleanor Roosevelt in ability, energy, and devotion to causes than any of the intervening First Ladies. Lady Bird was an intel-

ligent and shrewd woman whose business acumen had turned
a modest inheritance from her mother into an impressive
multimillion-dollar empire. The Texas Broadcasting Cor-
poration—with Mrs. Johnson as chairman of the board until
L.B.J. became President—owned vast real estate holdings,
cattle ranches, and radio and television stations. When asked
by Henry Brandon, a *London Times* correspondent, about
her much-celebrated business sense, Mrs. Johnson modestly
replied: "I've tried to select good people who have helped
run the business interests I have and make it worth their
while to stay with us through the years, establishing strong
cords of friendship and interest with them."24 Despite her
refusal to accept the credit for the successful business, a
typical Lady Bird trait, her background suggested that she
came by her interest and ability in business naturally. Lady
Bird was raised in Harrison County, Texas. When she was
five, her mother died; thus her father, an ambitious mer-
chant and rancher, became her life model. Lady Bird, growing up in financial comfort, learned at first hand how to
conduct real estate deals and negotiate business transactions.

As a young girl, she developed a keen love of the land.
Whenever Lady Bird reminisced about her childhood, she
spoke in terms of wild Cherokee roses, hickory trees, and
violets. The natural environment of pine forests and wildflowers was as much a part of her sense of community as
were people. Thus it was quite natural that, as First Lady,
Lady Bird would concentrate her energies on conservation
and beautification projects. In fact, during the five years
that L.B.J. was President, she traveled more than 200,000
miles both at home and abroad. Most of her domestic travel
revolved around her special interests: she dedicated Redwood
National Park, formed the Committee for a More Beautiful
Capital, planted wildflowers along the Texas highways, and
was considered the inspiration for the 1965 Highway Beautification Act. While some critics believed that her interest in
beautification was insignificant in comparison to the great
social problems faced by America, some later commentators

appreciated the fact that Lady Bird's concern for the natural environment foreshadowed the much publicized ecology movement of the late sixties.

Lady Bird once said that she and Lyndon had "a feeling of closeness to the land."[25] This feeling included an understanding and a disapproval of strip mining, of wanton cutting down of trees, and of the evils of dumping industrial waste into the rivers of America.[26] Indeed, in a way that few Americans, men or women, could know, Lady Bird Johnson was a woman who had lived on the land and had observed its natural rhythms intimately. Although she did say that each person could materially improve the environment by planting flowers and each community could help by cleaning up its streets, she did not believe that this level of activity would do the needed job. The First Lady recognized the need for government regulation of polluters, but she believed that education and awareness on the part of the public could help significantly to accomplish a cleaner environment.

During her years as First Lady, Lady Bird took more than forty trips related to conservation and beautification, many of them with Interior Secretary Stewart Udall. She was photographed rafting down the Rio Grande, praising the city planners of Hartford, Connecticut, extolling the virtues of rural living, and eating dinner at a campfire in the wilds of Texas. The public shared Lady Bird's interest in beautification; more than four hundred letters a week were mailed to the White House on the subject. Liz Carpenter, the First Lady's press secretary, believed that the First Lady "made every woman feel that she too can do something for her community —and still be a conventional wife and mother. She got them up from the bridge tables."[27] Indeed, Lady Bird's quiet demeanor and retiring nature appealed to many American women. Surely she did not have the chic of a Jacqueline Kennedy, but this very fact made her appear more human to the populace. With the marriage of both of her daughters during her husband's presidency, Lady Bird also engaged in typically motherly activities and thereby cheered middle-

American women enormously. Being essentially Southern in background and values, she believed in the traditional roles for women, but at the same time she believed that women should be knowledgeable and capable in other areas of life.

In addition to her strong advocacy of the preservation of the natural environment, Lady Bird supported the Head Start program and generally publicized all her husband's Great Society proposals. *U.S. News and World Report* editorialized that "Lady Bird Johnson seems to have developed into a new phenomenon of American constitutional government: the unofficial, unpaid 'traveling saleslady' for the President."[28] If Congress lagged in providing funds for the education bill, Lady Bird went to Appalachia and publicized the dire need for federal aid to education there. She envisioned herself as the President's honest aide and as his loving critic. In her interview with Henry Brandon, she said that the President often consulted her, especially in matters connected with the environment and human welfare. When asked about the Vietnam War, she commented that she had faith in the country's leadership and prayed constantly that they could find an honorable way to end the war. On another occasion and in another context, Lady Bird said: "But we must keep our eyes and our hearts and our energies fixed on constructive areas and try to do something that will make this a happier, better educated land."[29] The First Lady could work only for the projects she knew something about and in which she could provide substantive aid. Otherwise, she relied on the knowledge and good judgment of others.

When the Johnsons left the White House in 1968, L.B.J. had been largely discredited because of his Vietnam policy. Perhaps when emotions died down and the war ended, critics could look over his domestic program and praise its constructive aspects; in 1968, however, this was not possible, as the war overrode all other considerations. But Lady Bird Johnson did score high marks in the judgment of many contemporary observers. *Time* said that "she left her mark not on the White House, as did Jacqueline Kennedy, but on the land beyond."[30] And Shana Alexander, the regular *Life* correspondent who had traveled frequently with Lady Bird, concluded (while observing Lady Bird in the Redwood National Park, during her last official trip) : "Somewhere in that strange forest on that last day I began to sense how much more Mrs. Johnson leaves behind her than daffodils coast-to-coast. Quite possibly she is the best First Lady we have ever had."[31] Alice Roosevelt Longworth, a wise old woman who had seen many First Ladies, believed that there never had been one to equal Mrs. Johnson. And CBS commentator Eric Sevareid added: "She has done nothing wrong and so much right, including the stimulation of a new, popular consciousness about the precious American land, a renewed awareness that our spychoses are not apt to be well ordered if their physical setting is ordered badly."[32] The *Christian Century* editorialized that there had not been much to praise during the last Johnson years except Lady Bird's keen efforts to stop the pollution of our environment. And for this, they concluded, the nation owed the retiring First Lady a significant debt.[33]

In many ways, then, Lady Bird Johnson resembled Eleanor Roosevelt. She did not preach feminism but she practiced it; she did not reject the traditional womanly roles but she expanded the definition of woman enormously and made herself a respected person, not just a role-bound woman. She worked quietly but forcefully and tirelessly for the causes in which she believed. Her husband, as well as the public at large, respected her opinion because it was based upon firsthand knowledge and devotion. Lyndon B. Johnson brought to his administration a deep respect for the potential of woman; this fact would come as no surprise to anyone who knew Lady Bird Johnson.

"It's a good time to be a woman," noted Katie Louchheim, a State Department official. During L.B.J.'s first year in office, he appointed women to seventy-five executive positions. Patricia Harris, a black woman law professor and government official, became the ambassador to Luxembourg; Bennetta Washington, a high school principal in Washington, became the head of the Women's Job Corps; and Ruth Van Cleve became the director of the Interior Department's Office of Territories. Mrs. Van Cleve was quoted as saying: "For years I was just a government lawyer in sensible shoes. Now I'm a national asset."[34] L.B.J. scouted and recruited capable women with an unprecedented diligence and sincerity. "A woman's place is not only in the home, but in the House, the Senate and throughout government service," he told one audience. To another, the President assured the men that "Men will always have a place in Government, as long as there are no women to fill the jobs." At a Cabinet meeting in January 1964, he declared that women were a national resource that should be utilized. In a memo written to department and agency heads, he said: "It is imperative that an intensive effort be made to fill top-level vacancies in your agency with women who, but for the historical bias against their sex, would be considered well-qualified."[35]

Lyndon Baines Johnson came by his admiration for women naturally. In addition to his most capable wife, his mother, Rebekah Baines Johnson, exerted a very powerful influence on him. Being raised with three sisters, he grew accustomed to seeing women act as effective human beings. L.B.J. called his wife and two daughters "can-do women," and believed in the full utilization of womanly talent in the service of the government. Through his active recruitment, Mary Bunting left the presidency of Radcliffe to become the first woman member of the Atomic Energy Commission, and Mrs. Elizabeth S. May became the first woman director of the Export-Import Bank. Aileen Hernandez, president of the National Organization for Women in 1970, served for eighteen months (1965-1966) as the only woman member of the Equal Employment Opportunities Commission. Liz Carpenter, Lady Bird Johnson's press secretary, also acted as a positive catalyst, constantly encouraging the President to appoint women to government positions. Because of these combined influences, the Johnson administration's record on

women in government became significant. In the three administrations prior to his, women received less than 4 percent of
the appointments to federal jobs paying more than $10,000.
In his first year as President alone, L.B.J. promoted 730
women into jobs paying more than $10,000.[36]

It was not easy, however, to convince capable women to
move to Washington. If their husbands had important positions elsewhere, the women were usually reluctant to move.
Thus L.B.J.'s women appointees were often Washington-
based. One interesting exception to this rule was Mrs. Virginia Mae Brown, whose husband willingly moved his law
office from West Virginia to Washington so she could become
the first woman Commissioner of the Interstate Commerce
Commission.

The general unwillingness of women to move to Washington aptly signified the prevailing cultural attitudes of professional women. Both men and women believed that it was
perfectly appropriate to move your family around the country in behalf of your husband's career but neither sex
believed it proper or even conceivable to do the same thing
for the advancement of the wife's career. One White House
aide noted that "The President learned that a lot of qualified
women are not bachelor girls or old maids or widows."[37]
That obstacle, and it was a major one, has not yet been
overcome. L.B.J. tried to provide job equality for women but
could not get around this cultural restriction. Within the
first year in office, he boosted 2,000 civil service women and
continually showed his interest in their future. Washington,
during the early years of L.B.J.'s tenure, before the nightmare of Vietnam blotted out all domestic concerns, resembled
the early New Deal days. Women, along with blacks and
chicanos, believed that the Great Society cared about them;
institutional discrimination seemed on its way out. If anyone
could do it, analysts argued, it was L.B.J. And the appearance
of impressive women in important positions seemed to con-
firm this belief.

The Civil Rights Act of 1964 contributed to the optimistic

feeling of many Americans. Not only did the act provide equal opportunity and an end to discrimination against black Americans, but the bill's Title VII included the proviso prohibiting job discrimination on the basis of sex. The sex provision had been included at the suggestion of Southern representative Howard Smith as an obstacle to the implementation of the bill, but it passed, and this title became a major legal weapon for women. The Equal Employment Opportunity Commission was established to implement Title VII. While over 33 percent of all the complaints in 1967 dealt with sex discrimination, during the year 1969-1970, the figure was down to 19 percent. Despite the decrease, the Commission had never anticipated that the sex discrimination clause would be utilized at all; the Commissioners were surprised to learn that women were passed over for promotion because of their sex, were not hired because they had young children, and did not receive the same fringe benefits as men did.[38]

Martha Griffiths, Democratic Congresswoman from Michigan, championed the enforcement of Title VII. She criticized the EEOC when they relaxed their guideline requiring the classified ad columns to desegregate. "I have never entered a door labeled 'men' and I doubt that Mr. Holcomb [acting chairman of the EEOC] has frequently entered the women's room."[39] Mrs. Griffiths was no stranger to discrimination. An attorney by profession, she became Michigan's first woman representative in Congress in 1954; she is also the first and only woman on the powerful House Ways and Means Committee. Mrs. Griffiths has objected to the inequity of the Social Security pension law which does not grant survivor's rights to her husband, clearly reflecting discrimination against women legislators. She has led the House fight for the equal rights amendment as well.

As women's complaints appeared before the EEOC, so did the employers' complaints on the unenforceability of the provision. When the Justice Department filed its first suit in 1970 under the sex discrimination clause of the Civil

Rights Act — against the Libbey-Owens-Ford Company, among others—L.O.F. Vice-President M. B. Burwell was quoted as saying: "One of the major problems is a basic conflict between the Civil Rights Act and Ohio's female protective laws. The federal law generally prohibits any different treatment of male and female employees, while Ohio law has various special requirements applicable only to female employees."[40] One Ohio law prevented women from lifting more than twenty-five pounds on the job, while another forbade women from working more than a nine-hour day or a forty-eight-hour week. In August 1969, the Equal Employment Opportunities Commission established the guideline that whenever there was a conflict between state laws and federal guidelines, the federal provision would apply and the state laws would be invalidated. However, it was still doubtful in 1970 whether this view would prevail in the courts; indeed, many states considered testing that criterion. In addition to the very important problem of enforcing the nondiscriminatory clause of Title VII, there were notable omissions in the sex discrimination title: for example, no mention was made of women in the teaching profession, the largest single profession for college-educated women. A future amendment to the title would be necessary to deal with this large group of women.[41]

L.B.J.'s personal actions, as well as the legislative enactment of the Civil Rights Act of 1964, reinforced the foundation laid during the Kennedy administration with the establishment of the Commission on the Status of Women and the Equal Pay Act of 1963. The joint actions of these two administrations, then, provided the legal weaponry and the philosophical commitment for the post-1967 militancy of feminists. A reform impulse often explodes into various issues simultaneously. Woman's rights reformers thrive in an atmosphere where other groups are also fighting for their rights. Each particular group gains support from the other, each assures its own legitimacy by the existence of the other, and each is intellectually dependent upon the

other. Women could interpret the Great Society's pledge to
the poor and the deprived of all ilks to include them, too.
The multifarious expressions of liberation in the last years
of the sixties grew out of the Kennedy-Johnson era's pledges
and actions toward minority groups. It was the very sympathy of these Presidents that encouraged the later protests,
thus validating the sociological truism that it is a period of
constructive change, rather than one of repression, that
usually leads to still more action. Positive commitment on
the part of the nation's leaders gives the needy the impression that even more will be done; there was, consequently,
a dramatic rise in confidence, assertiveness, and agitation
once recognition of the social problem was granted. The
recommendations of the Kennedy Commission, the women
appointees of the Johnson administration, and the creation
of the EEOC all buoyed the spirits of women reformers and
convinced them that accelerated and intensive effort would
result in more extensive reforms. With the militancy of the
civil rights movement as a model, the foundation for the
women's liberation movement was established in the
Kennedy-Johnson years.

Human Sexual Response, published in 1966 by William H.
Masters, a gynecologist, and Virginia E. Johnson, a psychologist, titillated America as the first Kinsey report had done
over a decade before. Venturing into the delicate area of
sexual behavior, Masters and Johnson, after eleven years
of study, concluded their research and presented their results. Written in very scientific, technical language, *Human
Sexual Response* was based upon the observation of 382
women and 312 men, from the ages of 18 to 89, engaged in
sexual activity. Ten thousand orgasms had been witnessed
and recorded. In contrast to Kinsey's method of interviews
and case studies, Masters and Johnson set up a laboratory
situation in which sexual intercourse and auto-manipulation
were observed by the scientists. Generally, the study confirmed the conclusions of Kinsey and other sexologists, but

its single-minded concentration on the physiological aspects of sex, complete with electrocardiograph machines, gave it a previously unknown dimension. Masters and Johnson also dealt with geriatric sex, a subject that had not received much attention before.

In terms of female sexuality, Masters and Johnson confirmed the fact that women, under the proper conditions, could experience orgasm as well as men—in fact, more frequently and within a shorter period of time. Although some scientific reviewers criticized the study, the scientific and lay community generally praised it for its comprehensiveness. The use of some prostitutes in the study made A. F. Guttmacher ask: "How applicable are findings and conclusions based on a restricted, atypical study universe to a large, unselected universe?"[42] The absence of psychological data (even though Dr. Johnson was a psychologist) and the emphasis upon the physiological also received some criticism. Any general reader who purchased a copy of *Human Sexual Response* hoping for erotica was surely disappointed. The book was a scientific study which contributed much to the woefully meager amount of serious information available on the subject of sex.

THE NEW MOVERS AND SHAKERS

The National Organization for Women (NOW), originally led by Betty Friedan, came into being in 1966. According to one source, many middle-class, educated women had participated in the various state committees formed as a result of the Report of the Commission on the Status of Women; but at a meeting with Department of Labor officials in 1966, they became frustrated by the lack of results.[43] They decided, therefore, to form their own organization and to lobby for "women's interests" themselves. NOW, called by some the NAACP of the woman's movement, dedicated itself to effecting legal changes in the system to provide women with equal opportunity. Just as the NAACP utilized the courts to test discrimination against black Americans, so NOW operated within the system to lobby for desired legislation and to test Title VII's provision on behalf of women. They pressured the Equal Employment Opportunities Commission to desegregate classified ads and worked in a number of states to repeal protective labor laws which inhibited women's promotions and job opportunities. From a modest beginning of three hundred middle-class women and a few sympathetic men, the organization boasted, in 1970, a membership of three thousand in sixty-two chapters.[44]

The NOW Bill of Rights in 1969 listed the following seven planks:

    I. Equal Rights Constitutional Amendment
   II. Enforce Law Banning Sex Discrimination in Employment
  III. Maternity Leave Rights in Employment and in Social Security Benefits
  IV. Tax Deduction for Home and Child Care Expenses for Working Parents
   V. Child Care Day Centers
  VI. Equal and Unsegregated Education
 VII. The Right of Women to Control Their Reproductive Lives[45]

Since the equal rights amendment was first introduced by Alice Paul's National Women's Party in 1923, it had repeatedly been submitted and rejected in Congress, often without a hearing in the appropriate subcommittee. NOW joined the growing bandwagon of those supporting the amendment, while opposition continued from the women's trade union movement. Many women's liberationists also opposed it because they supported protective labor laws, the right of women to gain alimony (reparations for unpaid labor, in their terms), and opposed the draft for both sexes.[46]

Most of the other items in the NOW platform were classic-liberal legislative reforms; NOW's members were primarily professional women who believed in legal, educational, and economic equality for women and used the traditional arsenal of methods to obtain their desired reforms: publicity, lobbying, education, and, on occasion, direct action. The most radical, and debatable, item in the legislative program was the right to birth control and abortion. While the advocacy of this measure in 1910 would have classified these "new feminists" (as they have been called) as radicals, the issue had become more acceptable by the middle sixties and the definition of radical proposals was often much more extreme than the advocacy of the right of a woman to control her own reproductive life. In 1970, Aileen Hernandez, a black lawyer, became NOW's president and tried to interest working-class working women, most notably black women, in the organization. Miss Hernandez called the struggle of blacks and that of women "part of the same revolution—the human revolution." She believed that black women could support day-care centers and the right to abortion. Men were the "common victims" of the society's oppression, she argued, and "the liberation of women will be the liberation of men as well."[47] Men's stereotyped views of themselves and of women would end, once liberation occurred. The success of Aileen Hernandez's bid for wider membership in NOW remains to be seen.

One of the most effective writers for NOW has been Alice S. Rossi, a sociologist at Goucher College. Mrs. Rossi, an active lobbyist for NOW, contributed an article to the 1964 issue of *Daedalus* on women, "Equality Between the Sexes: An Immodest Proposal," which stands as one of the most thoughtful essays of the sixties about women. Alice Rossi looked at the history of feminism in this country and declared that its failure was due to the narrow goals of the suffrage movement, the society's basic conservatism, and the barrage of psychoanalytic and child-raising literature assuring women that motherhood is a full-time job. As noted an authority as Dr. Benjamin Spock argued that

women should not leave their children for outside work and
that mothering was a totally consuming enterprise.

Alice Rossi's evidence showed that working mothers' children performed as well in school as did those of full-time
mothers; that juvenile delinquency did not increase among
them; and that the incidence of neurosis was probably less-
ened by the mother's absence from her child.[48] She also
explored other popularly held myths about women as mothers, and argued that women had become full-time wives and
mothers precisely at the point in history when they were
free of many household tasks and when school, church, and
various community organizations had taken their children
out of the home. Contrary to the myth, she contended,
women had never been *solely* mothers. Farmers' wives had
worked in the fields, and in the factories. Women had traditionally been too busy milking the cows, spinning the yarn,
and churning the milk to be full-time mothers. Only in a
technologically advanced society had this phenomenon occurred. Further, Mrs. Rossi suggested that women whose
life roles took them beyond the home could lead satisfying
lives and bring greater happiness to their marriages. Because
they would be secure as human beings, they could enjoy
sexual relations as equals. Contrary to the view that emancipated women would feminize men, Rossi argued that in
Sweden, for example, where the society had equalized all
human roles, sexuality has become more dramatic and
exciting.

Alice Rossi's essay examined a number of traditional
myths and found them untenable—most notably, the myth
of the "working mother producing troubled children," and
the myth of the "emancipated woman castrating men." Her
appeal was largely to middle-class women with professional
aspirations, but her message affected all classes of women.
At the core of the issue in every feminist piece, and it was
surely present in Alice Rossi's essay, was the question of
woman's identity. Who or what is a woman? Is she only a

wife and a mother? Or is she a human being? Charlotte Perkins Gilman had written an article in the 1910's asking that question, but at the time, most readers probably laughed and did not understand the profound nature of the question. By 1964, it was still being asked, but more and more women were no longer laughing.

Some of the women who would become leaders in women's liberation groups in 1967-1968 gained their first experience in the woman's movement in NOW. Ti-Grace Atkinson, for example, who later became a major spokeswoman for women's lib, had been the president of New York City's NOW chapter as well as its national fund-raiser in 1966-1967.[49] Anne Koedt, an artist and writer, also had been active in the New York chapter and left it in October 1968 with Ti-Grace Atkinson to form a more militant feminist group, the October 17th Movement. NOW's specific appeal to middle-class college-educated women left out a large segment of American women: poor women, uneducated women, and college-going young women who could not associate with the settled, professionally oriented image of NOW. Thus two of NOW's contributions to the woman's movement, besides its own activities and its very existence, were that it served as a training ground for future leaders of women's lib and as a contrasting organization, one that could be unfavorably looked at, and then rejected, in favor of more militant women's groups. Although the median age of NOW members is not known, an impressionistic guess would be that women of thirty, rather than twenty, form the central group.

The civil rights and New Left movements also provided the training ground for many women's liberationists. Roxanne Dunbar, one of women's lib's theoreticians, told how her initiation into radical feminism was in SDS meetings, where women were still relegated to the traditional clerical tasks. Bernadine Dohrn, the former interorganizational secretary of SDS, said: "In almost any woman you can unearth an incredible fury, . . . and it's an anger that can be a powerful radicalizing force. To date, our movement has not really made room for the enormous political potential of women's repression."[50]

Robin Morgan, the editor of a popular anthology of women's liberation literature and an active participant in the movement, began as a volunteer worker for CORE and moved from there to the peace movement, gaining direct-action experience in the April 1967 peace march to the United Nations, the march on the Pentagon in October 1968, the demonstration against Dean Rusk at the New York Hilton in November 1968, and the Columbia University student uprising in April 1968. In the course of her radical political activity, she discovered that the New Left movement "didn't really make room for women."

> A lot of women came in expecting a radically new scene. Like, here was a group of young people with a new politics, a new life style, a new sexual honesty and freedom. And still, the notion of liberated woman was someone who is indiscriminate about whom she sleeps with, not a realization that women don't want to be objects. A lot of Movement women might just as well have gone to Scarsdale.[51]

Robin Morgan's feminist zeal led her to disrupt the Miss America contest in Atlantic City in September 1968, aptly symbolizing the contrasting views of women. Jo Freeman, a graduate student in political science at the University of Chicago and creator of the first women's lib group and newsletter in 1967, also became a feminist after a stint in the civil rights movement. She came to Chicago and found life choices denied her because she was a woman. "For the first time," she said, "I had to face getting turned down simply for being a woman. It changed my life. I became a raging gut feminist."[52]

Women's liberation meetings began as underground affairs, only for the sympathetic. Chroniclers of the movement mark the middle of 1967 as its beginning date. Young women, usually white, middle-class, and college-attending, gathered together to discuss common problems. Much to their surprise, they found that many women shared their feelings of inferiority; they blamed the culture for indoctrinating them wrongly. "Consciousness-raising" became the term used to describe the slow, agonizing, but essential discussions that eventually led to woman's de-acculturation and to her new integration as a human being. Underground pamphlets and magazines erupted to provide both information and propaganda for the believers; *No More Fun and Games* was the title of a Boston women's lib magazine. The movement as a whole took the name Women's Liberation Front, imitative of the National Liberation Front, the Viet Cong movement in Vietnam. Small groups proliferated on many college campuses as well as in the big cities. In the fall of 1968, WLF held its first national convention and brought together two hundred women from twenty states and Canada on less than a month's notice.[53]

The movement has remained loosely organized, like other New Left groups. For example, the Women's International Terrorist Conspiracy from Hell (WITCH), one offshoot, is dedicated to guerrilla theater and specializes in staging dramatic happenings, such as a coven of witches dancing down Wall Street on Halloween to hex the financiers. The Women's Radical Action Project (WRAP), a Chicago affiliate of WLF led by Jo Freeman, was primarily composed of graduate students at the University of Chicago who worked to reform the university's policies toward women. In December 1968, the university's sociology department did not renew the contract of Marlene Dixon, an assistant professor of human development and an active feminist. This event caused WRAP as well as other groups to protest and to organize demonstrations on behalf of Professor Dixon. University buildings were occupied, demands were issued, and tension grew, following the pattern developed at Columbia University earlier in 1968 and at the University of California at Berkeley still earlier.

But to no avail. The University of Chicago, an academic institution that liked itself the way it was, refused to meet the
students' demands and Marlene Dixon left. She subsequently
went to McGill University in Montreal and spent her week-
ends flying to various places around the United States to
organize women's lib groups. In early 1970, she said that
interest in women's liberation was steadily increasing—and
in unlikely places such as Iowa City, which had a women's
lib group of 400.[54] Indeed, estimates on the overall membership of the Women's Liberation Front range from 10,000 to
500,000.[55]

The focus of each women's lib group varies; campus-based
groups can simply set up "rap" sessions where girls can
discuss their adjustment problems and try to "get themselves
together," or they can become political groups directed at
changing specific examples of discrimination within the university. Women's lib groups may ally with other New Left
groups to agitate for student representation on faculty committees, or women may go it alone and deal with such women's
issues as abortion and day-care centers. City-based women's
lib groups may, similarly, concern themselves only with consciousness-raising or become politically active in seeking desired "women's legislation," either alone or in alliance with
others. Most women's lib groups accept both the class and
sex analysis of the woman's dilemma in American society;
that is, they share the Marxist-Leninist perspective of the
evils of a capitalistic society, a society that discriminates
against women, workers, and black, brown, and yellow peoples; at the same time, they separate out women's problems
from all the rest and argue that sex, more than class, is the
major discriminatory factor against women. Thus women in
exclusively women's groups—and WLF does not allow male
members (in contrast to NOW, which welcomes all sympathetic people)—often deal specifically with women's problems
and work toward the end of sex oppression.

The feminist philosophers of the new feminist movement
are many. The New England Free Press, an underground

publisher, first presented the pamphlet writings of many women liberationists. *Notes from the First Year* was a collection of mimeographed feminist writings published in June 1968; it was followed by a second-year collection that circulated above ground. *Female Liberation as the Basis for Social Revolution* by Roxanne Dunbar was one of the leading article-pamphlets that received considerable publicity within the movement. One of the few working-class women leaders in the movement, Roxanne Dunbar was the daughter of an Oklahoma cowboy; her mother, she has reported, treated her sons and daughters alike. While still in college, Roxanne Dunbar married and had a child but found the wife-mother role totally restricting. She left her husband and one-year-old child and became active in the feminist movement after having read Simone de Beauvoir's *The Second Sex*. Now she understood the reason for her malaise and vowed to do something about it. She became the leader of the Boston Group, a militant woman's group that often wore military fatigues and boots; her writings first appeared in *No More Fun and Games*.[56] In *Female Liberation . . .*, she utilized the Marxist frame of reference within which to analyze the woman's dilemma in Western society. She sympathetically supported other oppressed groups working toward liberation and accepted the liberal actions of NOW as desirable, although she argued that NOW's methods could never bring about the desired social revolution. Radical women had to organize themselves for themselves, as their oppression was far worse than men's.

> I do not find men all that oppressed by this society, though I hear men and women all the time argue that men are just as oppressed. . . . Every White man in this country has been raised with a false sense of power.[57]

Roxanne Dunbar believed that female liberation was the most advanced revolutionary thought at this point in history.

"Ultimately, we want to destroy the three pillars of class and caste society—the family, private property, and the state— and their attendant evils—corporate capitalism, imperialism, war, racism, sexism, annihilation of the balance of nature."[58] But the first pressing aim of women—radical women, that is— was to organize, raise their own consciousness, and attack the discriminations against women in our society. The style, philosophy, and methods of female liberation were not entirely worked out, Roxanne Dunbar suggested. Women had to learn about themselves and stop acting like men; aggressive and competitive qualities had to be consciously replaced with cooperative, more humane ones. She associated all the evils of American society with masculine traits. Women, according to her, had always been powerless and thus passive. No one knows, of course, how women with power would behave. But Roxanne Dunbar believed that, with the proper education and awareness, women would use power differently than men use it. Because militant feminists accepted the communist philosophy, she claimed, they would build on this foundation a community of love, sharing, and reciprocity.

For an even more erudite treatment of the same point of view, women liberationists read Chemistry Professor Margaret Benston's *The Political Economy of Women's Liberation*.[59] For an amusing message with a social punch, women's lib readers found Pat Mainardi's *The Politics of Housework* quite appropriate. Pat Mainardi presented a typical husband-wife dialogue that captured the male view of housework; one sample of the husband's remarks and the wife's thoughts should suffice:

> I don't mind sharing the housework, but I don't do it very well. We should each do the things we're best at. . . .

Also meaning:

> Historically the lower classes (Blacks and women) have had hundreds of years doing menial jobs.

It would be a waste of manpower to train someone else to do them now.

Also meaning:

I don't like the dull stupid boring jobs, so you should do them.[60]

The use of the word "politics" in this context demonstrated a new feminist awareness: politics meant power in the broadest sense. The feminists believed that all human relationships were power relationships, with one member-group dominating and the other member-group being dominated. Kate Millett's *Sexual Politics* (1970) was an even more explicit reference to this concept. Who did the dirty work in the house was only one indication, among many, of power relationships in which women were manipulated and dominated by men. The female sex as a whole, according to this point of view, has been powerless and thus misused. Powerful men do not respect powerless women and do not know how to relate to them in other than the dominating posture.

The Myth of the Vaginal Orgasm by Anne Koedt was another popular women's lib pamphlet. Discussing the hushed subject of sex itself constituted a liberating act for women. In this piece, Anne Koedt, an active New York feminist, argued that, contrary to Freud's teachings, the clitoris and not the vagina is the center of women's sexual orgasm.

Today, with anatomy and Kinsey and Masters and Johnson, to mention just a few sources, there is *no* ignorance on the subject. There is, however, social reasons why this knowledge has not been accepted. We are living in a male power structure which does not want change in the area of women.[61]

Men maintained the myth of vaginal orgasm according to her, because it was an effective way of dominating and controlling women. Men in our culture depend upon the penis to prove their masculinity and importance; if they cannot penetrate women, they cannot dominate. Recognizing the sexual truth about women could lead to a greater variety of sexual experiences for women, including lesbian sexuality. "The establishment of clitoral orgasm as fact would threaten the heterosexual *institution.*"[62]

Thus, Anne Koedt synthesized her discussion of women's sexuality with politics and the power roles each sex plays in Western culture. Removing the vaginal orgasm myth would also remove, she believed, the inevitability of heterosexuality. This is not to say that all women would become lesbians, but rather that the range of sexual choices would be greatly expanded. This article received popular praise from other women's libbers precisely because it discussed boldly a subject women usually shied away from, and also because it joined the discussion to the larger oppressive social issues as perceived by radical feminists.

Racism, often compared with sexism in women's lib writings, provided another example of how the white power structure oppressed the underdog, the deprived, and the nonwhite races. Indeed, the concern with the powerful versus the powerless is a central theme running through most women's liberation literature. The self-image of powerless women is understandably low; in order to both elevate the woman's self-image and gain power, radical feminists have tried, in their writings and actions, to strip away the myths regarding women, to pave the way for their own liberation, and thus to help more and more women become capable of utilizing power effectively. The analogy to the black slave has been frequently used. Slaves think of themselves as slaves and thus are no threat to the established powers. Only when they change their self-concept can they begin the long process toward individual rehabilitation and then collective action. In the 1960's, as in the 1850's, feminists allied with blacks because they saw their interests as the same. In both periods, the feminists eventually decided to go it alone, but their sympathies remained with the blacks' struggle for equality.

Women's lib has produced, in addition to the propaganda writings, academic discussions on the subject of women. Naomi Weisstein, for example, a psychologist at Loyola University in Chicago, showed in *Kinder, Kuche, Kirche as Scientific Law: Psychology Constructs the Female* how professional psychologists are as bound to the traditional cultural definitions of women as are laymen. Carefully surveying the professional literature, Dr. Weisstein showed that the Freudian view of women has gone largely unchallenged, despite the fact that there is little or no hard evidence to support it.[63] Further, what have passed for scientific conclusions on human personality and sexuality were often based more on chance than on observation. One series of tests described by Dr. Weisstein concluded that experimenters with one hypothesis always found evidence to support their hypothesis, while experimenters with an opposing view similarly always found evidence to support theirs. Thus scientific evidence is at best a fragile expression of a particular scientist's view of a subject, with diligently won evidence to support it. Dr. Weisstein concluded:

> I don't know what immutable differences exist between men and women apart from differences in their genitals; perhaps there are some other unchangeable differences; probably there are a number of irrelevant differences. But it is clear that until social expectations for men and women are equal, until we provide equal respect for both men and women, our answers to this question will simply reflect our prejudices.[64]

The comprehensive overview of experiments conducted on human intelligence and personality, as reported by Dr. Weisstein, effectively demonstrated that, in the late 1960's, the evidence was still scarce and uncertain on what precisely were the differences between the sexes. For hundreds of years, of course, the obvious anatomical differences had been pointed to as justification for the cultural differences imposed upon both sexes. But feminists throughout the ages had challenged the immutability and validity of the claimed differences. If indeed women could think abstractly, if they could endure pain, if they could manipulate mechanical objects, then couldn't they engage in a whole variety of occupations traditionally designated as male? What if most of the supposed sexual differences were in fact created by the culture? Perhaps girls were bad at mathematics precisely because they were *expected* to be bad at mathematics; perhaps girls could compete in athletics; perhaps. . . . The possibilities became infinite once the mind admitted the possibility.

Eleanor Maccoby, psychologist at Stanford University, has been studying sex differences in children's learning ability for many years. Her work has enormous significance for the feminist philosophy and indeed for everyone interested in knowing how learning occurs. The crux of the feminist position rests on the assumption that, aside from woman's ability to bear children, there are no significant differences between the sexes. In a receptive culture, women could attain all creative and scientific accomplishments that men attain. In one key report on "Women's Intellect," Professor Maccoby reviewed the professional literature on the subject and noted that, in the area of abstract mathematical ability, girls are less analytical and more global in their thinking. They not only handle information, but perceive it, differently from boys.[65] In a number of tests given to school-age children, this conclusion has consistently emerged. The question then arises, Why is this so? Is it based upon innate sex differences or is it environmentally determined?

The evidence is not conclusive yet, Professor Maccoby stated, but there is considerable indication that child-raising practices play an enormous role in determining how children learn. Verbally gifted girls, for example, often have mothers who play a major role in helping them with their schoolwork and offering constant guidance in the learning process. Bright boys, on the other hand, are more often left alone to question, explore, and develop independent answers to questions by themselves. The researchers reviewed in Maccoby's study concluded that the early independence and self-determination of the boys aided significantly in producing analytical thinkers. Those girls who exhibited aggressive qualities, normally described as boyish, performed better on analytical tests. The few girls, then, who escaped the protective guidance of their mothers performed more like boys. Generally, the parents treated a bright daughter differently from a bright son, and this factor affected the kind of thinking and learning the child excelled in.

But Professor Maccoby was not willing to discount the importance of inherited sex traits. "I think it is quite possible that there are genetic factors that differentiate the two sexes and bear upon their intellectual performance other than what we have thought of as innate 'intelligence.' "[66] She went on to suggest that aggressiveness, in the sense of dominance, may very well be a more prominent trait in boys than in girls. If this is so, then the two sexes do not begin at equal starting points in the process of learning. But Professor Maccoby, a cautious scientific investigator, did not want to argue categorically for one side of the eternal dichotomy, heredity versus environment. She concluded with the hope that our culture would reevaluate its image of the woman, and consider that aggressively intelligent females are as healthy and desirable as aggressively intelligent males, and that independence in both sexes is a highly valuable quality.

Clearly, Professor Maccoby said, there were members of the female sex who displayed the same intelligence traits as the males, but the culture effectively restrained the development in the female portion of the population while it encouraged it in the male. Thus, even if the percentage of females born with analytical ability was lower than that of the males, females were not allowed to develop naturally, so very few women fulfilled their potential in this area. Research has not arrived yet at any definitive conclusion on this subject; but as Eleanor Maccoby suggested, value changes may significantly alter behavior. Women's lib advocates have quoted the portions of Professor Maccoby's work on how child-raising practices affected learning, but have conveniently ignored her thought that genetic factors may also contribute to learning differences.[67] At this stage, however, most studies identify different child-raising practices as a significant variable in producing different learning patterns. Until this variable is removed—that is, until both sexes are treated in the same way, in the home and the school—it will not be known whether the learning differences are genetic or environmental.

The book that most effectively synthesized the feminist position in the late 1960's was Kate Millett's *Sexual Politics*. Published in 1970, it aptly brought together the bulk of the women's complaint against Western society and articulated the battle cry of the seventies. It both summarized and activated the feminist position. In many ways reminiscent of Simone de Beauvoir in *The Second Sex*, Kate Millett surveyed traditional myths, anthropological writings on the origin of society, the work of literary giants, Freud's theories, women's life in Nazi Germany and the Soviet Union, and the history of women in the last two hundred years. Originally written as a doctoral dissertation in comparative literature at Columbia University, the book became a popular success. Kate Millett's credentials as a feminist spokeswoman were good; she helped to organize the first Columbia University-Barnard College women's liberation group. As a faculty member at Barnard, she worked to increase the number of women on the faculty and publicized the university's alleged discrimination against women. She also participated in a feminist teach-in on Valentine's Day 1970.

The fair-minded would find it hard to deny the basic validity of feminism after reading *Sexual Politics*. The awkward writing style could be criticized, as could the repetitive nature of the content. However, the message was undeniable: in a patriarchal society, men dominated in every way. Everywhere you looked, there was evidence of it—in the structure of government, the legal system, literature, and sexual attitudes. In a brief postscript, Kate Millett looked toward a future when the female sex would be liberated. Yet nothing short of a cultural revolution would accomplish this mighty goal; "for to actually change the quality of life is to transform personality, and this cannot be done without freeing humanity from the tyranny of sexual-social category and conformity to sexual stereotype—as well as abolishing racial caste and economic class."[68] How this can or will be done is not explained. While most women's lib literature was read by the few believers, *Sexual Politics* reached beyond them to a larger audience. If Kate Millett did not convince all middle-class men and women of the legitimacy of feminism, she at least presented the message with impressive quantities of evidence that lifted her book well above the propaganda level.

Sexual Politics also synthesized the class-sex analysis of the woman's dilemma. Kate Millett integrated a Marxist perspective with a sexist one, assuming that the end of capitalism was a necessary prerequisite to women's emancipation; but she believed as did Margaret Benston and Roxanne Dunbar, that socialism did not inevitably guarantee women's liberation. Her discussion of the Soviet Union showed how the feminist revolution, at first enacted under the early Bolsheviks, was replaced during Stalin's regime with bourgeois attitudes toward women. The current generation of radical feminists shared with the 1910 feminists the belief that socialism—with its emphasis upon the redistribution of wealth, sharing rather than competing for work and goods, and the equalization of all people—provided the essential foundation for successful feminism. The term "sexual politics" also fused the class-sex dichotomy. Just as Anne Koedt viewed the sexual relationship as an institution, with the male sex dominating, so too did Kate Millett see the metaphoric meaning of politics. Cultural attitudes toward women —and Millett raised the discussion above class and sex to encompass all Western culture—have determined the status and role of women in every area of their lives.

Criticism of the women's liberation movement has come

from many quarters, some expected and some unexpected. It was to be expected that conservative unreconstructed men would view women's lib with hostility; it was to be expected that television interviews would turn the subject into a joke, and that Dr. Spock would be bewildered by the attacks on him while he continued to assert the primacy of the motherly role. But it was *not* to be expected that anthropologist Lionel Tiger would sweepingly dismiss the feminist movement and argue that men needed male camaraderie and fraternal associations (he called it "male bonding"). Women who wanted to end sex segregation, Tiger declared, were unstable, unhealthy types. Margaret Mead also expressed dissatisfaction with the strident tones of women's lib and asserted that the woman's traditional roles should not be rejected. Another unexpected criticism of women's lib came from some black revolutionaries who argued that, at this point in time, black women should stand behind their men; they must unite with the black man's struggle for freedom. Some leading black women, of course, supported women's lib, most notably NOW president Aileen Hernandez and Congresswoman Shirley Chisholm. Mrs. Chisholm said that she experienced more discrimination as a woman than as a black in American society. But black poet Nikki Giovanni claimed that women's lib is "Just another attempt of white people to find out what black people are doing or to control what we are doing. . . ."[69]

It is ironic that the growing militancy and group assertiveness that characterized the sixties has led to a split within the liberation movement rather than a new unity among segments of it. Black liberation and women's liberation both want to achieve the emancipation of their respective groups. But the white middle-class composition of women's lib has made black militants suspicious of its motives. While Elizabeth Gurley Flynn and Kate Richards O'Hare had good working-class credentials, they could deal with middle-class women because of their shared philosophy. Their sex and their common commitment to feminism united them. Today, race has so effectively divided people that many black women will not ally with white women, despite their mutual cause and sex, precisely because the color of their skin is different. This new dimension makes it very hard to create broad alliances for the feminist movement. Indeed, militant feminists today may reject alliances with the more moderate NOW chapters as well. However, once each liberation movement has gained a measure of self-confidence, the stage will be set for new alliances both within as well as between movements. During the 1970's, black power and woman power may well unite with all the other liberation movements to work for human power.

TWO GENERATIONS OF FEMINISTS

At this point in our discussion, it might be fruitful to compare the feminists of the 1910 generation with those of the current generation. How similar are they? What can we learn about feminists from such a comparison? Both generations shared many things: both despised war, yet lived through one; both believed that capitalism needed serious modification; and both believed that women were among society's greatest victims. Thus they shared a general worldview. What of their personal traits and backgrounds? With the exception of Elizabeth Gurley Flynn, who was only twenty years old in 1910, and Jo Freeman, who was twenty-two in 1968, the women's ages ranged from the mid-twenties to the early forties. Betty Friedan, at forty-seven, is the oldest leader in the current women's liberation movement. Of course, *The Feminine Mystique,* which signified her personal emancipation from the cultural view of women, was published in 1963, when she was forty-two. She has said that she could never have achieved liberation if she had not first experienced suburban living as a wife and mother. In terms of education, the current feminists, including the single representative from the lower class, Roxanne Dunbar, are better educated than their predecessors. The radical feminists

TWO GENATIONS OF FEMINISTS

1910 FEMINISTS	AGE IN 1910	CLASS BACKGROUND	EDUCATION	PARENTAL ATTITUDES	MARITAL STATUS	IF MARRIED, HUSBAND'S ATTITUDE
Henrietta Rodman	32	M	C	?	M	+
Crystal Eastman	29	M	G	+	M	+++
Kate Richards O'Hare	32	L	HS	+	M	++
Rose Pastor Stokes	31	L	E	neutral	M	+
Emma Goldman	41	L	E	–	D	
Elizabeth Gurley Flynn	20	L	HS	+	D	–
Mary Anderson	37	L	E	?	S	
Agnes Nestor	30	L	E	?	S	
Grace Abbott	32	M	G	+	S	
Susan Glaspell	28	M	C	?	M	++
Mary Heaton Vorse	36	M	HS	+	M	++
Neith Boyce	33	M	C	?	M	+

Legend

Class background: upper = U; middle = M; lower = L

Education: elementary = E; high school = HS; college = C; graduate degrees = G

Parental attitude: positive = +; negative = –; unknown = ?

Marital status: married = M; single = S; divorced = D

If married, husband's attitude: positive = +; negative = –

1960 FEMINISTS	AGE IN 1968	CLASS BACKGROUND	EDUCATION	PARENTAL ATTITUDES	MARITAL STATUS	IF MARRIED HUSBAND'S ATTITUDE
Alice Rossi	47	M	G	?	M	+
Betty Friedan	42	M	C	−	D	−
Aileen Hernandez	29	M	G	+	D	
Ti-Grace Atkinson	29	M	G	−	D	−
Roxanne Dunbar	22	L	G	++	D	−
Jo Freeman	22	M	G	++	S	
Kate Millett[a]	34	M	G	−	M	+
Margaret Benston*			G	?		
Robin Morgan	26	upper M	C	?	M	+
Pat Mainardi*		painter by profession		?	M	
Anne Koedt*			C	?		
Naomi Weisstein*		M	G	?	M	+

[a] Father had been a contractor who deserted the family when she was 14 and mother had to go to work.

*Little biographical information available.

of 1910, Kate Richards O'Hare, Rose Pastor Stokes, and
Emma Goldman, had minimal formal educations; the two
latter were immigrants who came to this country as young
teenagers. Pragmatic feminists in the union movement, such
as Mary Anderson and Agnes Nestor, similarly had little
formal schooling. All the feminists represented in the current generation went to college and most of them graduated.

Of the twelve 1910 feminists, seven were married, two
divorced, and three single; of the twelve 1968 feminists (with
information on only nine of them), four are married, four
divorced, and one single. Two of the 1910 feminists who are
listed as married in 1910, Crystal Eastman and Kate Richards O'Hare, were divorced after 1910 but remarried immediately thereafter. The public expressions of the divorced
women liberationists of the sixties are more critical of the
institution of marriage, and more wary of its feasibility or
desirability, than those of their predecessors. Crystal Eastman believed in reforming the institution of marriage, but
she also believed in marriage. The current group of feminists
seem more willing to renounce marriage as an anachronistic
institution. On parents' attitudes toward their daughters,
the evidence is both incomplete and inconclusive. In the cases
of writers Susan Glaspell and Neith Boyce, their self-definition as writers may not have carried the onus that parents
would place upon a daughter who wanted to be a chemist
or lawyer. (Still, the discussion of Fannie Hurst's parents'
reaction to her writing would counter this view.) The only
registered negative parental reaction in the 1910 generation
was that of Emma Goldman's parents. In the current generation of feminists, the six for which there is information on
this subject are divided evenly, with three sets of parents
displaying positive attitudes toward their daughters' search
for autonomy and three sets reacting negatively.

Parental attitude, like so many other factors, is a very
difficult variable with which to deal. Women may break out
of the societal mold in rebellion to oppressive parents or
be encouraged to be feminists by supportive parents; en-

couraging parents are as likely to produce feminist daughters as are discouraging ones. In the case of husbands, the evidence seems more clear cut. Supportive husbands are extremely necessary if feminists are to express themselves; an uncooperative husband in a household with an aspiring and persistent feminist may strain the marriage to the breaking point. In the current generation of divorced feminists, this seems to be the situation. The class background of the 1910 feminists was evenly divided between middle- and lower-class representatives while the current crop is almost entirely middle class, with the exception of Roxanne Dunbar.

What conclusions, if any, can be drawn from this comparison? With a sampling of only twelve women from each period, generalizations must be tentative and cautious. However, many of these women represent types as well as unique personalities; that is, the women listed here, especially the 1910 group, represent the lower class radical-immigrant feminist, the middle-class feminist writer, and the organization feminist. One fact that seems to emerge from these limited data is that the current generation is more homogeneous than the previous one. It is the college-educated woman of the sixties, not the working-class woman or the high school graduate, who is interested in feminism. But the middle-class feminist of the sixties, most notably the radical women's libbers, often embraces the causes of the working class and identifies closely with the nonwhite minorities and the underdeveloped countries of the world. Thus the middle class still produces the most feminists, but while their predecessors spent their time trying to raise the standards and life conditions of lower-class women, the current generation exerts a great deal of energy in rejecting its own class origins.

How or why did these particular women come to feminism? In both generations, some were attracted first by the struggle of workers and later by women's issues. To O'Hare, Flynn, Stokes, Goldman, Anderson, Nestor, and Abbott, the workers' struggle became theirs too. Similarly, Ti-Grace

Atkinson and Roxanne Dunbar identify with the working class and its aspirations. While the temperance and suffrage movements engaged the energies of Kate O'Hare, Crystal Eastman, and Mary Heaton Vorse before they became feminists, the civil rights and the New Left movements were the first experiences in activism and reform work for Roxanne Dunbar, Jo Freeman, Naomi Weisstein, and Robin Morgan. Initiation in a reform movement other than feminism seemed to be a natural path for many feminists, and during their activities with those particular movements, they underwent a very revelatory and disturbing discovery: their male comrades shared the society's values about women. The result was separation and self-assertion. Bright college girls who are denied equal academic opportunities might undergo an analogous experience. It is the rare woman who can achieve self-liberation without having experienced some external form of discrimination. Crystal Eastman and Henrietta Rodman, for example, were two unusual women who had great personal freedom of expression and action but who knew that their life opportunities were uncommon, so they dedicated themselves to freeing other women.

Thus no single portrait of a feminist emerges from these brief collective biographies. Opposite life experiences may contribute to the creation of a feminist: an encouraging father or a discouraging one; a sympathetic husband or no husband at all; advantageous educational opportunities or a lack of them. They were and are remarkable women precisely because they chose not to follow the majority. The movers and shakers in each generation are the minority who question, who step aside from the dominant group, and who ponder alternative ways to live and solve problems. The generation of the 1960's had a distinct advantage over their sisters of the 1910's in being able to gain publicity and often prominence for their opinions and their personalities.

The current generation does not have to waste large amounts of time presenting their views to the public in the way that the earlier groups did. The danger in instant celebrity, of course, is that the fame may corrupt, or become an end in itself, or more likely require time-consuming appearances in order to preserve that status. Crystal Eastman had to organize carefully, marshal her support, constantly encourage her followers, and ingeniously work to make her case known. In her time, public obstinance and apathy surely caused unending frustration, but the opposite—public familiarity—may also have undesirable consequences. Messages become chic and old-hat in an amazingly short time. If support comes slowly, but from personal and organizational contacts rather than from exposure on television, it may be longer lasting. Personal participation in feminist activities, in other words, has been the goal for both generations; whether it can come into being more effectively through a discussion on a TV talk show or through the presence of women in a meeting is not conclusively known. The feminists of the 1910's did not have to worry about the problems of fame; this generation, however, may have to learn how to turn the public's knowledge of their names and philosophy into a positive commitment toward feminism.

The activities of both generations also have much in common. The Feminist Alliance under Henrietta Rodman's leadership resembled some women's lib groups. While the Alliance demonstrated against the New York Board of Education's discriminatory practices toward married women teachers, women's lib groups have marched against university discrimination against women faculty and students. The Feminist Alliance ball of 1915, complete with costumes depicting emancipated women of all times, sounds reminiscent of some of WITCH's dramatic adventures. Crystal Eastman's New York Woman's Peace Party tried to mobilize women against the First World War, as women's lib and Women Strike for Peace organized women against the arms race and Vietnam. The writings of Kate Richards O'Hare, Rose Pastor Stokes, and Elizabeth Gurley Flynn shared the socialist theme with those of Roxanne Dunbar, Margaret Benston, and Kate Millett. Crystal Eastman, as a lawyer-feminist, resembled Aileen Hernandez in many ways.

Both generations of feminists also shared a sense of

community. Just as the Greenwich Village feminists and the settlement house workers had their respective groups of supporters and co-workers, so too do the current women's lib groups have their comrades in arms. This is a very important feature for any reform group: knowing that others share your views and your concerns. Today, the feminists' language may be bolder and more bitter, and the rhetoric may be more dramatic, but the essential plea and message have not changed substantially. Trade union women, such as Mary Anderson, Agnes Nestor, and Rose Schneiderman, may be absent from the current feminist ranks because of the very success of the first generation of union women. Although women are still underrepresented in union leadership, their militancy has disappeared and been replaced by a pragmatic focusing on the bread-and-butter labor issues. Trade union women have fought all efforts to repeal protective labor laws in the various states and have not joined either NOW or women's liberation. Students for a Democratic Society sent women organizers into the factories only to find the women unresponsive to their urgings and unwilling to give up the economic benefits gained from a steady job.

Sexual knowledge has increased significantly during this century and has made many of the hopes of the feminists a feasible reality. The 1910 feminists could talk about the right to birth-control information, but they could not guarantee the results; the leading gynecologists of the day still were not sure when conception occurred in the woman's monthly cycle. The Pill, introduced in the mid-sixties, became the first truly effective contraceptive in woman's history. Although controversy still surrounds it, with many respected doctors arguing that the negative side effects nullify its positive advantage, the Pill is being utilized by millions of American women. Knowledge of woman's sexual needs has also increased. Thanks to Kinsey and to Masters and Johnson, women have come to understand the natural sexual feelings they possess and their right to sexual expression.

Indeed, the woman, not as sexual temptress to man (the traditional image) but rather as a naturally sexual creature entitled to her own sexual fulfillment, has emerged for the first time in human history.

The importance, the implications, and the implementation of this new awareness are just becoming apparent. Freer sexual relations and cohabitation on the college campus are all part of the liberation gained from the Pill; whether the rise in premarital sexual relations will alter basic life patterns—that is, whether marriage will be delayed or denied and whether the divorce and remarriage rate will rise still faster—remains to be seen. Whether, in fact, sexual freedom on the part of the young truly reflects a profound new awareness of the natural sexuality of the woman as well as the feminist concern with the woman's right to be an independent being is unclear. Just as the flapper of the twenties distorted woman's emancipation to mean freedom to wear lipstick, flirt, and drink in public, so the so-called sexually free girl of the seventies may misunderstand the significance of the newfound freedom from pregnancy and the more relaxed public attitude; sexual freedom for women may mean sexual promiscuity in much the same way that it has for men.

Some feminist groups have been very concerned with this subject and have counseled their members that the new knowledge and technology regarding women's sexuality should become the basis for a new morality—not an imitation of male sexual morality. Women should not use men sexually any more than men should use women. The feminist goal is sexual relations based on mutual love and respect, with neither party dominating the other. The sexual politics of centuries should be replaced, according to the feminist view, with sexual equality. Some extreme feminists, who believe that men are incapable of respectful love in capitalistic cultures, advocate lesbianism or autoeroticism. But they are the minority; the majority of feminists look forward to healthy heterosexuality in a society of human equals. Until women are no longer treated as sexual objects, the feminists argue, in no society, capitalistic or socialistic, can true feminism be practiced. The new sexual knowledge, however, has provided a *basis* for the necessary reconsideration of human behavior.

THE PSYCHIC VIEW

The three faces of Eve, mentioned earlier, symbolized the deep psychological problems faced by many women in our society. Psychiatry, psychotherapy, sensitivity groups, and gestalt therapy have all arisen to help both sexes learn how to cope in frustrating America. To the middle-class Viennese women who told their tales of woe to Freud and to the middle-class white women who went to chic analysts on Park Avenue in the mid-sixties, the psychiatric message has been the same: adjust to your womanly lot in life. For the first time, however, feminists as well as all liberationists have challenged this established truism as well as many others. Perhaps it was society that was sick, they reasoned, not the woman. Perhaps it was the culture that deadened human energy and creativity, and not the individual rebel. This line of reasoning led to many young women's psychic emancipation as well as to the desperation of many. Self-knowledge is surely essential to individual autonomy but the culturally powerful means available to restrict women's choices may still prevent women from realizing their powers, thus causing new sources of frustration. If a woman knows what the trouble is and resolves to "get her head together," to use a popular colloquialism, she may still be thwarted in the pursuit of her goal. Society's rules have not yet been changed substantially. Married women especially suffer conflicts between their career, motherhood, and wifehood. It is still tremendously difficult, in the early 1970's, for a woman to fulfill multiple roles effectively.

To most feminists, career opportunities are crucial for the self-development of women. But in the twentieth century, more precisely during the last decade, a more sophisticated understanding of the relationship between self-image and career performance has been discovered. Before women can become effective career women/mothers/wives, they must become whole human beings. Modern psychology has demonstrated that a person with low self-esteem is a poor learner, an unpopular peer at school, and often a maladjusted adult. For feminists, this lesson explains woman's passivity, lack of drive, and unimpressive performance in the external world. Woman undervalues herself, has low self-esteem. Because society has effectively taught her that her capabilities are limited and well defined, and her life role predetermined, the woman in our society is never given the chance to explore her own depths to determine who or what she is. If she is boisterous and outgoing, she is criticized for being boyish; if she enjoys manual labor, she is considered masculine.

Men, too, are restricted by the culture's value system. There are behavioral patterns that they are obligated to adopt and others that they must avoid. A boy has his toys and a girl hers. But when it comes to lifework, an ongoing adult commitment to meaningful work, men do have greater opportunities than women, and they can channel their appropriate personality traits into the fulfillment of their professional roles. A woman's personality develops only as she pursues her wifely and maternal functions. Neither her children nor her casual social contacts give her a wide range of opportunities to explore her human potential. Although child raising is a challenging and often difficult job, many forces compete with mothers in our society for attention to, and authority over, their children. Further, although our culture has a Mother's Day and claims to love Mom, it does not reward motherhood in the way it rewards its soldiers, businessmen, and government officials. Experts try to help mothers raise their children, but mothers often suspect that this is an art rather than a science. Moreover, after the age of five, child raising is no longer a full-time occupation. What is a mother to do with the awkward hours from 9 to 12 P.M. and 1 to 4 P.M.? A father knows that he is many things and his eighteen-hour day can be efficiently divided so as to provide time to fulfill the roles of father, husband, worker, comrade, and son (with the role of worker consuming most of his time). The mother may also be a cook and a chauffeur, but these activities are part of her motherly role. She may be a PTA volunteer, but that is because she is Johnny's mother. Her identity is inextricably bound up with her one major role. And in an age when women are having fewer children and are living longer, filling up her time becomes a serious social as well as psychological problem. Who are women after their children leave them? What are they to do with forty years of their lives? What inner resources do they have after thirty years of indoctrination into the traditional womanly roles? Questions such as these, and the extreme difficulty in answering them, have produced a rise in the demand for psychiatrists, analysts, and other therapists.

Two very different but powerful recent books by woman writers have expressed women's psychological torment. The identity crisis, familiar to all readers of twentieth-century fiction, has taken on a new and unique dimension in the case of women. How can women who want to identify with the age-old roles also aspire to other human roles? Sylvia Plath, a poet whose work was highly respected by the literary elite when it first appeared in the late fifties and early sixties, has become, in the 1970's, a symbol of the tragic loss that our culture has perpetrated upon women. Enormously talented, a great scholar and winner of many literary awards, Sylvia Plath in her poetry expressed a total all-consuming concern for death that finally ended in her own suicide. The search for self was one of her major themes. In a poem entitled "The Applicant," a woman is described as "Naked as paper to start . . ." but "A living doll, everywhere you look. / It can sew, it can cook. / It can talk, talk, talk."[70]

In her posthumously published autobiographical novel, *The Bell Jar,*[71] Sylvia Plath defined her problem, or at least one of her problems, in terms that every feminist could understand: "The trouble was, I hated the idea of serving men in any way. I wanted to dictate my own thrilling letters."[72] Her poetry, of course, was her own unique genius; she did not share it with anyone else—genius is individual and inimitable. However, one of her thematic expressions, describing her own very personal trouble, was a feminist concern.

> From the tip of every branch, like a fat purple fig, a wonderful future beckoned and winked. One fig was a husband and a happy home and children, and another fig was a famous poet and another fig was a brilliant professor, and another fig was Ee Gee, the amazing editor, and another fig was Europe and Africa and South America, and another fig was Constantine and Socrates and Attila and a pack of other lovers with queer names and offbeat professions, and another fig was an Olympic lady crew champion, and beyond and above these figs were many more figs I couldn't quite make out.
>
> I saw myself sitting in the crotch of this fig tree, starving to death, just because I couldn't make up my mind which of the figs I would choose. I wanted each and every one of them, but choosing one meant losing all the rest, and, as I sat there, unable to decide, the figs began to wrinkle, and go black, and, one by one, they plopped to the ground at my feet.[73]

This passage succinctly captures, in dramatic and vivid form, the woman's dilemma. Sylvia Plath's psychological hell was familiar to many American women. But it took her genius to state it.

Such Good Friends by Lois Gould, a popular novel and movie of 1970-1971 cannot be compared in many significant ways with Sylvia Plath's writings. It is not as well written, and the level of thought and imagery is pedestrian in comparison to Sylvia Plath's; but its essential preoccupation with the psychological suffering and torture endured by a questioning woman makes it noteworthy. In this case, woman as sexual object is dealt with extensively by a woman writer who writes frankly and graphically. Lois Gould deals with the woman's identity crisis by sardonically describing the typical male view, the dominant view of woman, and the desperate and limited ways women have had to respond to the sexual tyranny imposed on them by men. The protagonist in the novel, Julie Messinger, achieved many bitter awarenesses during the course of the story, the major one being that she had been manipulated and made to feel guilty in her relationship with her husband, when all along he was the culpable party. Her husband, Richard, used to recite:

> "Higamous, Hogamous, Hogamous, Higamous, men are polygamous; Higamous, Hogamous, women monogamous." He also said that women were flowers; they were supposed to stay in place and look open and beautiful for the bee. . . . Screw male arrogance! Nobody gets to plant me in any mud-pile, cooling my rooted heels while he buzzes around on his fuzzy little wings. Knock, knock, it's your winged Messinger; you know you got the best nectar in this whole tulip bed, baby.[74]

How are women to respond to the male's sexual aggressiveness? They can compete with him at his own game, but in so doing acknowledge the validity of the game, or they can become indignant and be repelled by men altogether. Or finally, they can become angry and self-assertive. The woman may end up rejecting the male definition of sexuality, but that does not necessarily provide her with an alternative course. Julie Messinger described how she behaved masochistically at times, trying hard to interest her husband, and blaming herself for his lack of interest in her, never knowing that he was having an affair with another woman. She called that period in her life the "Story of O" period: "Learn masochism at home. Lesson 1: You are a thing. A thing does not expect pleasure."[75] Woman as a dehumanized object had been stated as fact in many feminist writings, but its portrayal in *Such Good Friends* heightens and deepens one's understanding. Pornography, written by and for men, had always been the best example of antifeminism. Julie Messinger often behaved in degrading ways sexually and appeared to satisfy the male sexual fantasies common in pornography. By having her heroine act out, in an aggressive manner, sexual behavior desired by men, Lois Gould showed how women had become captives of the same sick sexual fantasies as men. The sexual hangups of women, she seemed to be saying, are precisely tied to men's sexual hangups, and both sexes have to alter their views radically before wholesomeness can be returned to heterosexual activity. A woman can never build a healthy personality until she, and her husband-lover, come to terms with the meaning of sexual relations. Psychic wholeness, then, cannot be achieved until both sexes know who they are as human beings.

Fiction often captures the visceral sense of a problem in a way that factual studies cannot. *The Bell Jar* and *Such Good Friends*, each very different from the other, contributed mightily to the continuing discussion on women. *Such Good Friends* showed the new awareness of contemporary society in the psychosexual dimension of life and its critical relationship to woman's identity. Sylvia Plath's poetry and prose captured the dilemma faced by an enormously talented young woman who wanted motherhood, the love of a man, and the all-consuming life of a poet. That she did not succeed in effecting a workable synthesis was tragic; that society does not recognize the seriousness of the problem is also tragic.

CONCLUSION

As the sixties drew to a close, certain material changes

occurred in our society's institutional arrangements regarding women—but attitudinal shifts were not as apparent. In a study of women college students, for example, the researcher selected two articles on education and reprinted them in two sets, inserting fictitious author names, in one set a male and in the other a female. The college girls read both, but overwhelmingly chose the article by the male author as the superior one—even though the subject matter of the articles was very much alike and in a traditionally feminine field. "Women seem to think," commented the author of the study, "that men are better at everything—including elementary school teaching and dietetics!"[76]

The college woman's self-image in 1968, then, was still very low—and this is the crux of the matter. As women's lib groups discovered, self-assurance is fundamental to the liberation of women. If women who attended college in the late sixties still believed that they were intellectually inferior to men in every area, then a lot of work had to be done to raise their self-esteem. The revolution in self-images which would eventually result in attitudinal changes throughout society had not taken place yet. If college-aged young women still held traditional views about themselves, what about the over-thirty women and the lower-class women?

In 1970, as a husband-wife team of psychologists pointed out, "politically interested *women* join the League of Women Voters; politically interested *men* serve in legislatures."[77] The cultural definition of roles along sex lines has not changed substantially throughout the century. A look at opinion polls, moreover, suggests that women are as adamant as men in their unwillingness to change the traditional roles. In a recent Roper Poll, 74 percent of the women and 71 percent of the men said that women should have equal job opportunities with men; but when asked about free, low-cost childcare centers for working women, only 68 percent of the women and 61 percent of the men approved. In answer to the statement, "The wife should be the breadwinner if she is a better wage earner than her husband," only 10 percent of the women and 22 percent of the men agreed.[78] A 1970 study of the American Association of University Women showed that 60 percent of the men and 43 percent of the women polled were still committed to woman's role as wife and mother.[79] Altering the woman-as-homemaker image is a mighty task. In the early 1970's, it had not been accomplished.

But a number of material changes had occurred which may have repercussions in the future. The legal changes of the sixties, most notably the Equal Pay Act of 1963 and the Civil Rights Act of 1964 (Title VII), provide the necessary base upon which women can change their status in our society. Some evidence that the courts will interpret the laws along feminist lines is already evident. In 1969, the United States Court of Appeals for the Seventh Circuit reversed a lower court's decision and upheld the right of three women employees to work on a job requiring the lifting of weights in excess of thirty-five pounds (*Sellers et al.* v. *Colgate-Palmolive*). Colgate-Palmolive had fired the three women in accordance with an Indiana protective labor law prohibiting such a practice. The Court also said that the company had to inform all employees that they had the right to apply for more strenuous jobs than they had. Considering the fact that all the Colgate-Palmolive men were paid at wage rates which began at the highest rate payable to women, this decision was very significant.[80]

In a Supreme Court decision handed down late in 1971, the Fourteenth Amendment's equal protection clause was used for the first time in behalf of women's rights. The Court unanimously struck down an Idaho law which gave mandatory preference to men over women in the selection of administrators for an estate. Chief Justice Burger said that "By providing dissimilar treatment for men and women who are thus similarly situated, the challenged law violates the Equal Protection Clause."[81] Advocates of the equal rights amendment had been arguing for fifty years that the Fourteenth Amendment would not protect women; this decision may require them to change their opinion. Whether the Court will extend this interpretation in the future and consider the equal protection clause applicable to all areas of women's rights is not yet known. If it in fact does so interpret, then all discriminatory laws will be eliminated from the law books.

The workers for the equal rights amendment had a brief occasion to take heart in 1970 when the House of Representatives passed the amendment by a vote of 350 to 16; in August 1970, it looked as if the long struggle for the amendment, begun by Alice Paul in 1923, was to end successfully. Indeed, Miss Paul, at the age of eighty-six, was still working for its passage. But in October of that year, the Senate added so many restrictive clauses to the amendment that they crippled it. In the second session of Congress in 1971, the House again passed the amendment, 354 to 23, but the Senate judiciary subcommittee, the home of many opponents of the amendment, approved Senator Sam Ervin's (D., N.C.) substitute proposal, which stated that neither the federal nor the state governments should make any legal distinction between the rights and responsibilities of both sexes except on the basis "of physiological or functional differences." This exception, of course, nullified the whole intent of the amendment.[82] How do you interpret functional differences if not in cultural terms? In early 1972, victory finally came to the advocates of the amendment. The unadulterated version was passed by both houses of Congress and sent to the states for ratification. Perhaps the combined effect of the equal rights amendment and a more liberal judicial interpretation of the Fourteenth Amendment will finally erase all the legal inequities against women in the coming decade.

The divorce and abortion laws of this country also underwent a significant liberalization during the late sixties. The law, always lagging behind social custom, eventually catches up with the common practice of the society. The divorce rate, for example, has been steadily rising throughout this century. But it has been very difficult in most states of the

United States to obtain an easy, no-fault divorce. Nevada, known for its quickie divorces, became a major provider for those who could afford the trip. In the late sixties, however, various states looked at their divorce laws, most of which had been written a hundred years earlier, and revised them extensively. New York, which had allowed divorce only in case of adultery, revised its law in 1967 and established a no-fault principle; it called divorce "dissolution," and made it very easy for a married couple to end their marriage. California, Colorado, Florida, Iowa, Michigan, New Jersey, Oregon, and Texas also instituted no-fault divorce laws during this same period. The result is that Nevada's divorce business has decreased, and while the divorce rate has not risen dramatically, it has simply become easier for people to obtain divorces in their own states. Thus a phenomenon that exists has been recognized and obstacles to its accomplishment have been removed.

Abortion laws have been revised in the last decade as well. Abortion touches one of the most delicate and sensitive areas of human life. From the feminist perspective, abortion, or rather the right to abort legally, is an extension of the right of a woman to control her own body. The fight for birth-control information in the 1910's was a first step in the direction of the woman's right to determine whether she becomes a mother or not. If contraceptives prove ineffective, the argument goes, then abortion becomes necessary. Feminists argue that the moral question of whether the fetus is a living thing must be decided individually. Obviously, women who believe that the fetus is a life will not permit themselves to abort.

For the women who desire abortion in our society, the various state laws have, until recently, made it virtually impossible. That does not mean women have not had abortions. Over a million illegal abortions occur in the United States every year, but women often risk their lives in the process. Most states still permit abortion only if the mother's life is directly endangered. By 1970, ten states had expanded the conditions under which they would grant abortions. The major new provision is the inclusion of the woman's mental health as a reason for aborting.

In 1965, in the case of *Griswold* v. *Connecticut*, the Supreme Court ruled that a woman had a constitutional right to decide whether and when she was to have a child. In so doing, they overturned the Connecticut law which forbade the use of contraceptives in that state. Indeed, as late as 1970 two large states, Massachusetts and Wisconsin, limited the distribution of contraceptives to married persons, and Massachusetts permitted married people to buy contraceptives only with a doctor's prescription. Thus some states have antiquated laws regarding contraceptives as well as abortion. New York State in 1970 repealed its abortion law and made the decision on an abortion a matter for the woman and her physician. Washington and Hawaii are the only other states that have repealed all abortion laws from their statute books. As a result, 87,530 abortions were performed in the hospitals of New York during 1970, about one abortion for every two births in the state.[83] (In July 1970, however, New York permitted nonresident women to obtain abortions, so the statistics go beyond the population of New York State.) In 1970, 250,000 American women had legal abortions in contrast to 6,000 only five years before. The Supreme Court of California in the *Belous* case declared the state's anti-abortion law unconstitutional; one of the reasons for the decision was the abridgement of the woman's right "to choose to bear children," a fundamental right protected by the Constitution.[84]

The judicial branch of the federal government, with the aid of the U.S. Congress, then, broadened its interpretation of individual rights in the 1960's; woman's right to liberty and privacy became a guaranteed right and aided tremendously in furthering her liberation from social restrictions. But just as attitudes toward social roles have not changed significantly among the mainstream of American women, neither have they changed toward abortion. The woman's right to abort is recognized as unequivocal in New York,

Washington, and Hawaii but nowhere else as yet. Restrictive conditions still exist in most state abortion laws. The controversy over this issue has not yet ended, but it is a considerable part of the feminist's long struggle for autonomy.

The administration of Richard M. Nixon in 1969 did not augur well for women's rights. President Nixon appointed thirteen women to administrative positions out of a total of three hundred available posts; these included Mr. Nixon's personal and Mrs. Nixon's press and social secretaries.[85] Mrs. Dorothy Elston, Treasurer of the United States, represented the traditional woman's point of view in the Nixon administration. She acknowledged that the world of politics, government, and economics was a man's world, but rather than register dismay, indignation, or the hope for change, she said that "Men have better contacts to, and are more interested in, economics and politics. . . ." Although Mrs. Elston admitted that women were not represented at the Cabinet level, she believed that there were a sufficient number of women at the lower echelons of government. Patricia Hitt, Assistant Secretary of Health, Education, and Welfare, agreed with the Treasurer and said: "Frankly, I couldn't give you a single, solitary woman who has the training, background, and ability to fill one of those cabinet posts."[86]

When liberated woman journalist Gloria Steinem asked Mrs. Pat Nixon whom she identified with, other than her husband and daughters, the reply was given in a low and resentful voice:

> I never had time to think about things like that—
> who I wanted to be, or who I admired, or to have
> ideas. I never had time to dream about being anyone
> else. . . . I've never had it easy. I'm not like all you
> . . . all those people who had it so easy.[87]

Mrs. Nixon did not appreciate women's liberation; indeed, she did not even understand the nature of the question.

Thinking about who you are and what you are seemed to the First Lady to be frivolous, upper-middle-class nonsense—the kind of activity rich kids participate in, but surely not a worthwhile endeavor for serious-minded, hard-working, poor girls. Mrs. Nixon's daughters shared her perspective and typified the traditionally disposed women of our culture who find total happiness, and their true reason for being, in marriage. President Nixon seemed to agree with his wife and daughters. He made no effort to continue L.B.J.'s policy of recruiting women into high governmental positions. When he had the opportunity to nominate two Supreme Court justices in 1971, NOW as well as women's liberation groups advocated well-qualified women. President Nixon rejected the opportunity and nominated two men.

At the close of the 1960's, neither the White House nor the public at large believed that there was a woman's problem, women's lib notwithstanding. The shrill tones of women's liberationists confirmed the doubtfuls' view that these women were extremists and not typical of American women. A few women were beginning to challenge, through the courts, established laws in the areas of job discrimination and sexual freedom; but popular attitudes, as reflected in Mr. Nixon's middle-American women appointees, were that everything was just fine. Yet the hard statistical evidence was undeniable: women had not gained a significant place in the professions; indeed, they were even beginning to lose their foothold in traditional womanly professions, such as teaching. Working women earned from 10 to 40 percent less than men with the same qualifications. Only 3 percent of the women who work full time earn more than $10,000 a year, in comparison with 28 percent of the men.[88] There is no area, in fact, where one can look without seeing women treated in an inferior way. Women are denied entrance to medical and law schools, often over less qualified male candidates. As a sex, they receive less pay in the factories of America than men do, and are denied promotional opportunities because of restrictive labor laws.

Many of the feminists described in this book, especially those of the 1910 and 1960 generation, synthesized—in a difficult, exciting, and inimitable way—the individualistic, anarchistic tradition of reformer with the social, collectivistic type. That is, they merged a concern for self-realization with an urge to help the masses. There have always been these two dominant strains in the reformer mentality in America: the romantic anarchist, whose primary goal is individual fulfillment, and the social reformer, who envisions people within groups and hopes to elevate all interest groups to a common level of well-being. Henrietta Rodman, for example, was an iconoclast and socialist; she resolved this seeming paradox in her own life by living according to her own wishes, relentlessly relishing new experiences at the same time that she worked for the social uplift of working-class and professional working women. She had effected a revolution within herself; now she had to help other women revolt. Similarly, Kate Millett and many of her colleagues speak in mystical, romantic terms about individual actualization while working for the collective good of the working class. After feminists undergo a personal transformation, they often transfer their forces to helping other women achieve the same awareness.

But experiencing an agonizing self-appraisal and drastically altering your life style is not easy, certainly not a mass phenomenon. Feminists often sound like religious zealots or prophets precisely because they believe that they have seen the light—they have had a transforming experience that they want to share with others. Yet zealots have always been distrusted and, with few exceptions, gained few converts. Given this bleak prospect, how can the feminist utopia become a reality?

The first step toward positive feminist change is personal dissatisfaction. The next step is serious evaluation of the causes of the discontent, and then the planning of a constructive program to improve the situation. This is a rational

analysis of how change *should* occur. But human beings do
not always behave in the most reasonable, thoughtful way.
The signs of discontented American women are many: the
rising rates of alcoholism, adultery, and divorce all signify
women's unhappiness. Thus many women are at the first
stage, ready for meaningful change. But instead of taking
the second step, analyzing the reasons for their dissatisfaction, they continue to express it in drinking, or pro-
miscuous sex, or boring, time-killing activities. They do not
redefine their lives in healthy, constructive ways.

It is at this point that the educative message of feminism
can be particularly helpful to the majority of American
women—that is, to the non-college-attending young women,
to the married or unmarried women who work, and to the
stay-at-home mothers under and over thirty. (The young
woman who goes to college is exposed to feminism far more
than the rest of womankind. This is not to say that all college
girls accept and practice feminism, but rather that its message is communicated to them.) Ultimately, each woman has
the right and responsibility to decide for herself what aspect,
if any, of feminism she chooses to adopt.

It is the feminist as educator, as articulator of the problem
and the solution, who is central to the success of feminism.
Surely the 1910 and 1970 feminists have behaved as propagandists. But success has still eluded them. They have followed the traditional reformer pattern in this country; they
have organized, publicized the injustices, and lobbied for
their remedies. Why have they not succeeded? A key to
the answer may be found in the absurdly long time it took
to gain woman's suffrage. With the exception of the abolition
of slavery, no reform has ever taken longer to accomplish in
this society. Why? At least two significant reasons, I think,
can be seen. First, the culturally pragmatic American intuitively knew that suffrage was not a one-shot deal; that is,
it was not the end of reform but rather the beginning. Passage of a pure food and drug bill disposes of a serious problem neatly and finally in the minds of Americans; but allow-

ing women to vote raises new problems that need solving and creates new conditions for reform. Traditionalists—and the majority of Americans are traditionalists when the issue is long-held values—feared what would happen when women became active politically. Political democracy might be a fine rhetorical sentiment, but if it upset the home and the customary roles of wife and mother, it had to be avoided at all costs. Women, as has been suggested before, shared the male fear and anxiety; and it took a few energetic and determined women many generations to convince enough other women of the importance of suffrage to mount a truly impressive national campaign. The second reason, then, arises out of the first: it is time consuming to reeducate and organize. Both women and men had to be reeducated before suffrage could be accomplished.

Since it takes a long time to reeducate people and to organize them, the most extreme feminist demands will take even longer to accomplish. Short-term, specific feminist changes are already coming about. As already described, the law courts and the legislatures have begun to erase specific examples of discrimination. But the presence of a favorable law does not insure its usage. Nor does it lead inevitably to changes in attitudes and behavior. And these parts of the solution are the most difficult and the most important to bring about. Providing equal educational opportunity does not guarantee that women will take advantage of that opportunity. The assumption, of course—yet untested and therefore unproven—is that equal opportunity will lead eventually to equal expression and accomplishment. Children under ten years old today will undoubtedly grow up in a more equitable atmosphere than any American generation heretofore. The success of feminism will be seen in *their* behavior as well as in their children's.

Another problem, typical of every reform movement, is the tendency of its critics to judge it too quickly. The civil rights movement was called a failure before a generation had a chance to live under the Civil Rights Act of 1964; and hostile observers quickly denounced the women's liberation movement. But in both cases the evidence is not yet in. The increased life possibilities for both black Americans and women will not be fully realized immediately. Sympathetic conditions, conditions under which the positive laws are enforced fully—not a small matter—are crucial to success. Time and a favorable environment, therefore, are the two additional ingredients for the success of feminism. The woman's and the black Americans' movements are both revolutionary-reform movements in American history. They are the only organized movements that have tried to change important values and actions within the system. Their goals are revolutionary in the sense of radically altering people's views of themselves and others, but their methods are reformist; even the radical feminists described in this study always operated within the legal, legislative, and propaganda traditions of America. Jo Freeman, a political scientist by training and a major writer in women's liberation today, has talked about the "radical paradox" of the young feminists who say, "You shouldn't do anything unless it changes the whole structure of the system, and you can't change the whole structure of the system so you can't do anything."[89] The members of NOW, as well as most of the 1910 generation of feminists, did not subscribe to this view. They never resolved the paradox of how you revolutionize a society while operating within it, but simply acted on the belief that an informed America would end all discrimination against women. In other words, they believed that America could experience another revolution without an accompanying chaos and human loss.

Most feminists of the past, like many of the present, did not hold a rigid, doctrinaire view of proper and improper methods to achieve the feminist society. They accepted the need to work for specific feminist causes while propagandizing for cultural change. It is precisely the delicate balance of revolutionary aims with reform means that makes the feminist crusade so challenging and difficult to accomplish, but that also makes its possibilities for success much greater.

Without a well-defined formula, feminists can attack specific injustices of society at the same time that they can pray for a sudden, revolutionary change in human values.

In the late sixties, observers of the family institution noted that significant changes had already taken place. Just as economic rhetoric lags noticeably behind the practice—and laissez faire has not existed for at least 150 years—so the traditional family has already undergone significant changes. The extended family of agricultural America has been replaced by the nuclear family in an urban, industrial center. The family structure is a dynamic one, not static and immovable. Many factors have revolutionized the twentieth-century family structure: apartment dwelling, suburban living, and compulsory education, to name a few. Indeed, every decade in this century has witnessed tremendous shifts and/or strains on the family. War, depression, war again, sudden consumer prosperity, inflation, Vietnam, and more inflation have all affected the parent-child environment. The mother has given up many of her traditional roles in modern America. The question is, What does she replace them with? Indeed, this is part of a larger question: What will be the quantity and quality of work in the last part of the twentieth century? How will all healthy human beings, living longer in an automated society, spend their days? Leisure is a major social problem. The woman's dilemma, then, cannot be viewed in a vacuum—it is part of a major societal readjustment that can and should occur. But in this area, as in the view of women, values die hard. Americans consider work to be as sacred as the idea of woman as wife and mother. However, the fact of changed practices forces people to reevaluate their attitudes. For example, the increased number of divorces has made more and more people tolerant of divorce; the reality that more and more women are working requires a reevaluation of woman's role; and the shorter and shorter work weeks make people think about the meaning of work and life.

Television has brought feminism before the public, frequently oversimplifying its philosophy and promoting a false understanding of the issues. But public awareness is an essential first step to positive action. Henrietta Rodman never reached the audience of Kate Millett. No feminist tract ever rivaled the sales of *The Feminine Mystique* and *Sexual Politics*. The mass media, then, with all their dangers, offer modern-day feminists a great opportunity to publicize and explain their views. While pragmatic feminists work for the passage of equitable laws, or for the removal of unjust ones, the visionaries preach the new order on television and in books and magazines. It is the simultaneous activities of both the pragmatists and the visionaries that make the 1970's exciting for feminists.

Young feminists have more years to give to the struggle than their elders. They too have experienced a debilitating war and have been lured by the affluence of American society. But those few who read history may learn a lesson from the past: they will not be fooled by the various false freedoms placed before them, and they will use the biographies of earlier feminists as models for their own behavior. They will practice what they preach and never lose sight of the ultimate goal—a human society in which cooperation, rather than aggression, dominates. And in so doing, they will be carrying on the feminist philosophy. Leaders are, by definition, the few; everyone cannot exhibit (because we do not all possess) traits of remarkable skill, intelligence, energy, and bravery. But all women can, argue the feminists, recognize their own self-interest and change their behavior accordingly. All women may not be able to lead the feminist movement, but they can follow the feminists' lead. Women can change their life roles and experiences; they can shift their emphasis, take on new responsibilities as people, and alter the family structure. Indeed, the success and effectiveness of reform leaders lie in their ability to sway the many and acquire followers. The feminists of 1910 did not succeed in reaching this goal; maybe their sisters of the seventies will.

When the twentieth century began, social critics and prophets alike predicted that it was going to be a woman's century. All the signs were there. More women were working, going to school, and exhibiting signs of independence. Women lawyers and doctors, a never-before-observed phenomenon in America, were much in evidence. Women were destined to participate in every major area of life. The prophecy chilled the bones of the traditionalists and thrilled the idealists. But the fearful should not have worried; the optimistic predictions of the idealists never materialized. Women never achieved their due place in the twentieth-century sun. What happened? Why didn't the long-awaited egalitarianism come to pass? The answer, it seems to me, and I hope this study has suggested it, is that cultural attitudes are powerful and live a long and enduring life. Values change very slowly; even when challenged by a vocal minority (the usual way social change occurs), the value of woman as homemaker has lived on.

American reformers, even most radical thinkers, have never been, and still are not, revolutionaries. The changes desired by most activist reformers have never penetrated the fundamental structure of White Anglo-Saxon Protestant America. The sanctity of the home, of Mom, of private property, of the pursuit of happiness, and of profit has always been primal and everlasting. Americans have always felt, whether they could articulate it or not, that feminism threatened the sacred structure of American life. And they were right. If implemented, feminism would overhaul the institutions of the family, the school, and the factory. Child-raising practices, school curriculums, job opportunity, and life's work would be radically altered to meet feminist demands. Thus the resistance of the overwhelming majority of Americans to feminism is an understandable response—a response based upon content (or at least not serious discontent) with the status quo and extreme fear and anxiety about the future if the desired changes were executed. Under feminism, life would not be as it has always been. Men and women as well as children would behave differently, worship different gods, spend their time in new ways, and altogether live according to a different set of goals and expectations.

Feminism will come to life for the majority (a minority

always has practiced it and will continue to do so) only when the values of the American culture have been radicalized; when work is no longer defined as manly if it is outside the home and womanly if it is inside; when true individualism, rather than the pious hypocrisies that substitute for it, is practiced within a socially responsible environment; and when human worth is determined by human accomplishment and sex is no longer the fundamental starting point for deciding human destinies.

Given the nature of humans, in whom the will to dominance is strong, feminism's only hope, apparently, is that human beings can produce a society made up of psychically sound people, of human beings who do not receive personal satisfaction and security from exploiting and dominating others. An individual's worth and sense of self, in a feminist society, would be based upon his or her resources, interests, and achievements, not on the ability to use, misuse, and manipulate others. In short, the feminist utopia would also be a humanistic utopia, one in which neither color, creed, nor sex would determine a person's status; rather, people would be treated equally *as people*. Truly, the feminist vision is idealistic, but in a world in which cooperation is crucial to basic survival, the ideal may become real. That is not simply the feminist's hope—it is humanity's only hope.

Notes

1. Phillip K. Hastings, "Hows and Howevers of the Woman Voter," *New York Times Magazine,* June 12, 1960, pp. 14 ff.

2. Janice Law Recker, "Women in U.S. History High School Textbooks," *Social Education,* March 1971, pp. 249-260, 338.

3. Lindley J. Stiles, "Women, Wisdom, and Education," *Northwestern Review,* Spring 1966, pp. 25-27.

4. Hastings, "Hows and Howevers of the Woman Voter."

5. Katherine Anne Porter, "Her Legend Will Live," *Ladies' Home Journal,* March 1964, pp. 58-59.

6. Theodore F. Sorensen, *Kennedy* (New York, Harper Row, 1965), p. 252.

7. *U.S. President, Public Papers of the Presidents of the*

United States (Washington, Office of the Federal Register, National Archives, 1961-1963), p. 797.

8. *Ibid.*, pp. 799-800.

9. *Ibid.*, p. 800.

10. *Ibid.*, 98-103, 465.

11. *Ibid.*, pp. 780-781.

12. *American Women: The Report of the President's Commission on the Status of Women and Other Publications of the Commission* (New York, Scribner's, 1965).

13. James Reston, "Washington," *New York Times,* January 17, 1962, p. 32.

14. Stephanie Gervis, "Women Speak Out for Peace," *Nation,* 193 (December 30, 1961), 526.

15. "Who Really Cares for Peace?" *Christian Century,* 79 (May 23, 1962), 648.

16. Midge Decter, "The Peace Ladies," *Harper's,* 227 (March 1963), 51.

17. *Ibid.*, p. 52.

18. "Who Really Cares for Peace?" p. 648.

19. *New York Times,* December 14, 1962, p. 1.

20. *Ibid.*, December 8, 1964, p. 12; December 12, 1964, p. 19; January 9, 1965, p. 3; August 3, 1966, p. 12.

21. *Ibid.*, November 2, 1963, p. 10.

22. Lucy Freeman, *New York Times Book Review,* April 7, 1963, p. 46.

23. Louis Harris, "The Women's Vote," *Newsweek,* 64 (September 21, 1964), 32.

24. Henry Brandon, "A Talk with the First Lady," *New York Times Magazine,* September 10, 1967, p. 48.

25. *Ibid.*, p. 170.

26. See "Ways to Beautify America," *U.S. News and World Report,* 58 (February 22, 1965), 72-76+, and "The Land," *Time,* 88 (September 30, 1966), 53-54.

27. *Time,* 92 (November 29, 1968), 14.

28. "Mrs. LBJ: Saleslady for 'Great Society,'" *U.S. News and World Report,* 62 (March 27, 1967), 22.

29. Quoted in *U.S. News and World Report,* 64 (January 29, 1968), 13.

30. *Time,* 92 (November 29, 1968), 14.

31. Shana Alexander, "The Best First Lady," *Life,* 65 (December 13, 1968), 22B.

32. Quoted in "Lady Beautiful," *Christian Century,* 85 (November 27, 1968), 1523.

33. *Ibid.*

34. Quoted in Marion K. Sanders, "The New American Female," *Harper's,* 231 (July 1965), 37-43.

35. Peter Lisagor and Marguerite Higgins, "L.B.J.'s Hunt for Woman Power," *Saturday Evening Post*, 237 (June 27, 1964), 86.

36. *Ibid.*, pp. 86-87.

37. *Ibid.*, p. 87.

38. "From the Women: And What About Our Job Rights?" *U.S. News and World Report*, 61 (July 4, 1967), 61-62; and 69 (August 3, 1970), 51-52.

39. *Ibid.*, 61 (July 4, 1967), 61.

40. *Ibid.*, 69 (August 3, 1970), 51-52.

41. Alice S. Rossi, "Job Discrimination," *Atlantic Monthly*, March 1970, p. 101. In March 1972, the Act was amended to include educational institutions.

42. A. F. Guttmacher in the *New York Times Book Review*, May 29, 1966, p. 18.

43. Alice S. Rossi, "Women Liberation," *ADA World Magazine*, January 1971, p. 5M.

44. Jo Freeman, "The New Feminists," *Nation*, February 24, 1969, p. 241; *New York Times*, May 2, 1970, p. 36; NOW newsletters.

45. Mimeographed sheet entitled "National Organization for Women (NOW) Bill of Rights for 1969."

46. Robin Morgan, "The Media and Male Chauvinism," *New York Times*, December 22, 1970, p. 33.

47. *New York Times*, May 2, 1970, p. 36.

48. Alice S. Rossi, "Equality Between the Sexes: An Immodest Proposal," *Daedalus*, Journal of the American Academy of Arts and Sciences, 93 (Spring 1964), 607-652.

49. Helen Dudar, "Women's Lib: The War on 'Sexism,' " *Newsweek*, March 23, 1970, p. 72.

50. Peter Babcox, "Meet the Women of the Revolution, 1969," *New York Times Magazine*, February 9, 1969, p. 34.

51. *Ibid.*, pp. 86-88.

52. Dudar, "Women's Lib . . .," p. 73.

53. Freeman, "The New Feminists," p. 242.

54. Both Helen Dudar's article and Jo Freeman's, already cited, discuss the Marlene Dixon affair.

55. Dudar, "Women's Lib . . .," p. 74.

56. *Newsweek*, March 23, 1970, p. 73.

57. Roxanne Dunbar, *Female Liberation as the Basis for Social Revolution* (New England Free Press Pamphlet, 1969), p. 3.

58. *Ibid.*, p. 4.

59. See Chapter One of this book for an account of Margaret Benston's views.

60. Pat Mainardi, *The Politics of Housework* (New England Free Press Pamphlet, 1970), p. 1.

61. Anne Koedt, *The Myth of the Vaginal Orgasm* (New England Free Press, 1970), p. 2.

62. *Ibid.*, p. 5.

63. Naomi Weisstein, *Kinder, Kuche, Kirche as Scientific Law: Psychology Constricts the Female* (New England Free Press, 1970).

64. *Ibid.*, p. 6.

65. The following discussion is based upon Eleanor Maccoby's "Woman's Intellect," in *The Potential of Woman*, Seymour M. Farber and Roger H. L. Wilson, eds. (New York, McGraw-Hill, 1963), pp. 24-39.

66. *Ibid.*, p. 37.

67. In *Sexual Politics* (New York, Doubleday, 1970), Kate Millett quotes Eleanor Maccoby for support but does not register her reservations; Jo Freeman, in an unpublished essay, "The Building of the Guilded Cage," also quotes only part of Maccoby's view, the part that supports environmental determinism.

68. Millett, *Sexual Politics*, p. 363.

69. Quoted in Helen H. King, "The Black Woman and Women's Lib," *Ebony*, March 1971, p. 74.

70. Sylvia Plath, *Ariel* (New York, Harper Row, 1961), p. 5.

71. Sylvia Plath, *The Bell Jar* (New York, Harper Row, 1971).

72. *Ibid.*, p. 83.

73. *Ibid.*, pp. 84-85.

74. Lois Gould, *Such Good Friends* (New York, Dell Paperback, 1970), p. 139.

75. *Ibid.*, p. 152.

76. Philip Goldberg, "Are Women Prejudiced Against Women?" *TransAction*, April 1968, p. 30.

77. Sandra L. Bem and Daryl J. Bem, "We're All Nonconscious Sexists," *Psychology Today*, November 1970, p. 26.

78. "A Special Roper Poll on Women's Rights," *Parade Magazine*, September 26, 1971, p. 4.

79. *New York Times*, June 10, 1970, p. 42.

80. Alice S. Rossi, "Job Discrimination," p. 101.

81. *Chicago Sun-Times*, November 23, 1971, p. 6.

82. *Ibid.*

83. *Chicago Daily News*, November 20-21, 1971, p. 1.

84. Harriet F. Pilpel, "The Voluntary Approach: Population Control," *Civil Liberties*, November 1971, p. 3.

85. Paula Stern, "When's It Going to Be Ladies' Day?" *New Republic*, July 5, 1969, p. 14.

86. *Ibid.*, pp. 14-15.

87. "Thinking Man's Shrimpton," *Time*, 93 (January 3, 1969), 38.

88. In 1970, only two of the 13,000 posts of superintendent of schools were held by women, even though they hold 13 percent of the doctorates in educational administration. Only 4 percent of high school principalships were held by women, even though women made up 68 percent of public education teachers. Statistics on women in professions can be found in many sources. See, for example, "Women in Science," *Science,* October 9, 1970, p. 201.

89. *New York Times,* March 23, 1970, p. 32.

A NOTE ON SOURCES

With the exceptions that will be noted shortly, this book was based primarily upon published, rather than unpublished, sources. The fictional writings of all of the women novelists described, the autobiographies and biographies of the women treated, and the magazine and newspaper sources utilized were all available to the researcher.

The manuscript collections that were consulted in the preparation of *Movers and Shakers* include the Mary Heaton Vorse papers in Wayne State University's Archives of Labor History and Urban Affairs and Agnes Nestor's papers at the Chicago Historical Society. The various Greenwich Village feminists' papers—Neith Boyce and Hutchin Hapgood's papers in Yale University's Collections of American Literature as well as the papers of the Woman's Peace Party, New York Branch, and the American Union Against Militarism—both in the Swarthmore Peace Collection, Swarthmore College—were particularly helpful. Two of the most important Village feminists, Crystal Eastman and Henrietta Rodman, did not leave collected papers, so information about them had to be gathered from a variety of sources.

Many of the women discussed in this book are still living, and hence their papers are not available for scholarly investigation. These include Margaret Mead, Freda Kirchwey, and of course the whole group of women liberationists of the sixties. Eleanor Roosevelt's papers have not been open except to Joseph Lash, whose book *Eleanor and Franklin* (New York, 1971) aided me enormously.

AUTOBIOGRAPHIES

As the footnotes reflect, a fair number of autobiographies by these feminists have appeared. Mary Anderson's *Woman at Work* (Minneapolis, 1951), Elizabeth Gurley Flynn's *I Speak My Own Piece* (New York, 1935), Charlotte Perkins Gilman's *The Living of Charlotte Perkins Gilman* (New York, 1935), Susan Glaspell's *The Road to the Temple* (New York, 1927), Emma Goldman's *Living My Life,* two volumes (New York, 1931), Hutchins Hapgood, *A Victorian in the Modern World* (New York, 1939), Fannie Hurst's *Anatomy of Me* (New York, 1958), Mary McCarthy's *Memories of a Catholic Girlhood* (New York, 1957), Margaret Sanger's *An Autobiography* (New York, 1938), Rose Schneiderman's *All for One* (New York, 1967), Ida Tarbell's *All in the Day's Work* (New York, 1939), and Mary Heaton Vorse's *A Footnote to Folly* (New York, 1935) are all noteworthy. I was not able to obtain Sam Ornitz' compilation of Rose Pastor Stoke's unpublished autobiography, entitled *An Anonymous Autobiography.*

BIOGRAPHIES

A great deal of work is yet to be done on the feminist writers and activists of this century. Floyd Dell's *Women as World Builders: Studies in Modern Feminism* (Chicago, 1913) presents some brief portraits of little known feminists such as the Swedish feminist Ellen Key. August Derleth's *Still Small Voice: The Biography of Zona Gale* (New York, 1940) and Richard Drinnon's *Rebel in Paradise* (Chicago, 1961), a biography of Emma Goldman, provide important information on two quite different women. Joseph Lash's two-volume study of Eleanor Roosevelt is an excellent source: *Eleanor and Franklin* (New York, 1971) and *Eleanor: The Years Alone* (New York, 1972). There are two biographies of Margaret Sanger that are worth consulting: the revised

Ph.D. dissertation by David Kennedy entitled *Birth Control in America: The Career of Margaret Sanger* (New Haven, 1970) and the more popular *Margaret Sanger: Pioneer of the Future* by Emily Taft Douglas (New York, 1970). A number of current researchers are working on the life and activities of Elizabeth Gurley Flynn and Kate Richards O'Hare. Biographies of such important feminists as Crystal Eastman, Rose Pastor Stokes, Freda Kirchwey, Henrietta Rodman, and Mary Heaton Vorse still need to be written.

Some of my graduate students investigated such subjects as Alice Paul's activities in the 1930's (Paula Pfeffer), President Kennedy's views on women (Dorothy Cizmar), and Grace Abbott's career with the Immigrants Protective League in Chicago (Ellen Sherman). The papers they produced were the basis for my discussion of these respective subjects.

MAGAZINE ARTICLES

As noted throughout the book, *Movers and Shakers* has relied heavily on periodical literature. Besides the well-known middle-class magazines consulted, some of the less known but equally significant deserve mention. Kate Richards O'Hare's magazine *Social Revolution* (first called the *National Rip Saw* and published from 1904 to 1918) offers numerous instances of how the socialist-feminist blended the two ideologies. *The Masses,* the Greenwich Village magazine published from 1912 to 1917, dealt extensively with feminism, particularly before World War One.

Some of the women's magazines were also very helpful. Early in the century, the *Woman's Home Companion,* for example, published numerous pieces of fiction by such feminist writers as Susan Glaspell and Neith Boyce. Later in the century, Eleanor Roosevelt and Dorothy Thompson wrote regularly for the *Ladies' Home Journal* and provided substantive discussions of the woman's role in a magazine that was not known for its serious portrayal of the subject. Freda Kirchwey's *Nation*, generally known for its liberal intellectual political orientation, also contributed feminist literature, thanks to its outstanding woman editor and publisher.

PRIMARY SOURCES

The writings of all of the women featured in this book provided its significant basis. The novels of Susan Glaspell, Fannie Hurst, Lois Gould, and Sylvia Plath (whose novel, *The Bell Jar* [New York, 1971] may well be classified as autobiography) are all important primary sources. Pearl Buck's *Of Men and Women* (New York, 1941) and Mirra Komarovsky's *Women in the Modern World* (Boston, 1953), though less well known than Betty Friedan's *The Feminine Mystique* (New York, 1963) and Kate Millett's *Sexual Politics* (New York, 1970), are thoughtful and serious contributions to feminist thought; their worth is especially significant in terms of when they were produced. Three feminist plays that are virtually unknown to this generation, but surely deserve resurrection, are Rose Pastor Stokes's *The Woman Who Wouldn't* (New York, 1916), Zona Gale's *Miss Lulu Bett* (New York, 1920), which won the Pulitzer Prize that year, and Dorothy Parker and Arnaud D'Usseau's *The Ladies of the Corridor* (New York, 1952).

All the magazine writing of Margaret Mead, Eleanor Roosevelt, Mary Heaton Vorse, and the other women discussed here offers valuable information on the thematic concerns, as well as the style, of twentieth-century feminist writers. Because women have not been viewed as a "problem" by the overwhelming majority of Americans throughout this century, the quantity of material available is not as rich as the researcher would desire. In the 1960's, however, when a new interest in feminism, expressed as women's liberation, came into being, feminist spokeswomen were featured in newspapers, magazines, and on television programs. The quantity of women's liberation writings increased, and anthologies on women were published in great numbers.

The interest in women's literature, women's history, and women's psychology has continued in the early 1970's. Hopefully, *Movers and Shakers* is a positive contribution to our knowledge about feminist thinkers and activists. If it provokes other scholars to investigate the intellectual and social history of other outstanding women, the author will consider her efforts rewarded.

INDEX

Index

311